Penang Chinese Commerce in the 19th Century

ISEAS–Yusof Ishak Institute (formerly Institute of Southeast Asian Studies) was established as an autonomous organization in 1968. It is a regional centre dedicated to the study of socio-political, security and economic trends and developments in Southeast Asia and its wider geostrategic and economic environment. The Institute's research programmes are the Regional Economic Studies (RES, including ASEAN and APEC), Regional Strategic and Political Studies (RSPS), and Regional Social and Cultural Studies (RSCS).

ISEAS Publishing, an established academic press, has issued more than 2,000 books and journals. It is the largest scholarly publisher of research about Southeast Asia from within the region. ISEAS Publishing works with many other academic and trade publishers and distributors to disseminate important research and analyses from and about Southeast Asia to the rest of the world.

Penang Chinese Commerce in the 19th Century

The Rise and Fall of the Big Five

WONG YEE TUAN

YUSOF ISHAK INSTITUTE

First published in Singapore in 2015 by
ISEAS Publishing
30 Heng Mui Keng Terrace
Singapore 119614

E-mail: publish@iseas.edu.sg   • Website: bookshop.iseas.edu.sg

All rights reserved. No part of this publication may be reproduced, stored in a retrieval system, or transmitted in any form or by any means, electronic, mechanical, photocopying, recording or otherwise, without the prior permission of the ISEAS–Yusof Ishak Institute.

© 2015 ISEAS–Yusof Ishak Institute, Singapore

The responsibility for facts and opinions in this publication rests exclusively with the author and his interpretation do not necessarily reflect the views or the policy of the publisher or its supporters.

ISEAS Library Cataloguing-in-Publication Data

Wong, Yee Tuan.
   Penang Chinese Commerce in the 19th Century: The Rise and Fall of the Big Five.
   (Local history ; 24)
   1. Family-owned business enterprises—Malaysia—Pulau Pinang.
   2. Business networks—Malaysia—Pulau Pinang.
   3. Pulau Pinang (State)—Economic conditions—19th century.
   4. Pulau Pinang (State)—History—19th century.
   I. Title.
   II. Series: Local history and memoirs (Institute of Southeast Asian Studies) ; 24.
DS501 I595L no. 24 (2015)   2015

ISBN 978-981-4515-02-3 (soft cover)
ISBN 978-981-4515-03-0 (E-book PDF)

Typeset by International Typesetters Pte Ltd
Printed in Singapore by Mainland Press Pte Ltd

**For Si Shuk 四叔 (my late father)
in memory of his love, sacrifice, and foresight**

CONTENTS

List of Tables, Diagrams and Maps — xi
Acknowledgements — xv
Glossary — xvii
Abbreviations and Acronyms — xix
Notes on Spelling and Names — xxi
Notes on Currencies — xxi

1. **Introduction** — 1
   Why the Big Five Hokkien Families? — 3
   Methodology and Sources — 10
   Outline of the Book — 11

2. **Penang and the Big Five in Regional Context** — 14
   The Continuing Prosperity of Penang — 14
   Hokkien Merchants in Penang — 20
   Shipping and the Big Five — 21
   Entrepot Trade and the Big Five — 25
   Tin and the Big Five — 26
   Rice from Southern Burma and the Big Five — 29
   Coconut and Sugar and the Big Five — 30
   Pepper and the Big Five — 33
   Opium and the Big Five — 35
   Coolie Trade: Another Arm of the Big Five — 39
   Conclusion — 41

3. **Kith and Kin: The Big Five Familial Web**   47
   Agnatic Kinship of the Big Five Families   48
   Affinal Kinship of the Big Five   51
   Intermarriages among the Big Five   51
   Intermarriages between the Big Five and Other Families   53
   Conclusion   58

4. **Opium Farm Rivalry**   62
   Sworn Brotherhood *Hui*: The Ghee Hin and Kian Teik Tong   62
   The 1867 Penang Riot   69
   The Krabi Riot of 1878   74
   The 1879 Coolie Riot of Taiping   76
   The 1884 Plantation Coolies Revolt of Deli   78
   The Dominance of the Big Five and the Decline of the Ghee Hin   79
   Conclusion   81

5. **The Contest for 'White Gold'**   86
   Larut and the Big Five's Tin Mining Interests   87
   The Outbreak of Larut Wars: Tussles over Tin Mines   88
   The Involvement of Tan Kim Ching   89
   The Resurgence of the Big Five's Interests in Larut   93
   Another Front of the 'White Gold': Phuket and the Big Five   93
   'White Gold' from Southern Burma: The Big Five and the Ghee Hin   96
   Conclusion   98

6. **Western Mercantile Elite and Their Challenge to the Penang Chinese**   102
   From Liberalism to Management   102
   Western Merchants Prior to 1880s   103
   Straits Steamship Company and Straits Trading Company   106
   Royal Dutch Packet Company or Koninklijke Paketvaart Maatschappij (KPM)   113
   The Response of the Big Five to the Western Shipping and Trading Challenge: The Eastern Shipping Company   117
   Insurance Business: The Big Five versus the Westerners   122
   Implications of the Western Competition for the Big Five   129
   Conclusion   133

7. New Regional Order and the Decline of the Big Five	137
The Tin Industry	138
The Rubber Industry	144
The End of the Big Five Revenue Farms and the Rise of Government Monopolies	152
Centralized Land Policy	156
The Collapse of the Khaw Group and the Demise of the Big Business Empire	157
Family Feuds	159
Conclusion	163
8. Conclusion	170
Appendices	
Appendice 1	179
Appendice 2	186
Appendice 3	196
Bibliography	205
Index	219
About the Author	228

LIST OF TABLES, DIAGRAMS AND MAPS

Tables

Table 2.1	Penang's Import and Export of Straits Produce and Chinaware from and to the surrounding states, 1819–24 and 1835–40	18
Table 2.2	Ten Major Hokkien-owned Shipping and Trading Companies in Penang, 1860s–90s.	24
Table 2.3	Percentage Distribution of trade in Tin between Singapore and Penang, 1870–1910	26
Table 2.4	Coconut Estates of the Big Five and their Associates	31
Table 2.5	Import of Pepper from Sumatra (Aceh & Deli) and Export of Pepper from Penang (in piculs)	33
Table 2.6	The Annual Rental Rates of Penang Opium Farm 1860–1909	36
Table 2.7	Penang's Opium Revenue Farm Annual Rent as a Percentage of Total Revenue of Penang, 1876–1900	37
Table 4.1	Dialect Factions and Leaders of the Ghee Hin, 1860s–90s	64
Table 4.2	Business Involvement of the Ghee Hin Leaders, 1860s–90s	65

Table 4.3	Ghee Hin's Branches and Leaders in the Region, 1870s–90s	66
Table 4.4	The Leaders of the Kian Teik Tong or Toa Peh Kong, 1850s–60s	68
Table 4.5	Penang Opium Farm Annual Rent, 1855–70	74
Table 4.6	Perak's Major Revenue Farms and Farmers, 1880–82	80
Table 5.1	Leaders of Phuket's Kian Teik Tong	94
Table 5.2	List of Tin Mines controlled by Sit San's family in Lenya Township	96
Table 6.1	The Business Backgrounds and Family Relationship of the Singapore Hokkien Merchants	107
Table 6.2	The Shipping Agents of the Straits Steamship Company in Southeast Asia in 1920s	111
Table 6.3	The KPM's Four Shipping Lines to Sumatra	113
Table 6.4	The Family and Business Backgrounds of the Directors of Eastern Shipping Company	118
Table 6.5	The Board of Directors of the Penang Khean Guan Insurance Comoany, 1886	125
Table 6.6	The Financial Accounts of the Penang Khean Guan Insurance Co., 1886, 1891–1900, and 1905–6	127
Table 6.7	The Board of Directors of the Penang Khean Guan Insurance Company, 1897	128
Table 6.8	The Overseas Agents of the Penang Khean Guan Insurance Company	130
Table 7.1	Share of Malaysian and Siamese Tin Output held by Western and Chinese, 1906–1940 (in percentage)	143
Table 7.2	Number of Chinese, Javanese and Indian Workers in East Sumatra, 1883–1930	148

Table 7.3	Freight Capacity and Cost of Rail/Land/Water in Malaya	151
Table 7.4	Straits Settlements Government's Expenditure, 1900–5	155

Diagrams

Diagram 2.1	Brig Emma's Shipping Voyages and Cargoes	23
Diagram 3.1	The Intermarriages of the Five Families and Others Families in Penang	52

Maps

Map i	Penang and Its Surrounding States in the Nineteenth Century	xxii
Map 4.1	Areas in George Town (Penang) affected by the 1867 Riots	72
Map 7.1	Railway Network and the Distribution of Rubber in Malaya, 1924	150

ACKNOWLEDGEMENTS

Some content of this book have appeared as articles in *Asian Culture* and *Chinese Southern Diaspora Studies*. I would like to record my thanks to these journals for allowing me to reproduce them here.

This work succeeded to materialize with the advice, help and support given unreservedly by many people. Their contributions have added to its strengths in different ways while in no way absolving me from the responsibility for its weakness. First and foremost, I would like to express my wholehearted gratitude to my supervisory panel — Dr Li Tana, Dr Nola Cooke, Emeritus Professor David Marr, and Professor Carl A. Trocki. As a supervisor, Dr Li provided valuable guidance during the course of my academic pursuit. She not only gave lots of her time and comments which influenced my writing but also showed me how to strive for a good presentation. Her unique viewpoints always pushed me to improve my arguments. Her enthusiasm and tight supervision also facilitated the pace of my research. For all this, I am immensely indebted to her. Despite her role as a co-supervisor, Dr Cooke showed a strong interest in my work throughout the period. She generously and patiently commented all the draft chapters. Her insightful feedback and meticulous editing greatly helped to improve my writing. Without her assistance, I would not have been able to produce a readable scholastic work. All of them have had a great influence on the development, execution and writing up of this study, their intuition and knowledge have been invaluable, and I feel very fortunate and grateful to have them as my guiding light.

In regard to my field research, I would like to extend sincere thanks to a long list of people and institutes. Without them, my collection of data and information would have never been easy and smooth. In Hong Kong, thanks go to the University of Hong Kong for allowing me to use its libraries, with its excellent collections and facilities. The friendly service of the librarians made my research work enjoyable. To Ip Kwok Kwan,

I owe a real obligation for his friendship and help that made my stay in Hong Kong memorable. In Singapore, I thank the National University of Singapore and National Library of Singapore for the permissions to access their collection of materials. I am particularly grateful to Liu Yan, who helped me during my research at the National University of Singapore. I am sincerely thankful to Professor Ng Chin Keong and Dr Twang Peck Yang for being so generous with their time and dialogue. In Malaysia, my thanks go to the the National Archive of Malaysia, University of Malaya, Centre for Malaysian Chinese Studies in Kuala Lumpur as well as the Penang State Public Library in Penang. Of course, I cannot forget those individuals who had assisted my research. They are too many to name here but a number of acknowledgements must be made. Danny Wong Tze-Ken, a close friend of mine since 1998, deserves a word of appreciation. He never turned me away when I dropped by his office. In our conversations, he very generously shared with me his ideas, views and knowledge, which brought constant intellectual stimulation. I owe a debt of gratitude to Khoo Boon Dar and Lim Seng Haw, who helped me to obtain some very useful materials.

Special appreciation also goes to all the friends and informants in Penang. Among them, I am particularly grateful to Tan Yeow Wooi, who not only showed me around in George Town, but also brought me into contact with the Big Five clan *kongsis*. Without his help, I could have wasted a lot of time to obtain the needed information. Most of all, he selflessly devoted his time and personal collection to my research. His friendship has played a unique role in my academic pursuit, for our shared interest in the history of Penang and the Big Five. Heartfelt thanks are due to my friends in Canberra — Hoang Dat, Huang Zhi, Ng Kee Siong, Michael Churchman, and Lynnette Ng who rendered many needful helps to me and my family.

Last, but by no means least, I would like to express my deepest gratitude to my parents for their unstinting support and continuous encouragement. I am sure that they are delighted to see my work has eventually taken shape. I have accrued unrepayable debts for their total and unqualified love and support. For my wife, Phooi Yoke, I am forever indebted. I earnestly thank her for the encouragement, patience, understanding, and moral support and most of all for giving me the strength to believe in myself throughout the entire duration of this endeavour. My two beloved daughters, Ngi Chin and Ngi Xian, have been my great company during the revision of the manuscript.

Needless to say, I alone am responsible for all the errors and shortcomings in this book.

Yee Tuan
Penang
9 March 2015

GLOSSARY

Attap or Atap	Leaves of palms used for thatching.
Baba	A male descendant of the Chinese in the Straits Settlements who married the indigenous women. It also refers to creolized Chinese man.
Chandu	Opium prepared for smoking.
Chop	A trade name or trademark used by the Chinese businesses, it served as the name of the firm.
Coyan	A weight equivalent to approximately 1,334.7 kilograms.
Hui	A Chinese society or triad.
Kapitan	The head of the Chinese community, usually appointed by the government.
Kati	A weight equivalent to 0.60477 kilograms.
Kongsi	A partnership, company, secret society, or other shareholding socioeconomic grouping.
Orlong	An area equivalent to 1.333 acres.
Parang	A broad heavy knife used for slashing and chopping.
Picul or Pikul	A weight equivalent to approximately 60.48 kilograms.

Rupee	The basic Indian unit of currency; worth about one-half of a Spanish or Mexican silver dollar.
Seh	A Chinese family name or surname organization.
Singkeh	Literally "new guest" refers to a newly arrived Chinese immigrant from China.
Tahil	A weight equivalent to about 38 grams.
Towkay	A business owner or boss; used to refer to a merchant.

ABBREVIATIONS AND ACRONYMS

A.V.R.O.S.	Algemeene Vereeniging van Rubber Planters tier Osstkust van Sumatra (General Association of Rubber Planters of the East Coast of Sumatra)
CO	Colonial Office
KPM	Koninklijke Paketvaart Maatschappij (Royal Dutch Packet Company)
p., pp.	Page or pages in an article or book
PGSC	Pinang Gazette and Straits Chronicle
PAMA	The Penang Argus and Mercantile Advertiser
Rs	Rupee
Sp	Spanish Dollar
vol.	Volume

NOTES ON SPELLING AND NAMES

Throughout this book, the names for Chinese individuals, associations, and companies are mostly in the spelling used in the sources — Hokkien, Hakka, Teochew, or Cantonese. Where I was unable to discover the Chinese characters, I use only the transcripts. Except for the names of the places in China which are in *Hanyu Pinyin*.

NOTES ON CURRENCIES

The symbol of $ refers to Spanish dollar which was the standard currency used in the nineteenth-century Straits Settlements. From 1903 to 1934, Straits dollar replaced Spanish dollar as a standard unit of account for trade in the Straits Settlements and Southeast Asia.

$ 100	210.85 Sicca Rupees
$ 100	252.27 Dutch Guilders
$ 100	26.50 Sterling
$ 100	7 Sterling

MAP i
Map of Penang and Its Surrounding States in the Nineteenth Century

Source: John Crawfurd, *History of the Indian Archipelago: containing an account of the manners, arts, languages, religions, institutions, and commerce of its inhabitants,* vol. 1, no. 1 (Edinburgh, 1820).

1

INTRODUCTION

As a Hakka boy born and raised in Perak, despite its proximity, I only learned about Penang as a trading port established by Francis Light from school history texts. It was not until a trip in the year 2000 that I came to know Penang better personally. Walking around the streets of George Town, the business centre of Penang, I was amazed to see five temple-like *kongsi* houses standing magnificently in the middle of the town. These five *kongsis* are believed to have owned at least half of the shops and houses in the old part of George Town. More interestingly, they were once connected with each other by some secret passages and started the worst riots in the British colony at that time. Later, I came to know that a group of wealthy merchants from five Hokkien families founded these *kongsis* in the nineteenth century. Despite all this mythology, surprisingly, no one has ever seen fit to place them under a scholarly examination. Who were these Hokkien merchants and what roles did they play in Penang? How important were they? It was questions like these that stimulated me to ponder the relationship between those little-known Hokkien merchants and Penang about two centuries ago and to embark on researching the story about them.

In the existing literature, Penang's history has been framed within a colonial paradigm and studied from a top-down angle. The rise of Penang as a hub of commerce and trade, to many scholars, was due to the British free trade and free port policies as well as the legendary Francis Light. As L.A. Mills commented in 1925:

> During these years from 1786 to 1800 the population and trade of Penang were rapidly increasing… This seems to be traceable to three principal causes — the remarkable energy with which Light pushed

forward the development of the settlement, the great trust the natives had in him, and the system of free trade which prevailed until 1802 (Mills 1925, p. 42).

Seventy years later, echoing Mill's view, Sundara Raja remarked in 1997 that Francis Light, who promoted free trade, contributed greatly to making Penang a free port which stimulated vigorous trade and growing migrant settlement (Raja 1997, pp. 104–8). For these scholars it seems the colonial factor was central and sufficient in itself to explain the rise of Penang. But whether intentionally or not, these scholars have marginalized, if not actually dismissed, significant local elements such as the regional traders and their networks in the Penang story. I argue, on the contrary, that these local merchants played an indispensable role in transforming Penang into a major marketplace. This work thus shifts away from the colonial vantage point to focus on the crucial but much ignored local experience between the 1800s and 1890s.

Penang was established during the hundred years between 1740 and 1850, or the "Chinese century", as Anthony Reid terms it, when modern Southeast Asia was formed. This "Chinese century" witnessed a remarkable growth of Chinese activity in mining, agriculture and shipping in Southeast Asia.[1] To re-evaluate Penang within the "Chinese century", is not to write the colonial British out of Penang or the region, but to see how the interests of both colonial governments and the individual British merchants interacted, intertwined and operated in a wider regional arena. As Leonard Blussé has noted, Francis Light's occupation of Penang in 1786 was the first British attempt to incorporate the Chinese network in Southeast Asia (Blysse 1999 p. 127). This was why the British established their trading base in Penang, with the aim of engaging in and capitalizing on the trade connections of the Chinese merchants spreading across Kedah, Melaka, Selangor, southern Burma, southern Siam, Java and Sumatra. The rise of Penang was built upon such networks.

In his recent doctoral thesis, Philip King reveals the importance of southern Siam in the formation of Penang. He points out that Penang was closely connected to the east coast of southern Siam through overland routes; it was the "land track" that fostered the trans-peninsula trade that rendered Penang's prosperity (King 2006, pp. 61–71). Originally Kedah had controlled this route, but with the settlement of Penang, and Kedah's weakness, its advantages fell to the British. By demonstrating the active involvement of the British, Malays, Siamese and Chinese in the tin business of the Rahman polity, King convincingly argues that the central peninsula was a historically important centre rather than an inconsequential periphery of sociopolitical and economic development (King 2006, pp. 77–194). Most importantly, King's work erects the central peninsula as a regional category of analysis.

If King was interested in the land, my focus is on the maritime world and Penang's important connections with the Straits of Melaka and the Andaman Sea, reaching to Sumatra in the west and touching on southern Burma in the north. This water-based network of Penang's reached out to its maritime surroundings and the agricultural and mineral-rich states. Thanks to its seaward orientation, nineteenth-century Penang became a regional hub rather than a local entity. By identifying and carefully delineating the operations of its main Chinese business networks, we will show that Penang and the surrounding states formed an organic economic whole, for which Penang was the thriving regional entrepot. But this meant that the surrounding states, particularly southern Burma, southwestern Siamese coast, western Malay states, and the north and eastern coasts of Sumatra, also played an indispensable role in the formation of Penang. In this wide arena, a group of five dominant Hokkien merchant clans were particularly visible, and it is these people and their stories that I am particularly interested in exploring in this book.

WHY THE BIG FIVE HOKKIEN FAMILIES?

Examining the literature on the Chinese business in Southeast Asia, one often comes across the buzzwords — Chinese business networks. Many scholars have attributed the Chinese business prominence or success in the region to the web of dynamic and flexible business networks that they discerned around the Chinese. Scholars like Yoshihara Kunio S. Gordon Redding, Joel Kotkin, Michael Backman, Claudia Cragg and Yen Ching-hwang (Kunio 1988; Redding 1990; Kotkin 1993; Backman 1995; Cragg 1995; Yen 2002). have argued that the dynamism and flexibility of the Chinese business networks derived from a set of cultural traits that included the Confucian ethic, personal trust (*xin yong*), personal connection (*guan xi*), frugality, diligence and risk taking. Most importantly, they treat the business networks as Chinese entities in the context of modern nation-state. In this rich body of literature, the "Chinese" are usually presented as a homogenous group sharing common cultural values and single, defined heritage, which facilitated the formation of uniform business networks to serve commercial interests within a concrete nation-state system.

When one comes to explain the Chinese economic pre-eminence in the historical context of Southeast Asia, this model is insufficient and even impertinent. This is because the culturalist perspective and its narrow interpretations tend to obscure and generalize rather than clarify Chinese ethnicity and business networks in a historically fluid, transnational and multi-ethnic sphere like Southeast Asia. However, two scholars, Wu Xiao An and Mark Ravinder Frost (Wu 2003; Frost 2005, pp. 29–66), offer greater insights into the Chinese business networks in the nineteenth-century Southeast Asia. Moving away from the orthodox notion and stereotyped perspective, Wu presents the Chinese business networks as a synthesis of families, politics and business that was crucial not only for Chinese economic prominence but also for the formation of a Malay state, Kedah. Focusing on the Straits Chinese in Singapore, Frost shows that the Nanyang networks which based on junk trade, capital, kinship, and temple turned Singapore into an ever-expanding entrepot. It is clear that the Chinese business networks were not just a configuration of cultural traits, but rather a web of interconnected institutional, organizational, and familial elements.

While Wu confines his study of the networks to a small geographical setting (Penang and Kedah), Frost treats them as Straits Chinese-oriented and centring on Singapore. To expand and deepen our view of the extent and diversity of the Chinese business networks, I try to take a grass-roots view, to examine the "Chinese" according to dialect and locality (Hokkien, Cantonese, Hakka and Teochew) and trace their business networks both within and across ethnic and political boundaries. In other words, the scope of my investigation will extend across state borders, beyond ethnicities and sub-ethnic categories and across socio-economic classes, and although naturally centred on Penang it will also go beyond a limited geographical perspective. My goal is to locate the Penang Hokkien mercantile elite in its own historical context during the nineteenth century. To do so, I focus upon the five most important Hokkien mercantile families of the time, namely the Khoo 邱, the Cheah 谢, the Yeoh 杨, the Lim 林, and the Tan 陈 in Penang — the Big Five. They were all from Fujian province of coastal China.[2] The members of the Big Five were closely connected to each other through generations of intermarriages in their native land (Liu 2004, p. 103). They always banded together to venture on overseas trade and migration. After settling in Penang, the merchants of these five families set up their respective clan *kongsis* which became the largest congregations of consanguineal kin in Penang and Southeast Asia. Besides clan *kongsi*, they also founded and controlled all the major Hokkien temples and associations.

The Hokkien Kongsi, for instance, a loose common organization which was founded in 1856 served to coordinate all social welfare activities of the Hokkiens.³ It was this family network and dominant social role that rendered the five families the existence of essential and group identity. These five Hokkien families comprised merchants and capitalists who had moved about and conducted business in their region since at least the eighteenth century, not only as maritime traders but also as agriculturalists and miners. If not as important as influential Chinese in Singapore like Tan Kim Ching and Cheang Hong Lim, who operated on a higher and larger platform, the big five Hokkien families were in the middle rank of the Nanyang Chinese mercantile elite, ahead of better-known families like the Khaw 许 of Ranong, the Choong 莊 in Kedah, or the Wu 吳 in Songkla, who operated on a local basis.

Of course I am not the first historian to be drawn to these important economic actors. Existing works on this subject include Jennifer Cushman's *Family and State* (Cushman 1991), Wu Xiao An's *Chinese Business in the Making of a Malay State 1882–1941* (Wu 2003, p. 177). Chuleeporn Pongsupath's "The Mercantile Community of Penang and the Changing Pattern of Trade 1890–1940" (Pongsupath 1990), Phuwadol Songprasert's "The Development of Chinese Capital in Southern Siam 1868–1932" (Songprasert 1986), Neil Khor Jin Keong's *Economic Change and the Emergence of the Straits Chinese in Nineteenth-century Penang* (Khor 2006, pp. 59–83), and *Penang and Its Region: The Story of an Asian Entrepot*, edited by Yeoh Seng Guan, Loh Wei Leng, Khoo Salma Nasution and Neil Khor (Yeoh et al. 2009). Cushman's work focused on the Khaw family in the context of Penang–southern Siam relations. She provided a detailed analysis of the strategies used by the Khaw family — marriage, political and commercial alliances with Siamese nobility, Penang Chinese businessmen, and Australian entrepreneurs — in achieving their economic and political interests. Drawing from British, Thai, Australian primary source materials, plus interviews with family members, family genealogy, and secondary sources on overseas Chinese, Cushman revealed the process in which the Khaw family rose and declined as an influential economic force in northern Malaya and southern Siam from the 1830s to the 1920s.

Unlike Cushman, Songprasert relied mainly on the Thai archival materials to illustrate the intricate connections of the Penang-oriented Hokkien merchants with the southern Siamese states. He detailed the subtle interdependent relationships existing between three parties (the Penang Hokkien businessmen, the ruling power in Bangkok, and the local elites of the southern Siamese states) in the form of secret society memberships, business partnerships and patron-client relationships, from 1868 to 1932. Through such interlocking relationships, each party exerted influence in order to secure its own economic or political interests in the southern Siamese states. The Bangkok-based central government used the influential and wealthy Hokkien merchants and local Siamese elite to develop the economy of the southern Siamese states for state revenue and to maintain Siamese sovereignty in the Peninsula. The local Siamese elite and the Hokkien merchants, who had access to labour, technology and the market, needed the sanction of the central government to tap the tin mines and revenue farms. With these interdependent relationships, according to Songprasert, the businessmen of the Tan and the Khaw families were able to accumulate capital and expand their influence in the southern Siamese states.

Wu's work examines the role and function of Chinese business enterprise and its networks in the context of Penang–Kedah from 1882 to 1941. Using the leading Chinese families, particularly the Lim family of Penang and the Choong family of Kedah, Wu provides an absorbing account of the complex interplay between the Chinese businessmen, the Kedah ruling elites, the colonial government in Penang and the Siamese government. He observed the constantly changing pattern of alliances and opposition among the various groups as they manoeuvred for profits and power in their various economic and political relationships. With all this, Wu showed economic influence of the leading figures in the Lim and the Choong families and their vigorous involvement in the development of a western Malay state.

Using a similar time-span to Wu's, Pongsupath explored the relationship between changing trade patterns and developments within and between the two major mercantile communities — the Chinese and the Western traders of Penang. Her work elucidated two themes: how the regional entrepot trade of Penang during the late nineteenth century conditioned the rise of Penang Chinese economic influence and the changing pattern of trade and the transformation of the Penang port's function (from an entrepot centre to primarily a Malayan port) in the early twentieth century. This change undermined the leading commercial position of the Penang Chinese but increased the role and influence of Western interests. To illustrate the role and influence of the Penang Chinese mercantile community within the Penang dynamic trade pattern, Pongsupath referred to a group of prominent Chinese capitalists and merchants who were important for their involvement in shipping, planting, tin mining, and revenue farming.

By focusing on three Straits Chinese families — the Koh, the Khoo, and the Lim, Neil Khor unfolded the ways of cultural capital being created and utilized to form inter-family alliances in order to derive the necessary resources and influence for business pursuits and attainment of colonial socio-political status in Penang. The Koh family, with Peranakan Chinese heritage and close relationship with the British, assumed a leadership role over the Chinese community. To strengthen this leadership role and extend business interest into tin mining, the Koh family, through marriages, established alliance with the Khoo family, which controlled the powerful Hokkien secret society and tin mines in Perak and southern Siam. Similarly, the Khoo family constructed marriages with the Koh family to gain access to Peranankan culture and British patronage, which promised both commercial privilege and upward social mobility. The Lim family, which came to Penang in 1850s, identified the socioeconomically and politically importance of the Koh and the Khoo families and forged alliance with their family members through business partnership and marriages to achieve business success and gain entrance to Penang colonial culture.

Penang and Its Region contains five essays that touch on some Penang's businessmen and their networks. In her essay, Low Wei Leng sheds light on the rise of Chinese merchants in Penang's inter-regional and intra-regional trade and shipping in the mid-ninettenth century. Chuleeporn Virunha's work scrutinizes the Penang Chinese merchants, who built and controlled the intricate economic and commercial structure of Penang, and their ability to respond to the Western challenge from 1890 to 1940. The essay by Stepanie Chong Po Yin sets out to examine the Eu family that built Eu Yan Sang, a manufacturer and retailer of Chinese medicines in Malaya from 1876 to 1941. It traces the development of this family business from a local provision shop to a regional enterprise which had business interest extended to Singapore, Hong Kong, and China. Carl Trocki's essay looks at Koh Seang Tat's revenue farm networks expanding from Penang to other Southeast Asian states like Siam, Sumatra, and Saigon, and as far as to Hong Kong. Wu Xiao An's study on the Choong family reveals the significance of another Chinese family in the socioeconomic and political development of Penang and Kedah in the period of 1870s–1960s.

While all the six studies touch on the Big Five in some way and clearly demonstrate the preponderant and indispensable role of these Hokkien mercantile families in the economic development of the nineteenth-century Penang region, each author was predominantly focused on other concerns.

We cannot draw a clear picture of nineteenth-century Penang from their studies because even taken together they are missing a central factor, the interactions and activities of the key players, the Big Five. Without considering them collectively, the story of Penang remains fragmented and at times even mysterious.

Penang was closely connected to a sophisticated network of ports, frontier bazaars and agricultural or mineral-producing hinterlands largely because of the economic activities of the Big Five families and their close associates. Together they formed the most powerful and conspicuous economic force in the nineteenth-century Chinese community in Penang. As this book will show, not only were they maritime traders and shippers, they were also capitalists, agriculturalists and mine owners or financiers with extensive socioeconomic connections throughout the whole Penang-centred region. They controlled all the major economic sectors and dominated most of the socioeconomic organizations, which were the local community authorities. Most importantly, their family and partnership networks reached far beyond the Hokkien dialect networks, unlike what the conventional scholarship on overseas Chinese would have us believe. As will be seen in the following chapters, they were closely related to members of the Hakka, Cantonese, and Teochew dialect groups. But this was not all: Malay rulers, Indian chettiers, Siamese elites, Armenian businessmen, British government officers and individual merchants, and even Australian entrepreneurs were all at different times and places intimately involved with the Big Five and their commercial interests. The knitting together of all these elements together constituted the crucial factor holding together the economic structure and commercial mechanism of Penang and its surrounding states. It was not until the early twentieth century that the Big Five slowly succumbed to newly-assertive colonial political power and increased competition with Western capital, neither of which had seriously threatened its Penang-centred regional network for much of the previous century.

The Big Five naturally did not always form a solid bloc, without internal conflicts or competition among themselves. Rather, they functioned more as an interest group which was bound together by common economic pursuits in the Penang-centred region. As an interest group, they were prepared to compromise, accommodate, and negotiate their differences by creating alliances that helped them to achieve or maintain their business domination, whether as a minority in Malay states or in the face of British colonialism. Differences, like competition, conflict, and confrontation were not uncommon within each of the five families, in between the five families or with other families. What mattered was how the Big Five dealt with these problems. In their most successful decades, the Big Five adopted and manipulated a number of levers designed to counteract discord, including weaving complex webs of intermarriage, creating clan *kongsis*, sworn brotherhood *hui*, and joint business partnerships. Not only did these mechanisms often help to resolve such tensions, they also formalized and institutionalized the cooperative relationships between themselves and other families for various business ventures. On top of this, the Big Five also maintained the continuing links to China through the patronization of temples, schools and other foundations in their native villages and the purchase of titles and degrees from the Qing government.[4] As such, the Big Five played a leading and dynamic role in the formation of the regional business network which provides the key to new concepts, framework and new questions in the analysis of nineteenth-century Penang.

In summary, the Big Five give us an insight into the structure and workings of a web of business networks which reveal the dominant economic reality in Penang and its region. This web of networks consisted of a group of elite families, sworn brotherhood *hui*, *kongsis*, and commercial companies characterized by the inter-family alliances and cross-ethnic/sub-ethnic partnerships that controlled a cluster of transnational and interconnected business activities constituting the economic pillars of the Penang region. Unravelling such business networks allows us to break down conventional spatial categorization and view Penang and its surrounding states as one economically unified geographical region.

This work benefitted and built on the new scholarship on the Southeast Asian Chinese in the last two decades. Among them are Carl Trocki's *Opium and Empire* (1990), *The Rise and Fall of Revenue Farming*, edited by John Butcher and Howard Dick (1993), *"Secret Societies" Reconsidered: Perspectives on the social history of modern South China and Southeast Asia*, edited by David Ownby and Mary Somers Heidhues (1993), and James Rush's *Opium to Java* (1990). They provided broad contexts for the understanding of the Southeast Asian Chinese, and threw new lights onto the Chinese business world, particularly the opium revenue farms and revenue farming systems which were the crucial and integral part of the colonial economy. With this study, I seek to make a contribution to the existing literature on the Southeast Asian Chinese by illuminating three important aspects of Chinese capitalism and entrepreneurship in the nineteenth-century maritime Penang region. Penang, from which radiated of an extensive and multifaceted web of Hokkien business networks, became not only a regional entrepot and a base for the supply of capital and labour but also a springboard for its business and political elite to penetrate the surrounding states. Riding on the Penang-based Hokkien networks, these business elite were able to channel capital and transform the adjacent hinterlands into an agricultural and mining production powerhouse. On this foundation the European political elite were able to extend their political influence and consolidate colonial political control over the indigenous regimes. Second, the business networks they created, although centred on the Hokkien families in Penang, cut across dialect, ethnic and class boundaries and extended well beyond Penang. Their business partnerships, family relationships, and sworn brotherhood *hui* incorporated not only Hakka and Cantonese but also Europeans, Siamese, Malays, and Indians. Lastly, opium revenue farms, coolie brokers and *hui* served as the real key to understanding Penang's economy. Their economic and political role in the region and in the British empire were the absolute elements that linked all the economic activities into one integrated whole to generate wealth for the Chinese business families and provided financial wherewithal for the colonial powers to construct modern bureaucratic state structures in Southeast Asia.

METHODOLOGY AND SOURCES

In this book, I adopt a contextual and interactional approach to delineate and analyse the Big Five Hokkien families as a leading economic force in the transformation and development of Penang and its surrounding states from the nineteenth to the early twentieth centuries. The economic landscape of the Penang region was characterized by a range of vibrant economic activities, such as revenue farming, cash-crop planting, tin mining, and shipping and trading. It was in this setting that the Big Five established their sophisticated socioeconomic organizations and actively interacted with a kaleidoscope of Europeans and locals, exploiting all these economic opportunities and rose to become the dominant economic players. To help reconstruct and revive this historical context, I consulted a large volume of newspapers, including the *Pinang Gazette and Straits Chronicle (1838–1900)*, *The Penang Argus and Mercantile Advertiser (August 1867–March 1873)*, and *Penang Times (October 1882–March 1885)*. While these newspapers have been very much underutilized, my reading of them shows they contain particularly rich social, economic, and political information. Shipping activities, business transactions, trading statistics, and commercial company details also appeared frequently in their pages, as do social aspects, like marriages, festival celebrations, obituaries, riots, and court cases.

Although there were limited details on political affairs, some important government announcements, notices and reports were also publicly disseminated by them. By collecting and collating all this information and data from every issue of the newspapers, it became possible to detect a consistent and subtle pattern of business operations and interactions. To supplement the inadequacy of political information, I also consulted a number of archival collections (Straits Settlements Government Gazettes, Proceedings of the Straits Settlements Legislative Council, Proceedings of the Federal Council of the Federated Malay States, Straits Settlements Original Correspondence, and Straits Settlements miscellaneous papers and original correspondence) and a wide range of secondary sources. On top of these, I also made use of published and unpublished Chinese sources, such as family genealogies, temple records, personal papers and clan magazines, some of them collected from the family members of the Big Five.

OUTLINE OF THE BOOK

This chapter introduces an approach to Penang from the regional perspective. With this approach, Penang's Big Five Hokkien mercantile families (the Khoo, the Cheah, the Lim, the Yeoh, and the Tan), who possessed an extensive regional business network, become the focus. To trace the Big Five's regional business network, this study reveals new dimensions of ethnic interaction, economic cooperation and competition, state and family relationships that shaped Penang and the surrounding states.

Chapter Two demonstrates that Penang was a flourishing regional entrepot for the whole nineteenth century despite the rise of Singapore. Its prosperity was closely related to Singapore's entrepot trade and the enterprising Big Five Hokkien families, who dominated a wide range of business activities (shipping, entrepot trade, tin mining, revenue farming and coolie trading) and possessed extensive business connections with the surrounding states (southern Burma, southwestern Siam, western Malay states, and the northern and eastern Sumatra).

Chapter Three explores the family networks centring on the Big Five. These were the secret of success for the Big Five in establishing their business domination in the Penang region. The family networks of blood and matrimonial ties not only cut across state, dialect, and ethnic boundaries, but also spanned the generations. With this flexible and interlocking family network, the Big Five could use or rely on a substantial number of relatives to manage, secure, and advance their business interests in the region.

Chapter Four makes a close examination of the Big Five's most profitable business — opium farming. The Big Five not only grouped themselves under the umbrella of a sworn brotherhood *hui* (the Kian Teik Tong), but also established alliances with other *hui* like the Hai San, the Ho Seng, and the Indo-Malay Red Flag Societies to protect and pursue their opium farming businesses in the region. In order to gain the monopoly of the opium farms, the Big Five used their *hui* network to mobilize armed power and financial resources to compete with their arch rival, the Ghee Hin.

Chapter Five looks at tin mining — another lucrative business pursued by the Big Five in the nineteenth century. Larut (Perak), Phuket, and Mergui became magnets for tin traders and miners. By extending their *hui* network and capital, the Big Five were able to tap the rich tin reserves in the three states. In order to gain their control over the tin business, the Big Five had to compete and manoeuvre along with the Ghee Hin and the Singapore Hokkien mercantile elite.

Chapter Six explores the growing Western business challenge to the Big Five and the response of the Big Five towards the rising Western business competition at the turn of the century. The Royal Dutch Packet Company (KPM) and the British Straits Steamship Company and Straits Trading Company expanded their shipping, tin-trading and smelting interests in the region. In response to Western competition, the Big Five formed the Eastern Shipping Company and the Penang Khean Guan Insurance Company. At the turn of the century, the Big Five amalgamated these two with the other three companies to form a conglomerate — the Khaw Group, to strengthen their business competitiveness.

Chapter Seven rounds off by probing the rise of a new regional order and its impact on the Big Five in the early twentieth century. Equipped with large and unlimited capital, and employing new management skills and technology, Western mercantile interests succeeded in gaining control of the primary commodity production and trade, such as tin and rubber. Concurrently, the expansion of colonial bureaucratic machines and the imposition of restrictive legislation deprived the Big Five of economic privileges like revenue farming monopolies and easy access to landownership. This unfavourable economic and political order not only undermined the Big Five's economic bases but also crippled the Big Five's ability to operate as a powerful interest group.

Notes

1. Anthony Reid, "Chinese Trade and Southeast Asian Economic Expansion in the Later Eighteenth and Early Nineteenth Centuries: An Overview", in *Water Frontier: Commerce and the Chinese in the Lower Mekong Region, 1750–1880*, edited by Nola Cooke and Li Tana (Lanham: Rowman & Littlefield, 2004), pp. 22–32. See also Anthony Reid, "Introduction", in *The Last Stand of Asian Autonomies: Responses to Modernity in the Diverse States of Southeast Asia and Korea, 1750–1900*, edited by Anthony Reid (London and New York: Macmillan Press, 1997), pp. 11–14.
2. The Khoo, the Cheah, the Yeoh, and the Lim families originated from the Sandu (三都) district in Haicheng (海澄), county of the Zhangzhou (漳州) prefecture in Fujian Province, while the Tan family was composed of the members from Tongan (同安) in Fujian. 张少宽, "十九世纪槟华五大姓初探", 东方日报 *Dong Fang Ri Bao* [Oriental Daily News], 28 June 2000, p. A16.
3. Tan Kim Hong, "Organizational Structure and Development of Hokkien Kongsi, Penang", in *The Story of Hokkien Kongsi, Penang* (Penang: Hokkien Kongsi, 2014), p. 84.
4. *槟城龙山堂邱公司: 历史与建筑材料 Bincheng Longshantang Qiugongsi: Lishi Yu Jianzhu Cailiao* [Leong San Tong Khoo Kongsi: The History and Architecture] (槟城: 槟城龙山堂邱公司出版小组 [Penang: Leong San Tong Khoo Kongsi Publication Committee], 2003); 林氏敦本堂暨勉述堂: 壹百週年纪念刊 *Linshe Dunbentang Ji Mianshutang: Yibaizhounian Jiniankan* [Centenary Souvenir of Lim Kongsi Toon Pun Tong and Lim Sz Bian Soot Tong]; 石塘谢氏世德堂福侯公公司章程 *Shitang Xieshe Shidetang Fuhougong Gongsi Zhangcheng* [Rules and Regulations of Seh Cheah Kongsi]; Yen Ching-hwang, *Community and Politics: The Chinese in Colonial Singapore and Malaysia* (Singapore: Times Academic Press, 1995).

2

PENANG AND THE BIG FIVE IN THE REGIONAL CONTEXT

Most earlier works have long held that Penang's hey-day finished when Singapore emerged in 1819 at the tip of the Malay Peninsula. This new British colony was strategically situated and able to attract commerce and investment from both the region and the world. Thereafter, Penang was of no real importance, as the rise of Singapore necessarily reduced it to nothing but a local commercial centre. However, this chapter reveals that Penang continued as a flourishing regional hub for the whole of the nineteenth century, and was in some respects even more important than Singapore. It then goes on to discuss the operations of the leading Hokkien merchants, the Big Five, considering their various economic activities from shipping through to entrepot trade, commodity production, opium farming, to coolie trade, and how the Big Five dominated all these economic activities.

THE CONTINUING PROSPERITY OF PENANG

The foundation of Penang by the British in 1786 was mainly due to strategic and commercial interests. A series of events in the early 1780s — the active presence of French naval forces in Indian Ocean and their intention to secure the tin trade of the Tenasserim coast during the early 1780s, the closure of Dutch East Indies ports to British ships during 1782–83, and the Dutch conquest of Riau in 1784 — had made the British (East India Company) greatly aware of the dangerous stranglehold two hostile European powers had on their mercantile interests in Southeast

Asia.[1] This exigency prompted the British to establish a base in Penang, an island off the west coast of Kedah. Situated at the northern end of the Melaka Straits and on the periphery of the archipelago, Penang was in close proximity to some old trading ports. Aceh in northern Sumatra was nearby in the west, while Kedah and Perak in the western Malay states flanked the east of the island. To the north, it was open to Rangoon and Mergui in southern Burma and Phuket of southwestern Siam, Selangor and Melaka lay to the south. Penang, in the middle of this matrix of ports, developed rapidly as an entrepot. If Penang suffered a decline in trade when Singapore was established in 1819, it quickly rose as a centre of regional trade in the 1820s (Raman 1969/70, pp. 29–30; Freeman 2003, p. 139).

For many recent scholars, Penang's role as an entrepot was unsustainable and short-lived as Singapore's ascendancy grew. Khoo Kay Kim, for instance, has argued the fast-diminishing significance of Penang in serving as an entrepot port, given its moderate growth and decline of commerce in 1806–19 and growing British direct trade between India and China. In his work, *Malay Society*, he remarked that the lack of British shipping between Penang and China caused the downturn of Penang's trade which, in turn, degraded Penang as a port, so it only flourished for approximately the first twenty-five years after its establishment (Khoo 1991, pp. 64–65). Khoo then emphasized the founding of Singapore in 1819, with its more strategic location, and its galloping growth of trade that sealed the fate of Penang (Khoo 1991, pp. 66–68). Neither K.C. Tregonning nor C.D. Cowan had favourable views of Penang's prosperity after the establishment of Singapore, despite their other attempts to present the significance of Penang. Pointing to the descending trade figures of Penang in the period of 1821–30 and increasing direct British shipping between India and China in the period of 1813–34, they asserted that Penang was fading into insignificance (Tregonning 1965, p. 126; Cowan 1950, pp. 14–16). The impressive growth of Singapore's trade in that period, according to them, indicated Singapore was in fact replacing Penang. Tregonning observed:

> After 1819 Singapore replaced Penang as the entrepot port where goods could be transshipped, or where bills of lading could be altered, for private trade to England; and finally with the opium demand rising steadily, private traders on country ships could sail direct from India with full cargo (Tregonning 1965).

Cowan's view was equally unfavourable:

> The future of Penang at the end of 1819 was not bright. The annual deficit remained as high as ever. Trade, whilst a slight improvement was noticeable, was not good... by 1822 the value of trade of Singapore exceeded that of Penang, and it went on increasing at the same unprecedented rate, with occasional small recessions usually, it appears, due to the conditions of the China trade, which made up more than a third of the total trade of the port (Cowan 1950, p. 11).

The authority on Singapore history, Wong Lin Ken, also stated axiomatically:

> The location of Penang at the northern end of the Straits of Melaka was far inferior to that of Singapore, being open to fewer countries and forming a depot only for the northern ports of Sumatra and the west coast of the Malay Peninsula. In fact Penang was to a large extent a 'feeder' port of Singapore (Wong Lin Ken 1961, p. 86).

The consensus of these authorities, therefore, was that the rise of Singapore not only pushed Penang to the fringe but also eliminated its role as an entrepot port and reduced it to a mere dependency. Such view of Penang's fate is still unquestioningly upheld by Nordin Hussin's work of 2007 — *Trade and Society in the Straits of Melaka* (Hussin 2007). This, however, was only one side of the story of Penang's trade and commerce. It is true that Singapore did divert trade away from Penang and Melaka, but because of the flourishing trade and rapidly increased trade volume of Singapore, Penang also grew rapidly in this much improved environment. Furthermore, the existence of the Big Five made Penang different from Melaka, where most of the enterprising *Baba* Chinese had moved to Singapore (Lim How Seng 1995, p. 19; Turnbull 1972, p. 31; Trocki 2006, p. 47). Singapore was thus not a negative factor but a benefit for Penang. As an entrepot, Singapore radiated an arc of trading contacts with other states within Southeast Asia, of which the most important was the direct connection with Penang, which was already an established maritime hub. Penang acted not only as a distribution point for the commodities (China goods, opium) from Singapore to the surrounding states at the northern end of the Straits of Melaka but also as a collection point for Straits products (tin and pepper) for Singapore. Each fed the other, stimulating and being stimulated by their mutual flourishing trade. It was in this context that Penang continued to function as an entrepot centre for the local and native traders between Penang, North Sumatra, southern Burma, southwestern Siam, and western Malay states.

Although there is a scarcity of data on ship movements in and out of Penang in the 1820s and 1830s, the data on the quantity of Straits products and Chinaware imported and exported through Penang in the period of 1819–24 and 1832–40 shows no sign of decline whatsoever. Contrary to what the scholars cited above believed, after the rise of Singapore most of the commodities coming in and going out from Penang actually multiplied. Penang's trade with the regional states, such as Aceh, the Pedir Coast, Pegu, Moulmein and the East Coast of Sumatra, was particularly vigorous (see Table 2.1).

This pattern of trade and shipping continued to characterize Penang's maritime landscape from the 1840s onwards. In fact, such regional trading and shipping activities became so vigorous that Singapore could hardly compete in this sphere. For example, in 1843–44, 744 native and 60 square-rigged vessels entered Penang from Aceh, Deli, Moulmein, Pangha and the west side of the Peninsula; with the number of native and square-rigged vessels departing from Penang to the same states at 994 and sixty-one respectively (see Appendix 1). Compare this with Singapore, where the number of native vessels entering from or departing to those states was approximately 200–300 fewer than Penang; the number of square-rigged vessels arriving from or leaving for those states was also lower than Penang by thirteen to fourteen. For the subsequent years, Penang's native and square-rigged vessel traffic with those regional states experienced a more noticeable increase. In the ten years from 1846 to 1853, the number of incoming and outgoing native and square-rigged vessels between Penang, Sumatra, Moulmein, Pangha, and the west-side Peninsula exceeded 1,000. By contrast, Singapore's traffic borne by native and square-rigged vessels with those states remained sluggish and never exceeded 900. From the 1860s to mid-1890s, although there were some increases in the traffic of Singapore with those states, Penang remained as the entrepot centre for Perak, Kedah, the West Coast of Siam, and Burma. It was only in the 1890s that Singapore's shipping traffic with Sumatra overtook Penang.

It is clear that such a large amount of trade required a huge number of boats, both square-rigged vessels and native craft, to connect Penang and its region. But if a lot of shipping was involved, its control was surprisingly limited. Most of the shipping involved was owned and operated by a small number of Hokkien mercantile families in Penang. The next section examines the role of Hokkien merchants in this thriving regional entrepot.

TABLE 2.1
Penang's Import and Export of Straits Produce and Chinaware from and to the Surrounding States, 1819–24 and 1835–40

Import of Pepper, Betel Nuts and Bird's Nests from Aceh & the Pedir Coast

Year	Pepper (piculs)	Betel Nut (piculs)	Bird's Nests (catties)
1819–20	5,701	24,810	N/A
1820–21	5,628	30,890	50
1821–22	11,222	29,141	287
1822–23	4,786	38,155	455
1823–24	N/A	N/A	N/A

Import of Pepper (in piculs) from the Ports on the East Coast of Sumatra

Year	Deli	Bulu China	Langkat	Batubara	Sirdang
1819	2,342	315	95	59	217
1820	14,315	1,757	2,462	1,174	2,954
1821	10,672	870	4,965	578	180
1822	30,444	9,199	6,278	1,246	2,926

Imports of Tin, Rice and Pepper from Pungah

Year	Tin (piculs)	Rice (coyans)	Pepper (piculs)
1832–33	4,673	$49\frac{1}{2}$	25
1833–34	4,897	86	39
1834–35	8,555	220	314

Imports of Tin, Rice and Pepper from Kedah

Year	Tin (piculs)	Rice (coyans)	Pepper (piculs)
1832–33	618	28	50
1833–34	736	50	10
1834–35	597	244	7

Imports from the Coast of Pedir and Acheenese Ports on the East Coast of Sumatra

Year	Bees'-Wax (piculs)	Betel Nuts (piculs)	Rattans (piculs)
1835–36	56	64,104	4,975
1836–37	64	81,267	5,207
1837–38	164	98,406	6,394

Import of Rice and Sticlac from Moulmein		
Year	Rice (baskets)	Sticlac (piculs)
1837	60,940	34
1838	34,223	408
1839	55,675	670
1840	29,300	55

Export of Betel Nuts to Pegu	
Year	Betel Nuts (piculs)
1819–20	198
1820–21	504
1821–22	N/A
1822–23	619
1823–24	842

Export of Betel Nuts to Pungah	
Year	Betel Nuts (piculs)
1832–33	1,256
1833–34	854
1834–35	4,660

Export of China Ware, Betel Nuts and Sugar to Moulmein			
Year	China Ware (piculs)	Betel Nuts (piculs)	Sugar (piculs)
1837	74,000	324	197
1838	329,500	2,879	195
1839	179,500	3,285	547
1840	223,250	1,634	1,942

Note: N/A= Not Available

Sources: John Anderson, *Mission to the East Coast of Sumatra in 1823* (London: Oxford University Press, 1971*b*), pp. 422–24; John Anderson, *Acheen and the Ports on the North and East Coasts of Sumatra* (London: Oxford University Press, 1971*a*), pp. 229, 238; *The Maulmain Chronicle* 1837–40; *The Singapore Free Press and Mercantile Advertiser*, 24 December 1835, p. 3.

HOKKIEN MERCHANTS IN PENANG

Among the Chinese mercantile community of the Penang-centred economic region, the Hokkiens formed an essential component. They were the descendants of the Hokkien speakers (or south Fujianese people), who had enjoyed long and close trading relations in Southeast Asia since at least the fifteenth century. Over time, many of them had settled and established themselves as a merchant-trading community in Southeast Asian ports like Melaka, Kedah, Batavia, Manila, and Saigon.² In the seventeenth and eighteenth centuries, these Hokkiens emerged as the undisputed leaders in seafaring enterprises (Ng 1983, p. 1).

They moved from one port to another within Southeast Asia, becoming active internal migrants within the region. Individuals and families from this restless Hokkien group were among the early migrants to Penang, forming the community of tradesmen and capitalists of the island. Among them we find some of the most important family names in Penang's future. Koh Lay Huan 辜礼欢, a merchant and a Kapitan Cina of Kuala Muda in Kedah, brought his relatives and friends from Kedah to Penang in 1786 (Wong 1963, p. 13). Lim It Kim 林乙金, a planter and merchant who married a daughter of a Thai local chieftain, probably moved from southern Siam to Penang in early 1800s (Wu 2003, p. 40). Cheah Yeam or Eam 谢掩, who was a fisherman and trader, first landed in Bangan Dalam in Kedah and then moved to Penang.³ Khoo Cheng Lim 邱清临, who came to Melaka to work as a pepper plantation labourer and then became a general trader, migrated to Penang in 1830s and married Koh Qin Yean, the granddaughter of Koh Lay Huan (Yeap 1976, pp. 9–10; Wong 1963, p. 14). Tan Gaik Tam 陈玉淡, a trader and miner who built his wealth from tin mining in Phuket, based his family in Penang (Teoh 1997, pp. 36–38). Khaw Soo Cheang 许泗章, who established himself as a trader in Bencoolen, left Sumatra for Penang in the early 1820s.

It is generally believed that the Chinese in Nanyang came from China and started from nothing. But the above-mentioned people migrated directly to Penang from the surrounding states instead of China, and they were established traders. The example of Khaw Soo Cheang is a case in point. According to accounts by the Khaw family and Prince Damrong, Soo Cheang had migrated from China to Penang where he rose from humble beginnings there. Damrong recorded that Soo Cheang worked as a labourer; the family members describe Soo Cheang starting off as a pedlar of fruits and vegetables (Cushman 1991, p. 10). These two similar accounts seem to have convinced many scholars, including Jennifer Cushman, of Soo Cheang's rags-to-riches life. However, Soo Cheang was no penniless migrant when he came to Penang: he was an established businessman who already commanded some business concerns and connections. In 1816, Soo Cheang had left Amoy for Bencoolen (now Bengkulu), a coastal town in West Sumatra under British influence from 1685 to 1824. He settled there as a trader. But when Bencoolen was exchanged for Melaka with the Dutch under the Anglo–Dutch Treaty of 1824, Soo Cheang was persuaded by William Thomas Lewis of the Bengal Civil Service and Resident Councilor of Penang to move to Penang.[4] Upon his arrival at Penang, Soo Cheang entered into a partnership with the firm Chop 'Bian Hong' and traded with the Siamese provinces on the West Coast, principally with Pungah. Through the Penang–Pungah (Phang Nga) trade connection, Soo Cheang came into contact with the Siamese business and political circles, and they later helped facilitate the building of Soo Cheang's business empire on the southwestern coast of Siam.

With their pre-existing local knowledge and sound business backgrounds, these Hokkien merchants and traders made up the core group of Penang's Chinese community. They were either the main members of, or related closely to, the Big Five families (the Khoo, the Cheah, the Lim, the Yeoh, and the Tan). Not only were they able to participate individually in various economic activities, but they also established themselves collectively as a leading economic force in Penang and the surrounding states. How was the cluster of the five families able to achieve such regional ascendancy? The rest of this chapter answers that question by providing an overview of their numerous business interests. We will begin with shipping.

SHIPPING AND THE BIG FIVE

We saw earlier that many local craft of various types plied the seas between Penang and regional destinations. It is no exaggeration to say that shipping was the lifeline of the Hokkien merchants who were engaged in seafaring activities for a few centuries. The Hokkien merchants brought their junks when they moved from other places to Penang. Prior to 1830, junks were primarily used by the Hokkien merchants in Penang to carry their trade goods in maritime trade. For example, Lee Toah 李獺 (Che Toah) and Lim Siong Pan 林嵩泮 (Che Siong or Seong) owned at least two junks — *Lam Hin* plied between Penang and west coast of Sumatra in the 1810s

(Lee 1995, pp. 244, 257); another 225-ton junk built in Pungah, sailed between Pungah, Penang and the west coast of Sumatra transporting rice, bird's nests, tin, piece goods, and opium in the 1820s.[5] After 1830, junks were slowly phased out and replaced with square-rigged vessels, which offered a much more secure voyage. The 1850s and 1860s witnessed a growing number of schooners, brigs, and barks acquired and operated by the Hokkien merchants. While it is hard to pinpoint the exact number of those vessels and craft owned by Hokkien merchants and traders, by gauging from the shipping intelligence published in two local newspapers — *Pinang Gazette and Straits Chronicle* and *The Penang Argus and Mercantile Advertiser*, we can say with confidence that the Hokkien merchants owned and operated a substantial number of schooner and square-rigged vessels. In 1869, for example, a list of eighty-one ships (barque, brig, and schooner) was published in *The Penang Argus and Mercantile Advertiser*, and there were fifty-one vessels owned by the Chinese, who were mostly Hokkiens of the Big Five families. The Khoos, the Lims, and the Cheahs controlled the largest number of vessels. In view of this fleet of ships, it is clear that the Hokkien merchants and traders of the Big Five families were the leading players in Penang's bustling maritime traffic in the mid-nineteenth century.

Moving to Penang did make the Big Five more prominent in business, especially in shipping and trade, the backbone of Penang's economy. For example, Khoo Beng San's company, called Beng & Co., had two vessels — the 350-ton barque, the *Angelica* and the 189-ton brig, the *Cassador*, sending Straits produce such as tin, rattans, fish maws, shark fins, bird's nests and spices to Macao and bringing back Chinese goods like tea, brassware, paper umbrellas, Chinaware and tobacco to Penang in the 1820s–30s.[6] Lim Thong's 191-ton brig, the *Sakee*, regularly plied between Penang, Aceh, Melaka and Singapore in 1838.[7] The cargoes, which were shipped to Aceh, included European cloth, Indian cotton piece goods, and China goods. In return, the brig brought back mainly pepper that was further shipped to Singapore, India or China. Khoo Sim Keok 邱心菊 and Cheah Chow Phan 谢昭盼 jointly owned the bark *Adelaide* carrying tin, rice and betel nut from Penang to China, then bringing China goods back to Penang and southern Burma in 1840s–50s;[8] Khoo Thean Teik owned a brig, the *Emma*, sailing between Penang, Moulmein, Aceh, Takuapa, and Singapore in 1850s–60s.[9] After bringing different goods from these places into Penang, Thean Teik redistributed them to surrounding destinations.

For instance, Takuapa tin and Moulmein rice were shipped to Singapore; in return, muskets and China goods were carried back to Penang for sale to Aceh and Moulmein[10] (see Diagram 2.1).

Later the Big Five and the Hokkien merchants of other families established some major shipping and trading enterprises. From 1860s to 1890s, they controlled at least ten shipping and trading companies in Penang (see Table 2.2).

DIAGRAM 2.1
Brig Emma's Shipping Voyages and Cargoes

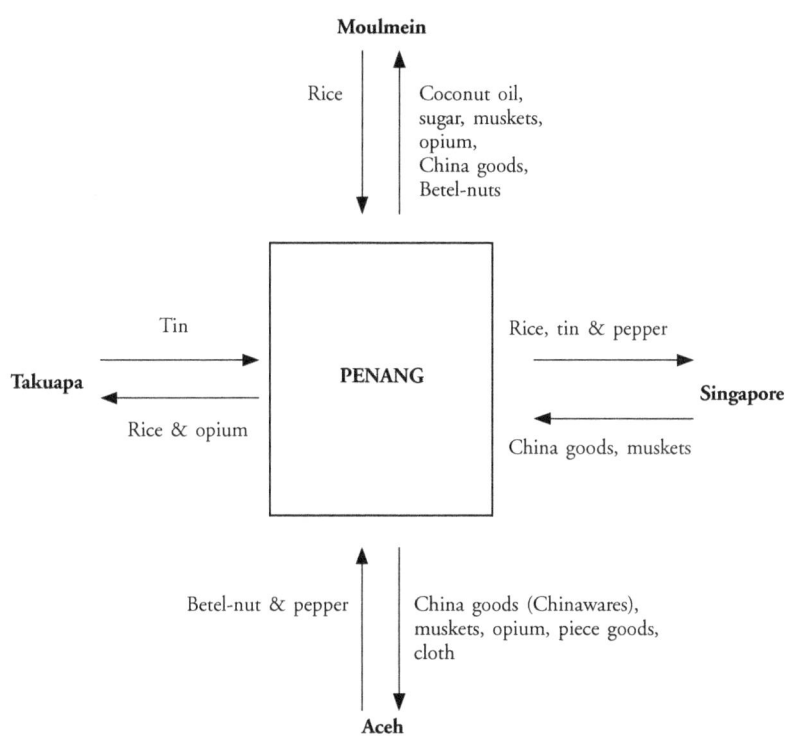

Source: Compiled from *Pinang Gazette and Straits Chronicle*, 30 April 1844, p. 3; 20 April 1850, p. 4; 29 June 1850, p. 4; 17 January 1852, p. 4; 14 February 17 July 1852, p. 3.

TABLE 2.2

Ten Major Hokkien-owned Shipping and Trading Companies in Penang, 1860s–90s

Name of Companies	Name of Partners
Kay Thye & Co.	Khoo Lek, Khoo Fwa Lam, Khoo Gek Hoo, Khoo Sek Gim, Khoo Kek Hai, Khoo Lim Taing, Khoo Chaing Kian, Khoo Chaing Tee, Khoo Bean Hio, Khoo Bean Tin, Khoo Bean Kheng, Koh Siang Tai, Koh Hay Neo, Lim Nee Neoh, and Ang Poh Beng
Ban Chin Hong &Co.	Ong Boon Kheng, Ong Loon Tek, Ong Beng Tek, Ong Sin Tek
Chong Moh & Co.	Khoo Hooah Tooi, Yeoh Cheng Kung, Cheah Chee Teong, Tan Swee Keat, Lim Teck Poh, Chuah Yu Kay, Lee Phee Yeow, Lee Phee Choon, Lee Un Hooi, Lee Kow Tooi, Goh Khuan Leang
Beng Brothers	Quah Beng Ky, Quah Beng Kung, Quah Beng Hoe, Quah Beng Kee
Koe Guan	Khaw Sim Kong, Khaw Sim Khim, Khaw Sim Tek
Hock Moh & Co.	Lim Eow Hong, Lee Haay Thye, Lee Teng See
Hock Chong & Co.	Lim Chong Seow, Lim Chong Thae, Lee Teng See
Khoo Oon Keong	Khoo Oon Keong
Leng Cheak & Co.	Lim Leng Cheak, Lim Pee Cheak, Lim Eow Hong, Lim Eow Thoon
Kong Hok Keok	Cheah Tek Soon & Chuah Yu Khay

Sources: *Pinang Gazette and Straits Chronicle*, 16 December 1879, p. 5; 30 December 1879, p. 3; 6 April 1886, p. 3; 28 June 1889, p. 6; 14 February 1890, p. 6; 1 October 1891, p. 7; *The Penang Directory for the year 1874 including that of Deli*, pp. 32–33; *The Penang Almanack and Directory for 1876*, pp. 30–33.

The Chong Moh & Co. 崇茂号, for example, was established by the merchants of the Big Five, the Lee family, the Chuah family, and the Goh family in the 1860s. It first operated four to five brigs and barques and later started to acquire steamships. By 1890, it emerged as the largest ship-owner and importer in Penang[11] and owned eight steamers, constantly plying between Penang, Singapore, Phuket, Rangoon, Deli, Aceh, Perak, Kedah, Calcutta, and China. It shipped coolies, China goods, Straits produce, and European and Indian merchandise in and out of Penang. Using Penang as a base, the company handled large transhipment trades in the region. In total, the merchants of the Big Five owned at least thirty steamers in this period of time. With such large fleet of ships, they succeeded in establishing criss-cross shipping and navigation pattern in the Melaka Straits, Eastern Indian Ocean, and South China Sea and gaining control of the major sea lanes in the region.

The Hokkien-owned vessels were thus not only involved in short and medium distance shipping, but also in the long distance trade. The shipping routes and navigation patterns of the Penang Hokkien vessels wove an extensive network which connected Penang to the surrounding maritime states as well as to China and India. The Big Five's transnational and transregional shipping patterns and trade were crucial in integrating Penang into the larger shipping and trading world and hence in maintaining Penang's position as a regional entrepot.

ENTREPOT TRADE AND THE BIG FIVE

Trade in Straits products, European manufactures, and Indian and China goods was one of the most lucrative businesses for the Penang Hokkiens and played a significant part in building up the wealth of the Penang Hokkien merchants and traders. The criss-cross voyages and the shipment of diverse cargoes did not occur without an underlying economic rationale. It all operated on the basis of cost advantage. With their vessels reaching different states, the Hokkien merchants were able to source tradable commodities at low prices from one place and then dispose of them at another place for higher prices; by shipping and trading a variety of cargoes, they made profits from different commodities instead of only from one. To secure the necessary large supply of popular and profitable commodities at low prices, many of the Hokkien merchants were also actively involved in financing and operating the agricultural and mining enterprises, which we will turn to later.

To show how the Big Five's profitable commercial dealings operated we can examine a list of trade goods — tin, rice, coconut, sugar, pepper, and opium, that flowed in and out of Penang. As the major imports and exports handled by the Big Five, they dominated the intra-regional and inter-regional trade. The economic value of these commodities was important in both the regional and international markets, allowing the Big Five to make tremendous profits by trading them regionally and internationally. In fact it is no exaggeration to say that the wealth of the Big Five and Penang's prosperity depended directly on these valuable commodities.

TIN AND THE BIG FIVE

To understand the importance of the Big Five in the tin mining business, it is important to have an overview of the tin import and export of Penang and Singapore between 1870 and 1910.

As shown Table 2.3, the amount of tin imported into Penang was always greater than Singapore, while the amount of tin export from Penang was competing closely with Singapore. The large import of tin to Penang was due to the increasing production of the tin mines in Perak

TABLE 2.3

Percentage Distribution of Trade in Tin between Singapore and Penang, 1870–1910

Year	Import of Tin		Export of Tin	
	Singapore	Penang	Singapore	Penang
1870	6.15	73.70	47.23	52.77
1875	6.15	71.18	40.89	59.11
1880	4.24	71.72	54.60	45.40
1885	15.31	69.79	33.16	66.84
1890	29.13	69.89	59.82	40.18
1895	31.57	68.43	62.00	38.00
1900	19.68	80.32	56.76	43.24
1905	39.55	60.45	48.00	52.00
1910	30.72	69.28	45.93	54.07

Source: Chiang Hai Ding, *A History of Straits Settlements Foreign Trade 1870–1915* (Singapore: National Museum, 1978), p. 188.

and Phuket from the late 1860s. Large quantities of tin from these two states flowed into Penang from 1868 to the late 1890s. On the other hand, Singapore's tin imports became more or less stagnant after 1850, mainly because the tin mines in Pahang, its main tin supplier, were neglected by the Straits capitalists for various reasons (Wong 1965, p. 31). To compensate, Singapore began to import tin from Penang in the 1860s. By 1890, the tin imported into Singapore took up 34.3 per cent of the total value of Penang's merchandise trade, making Singapore the largest customer for Penang tin (Pongsupath 1990, p. 60). In other words, Singapore re-exported Penang tin. Perak and Phuket, these two tin-rich states, transformed Penang into a port whose tin exports surpassed those of Singapore during the 1860s to 1890s.

The prominent Hokkien merchants and capitalists of the Big Five were the most dynamic force in this vibrant tin production and trade. Tin mining activities had been carried out in Phuket, Trang, and Pangha for centuries. Tan Gaik Tam or Tan Tam of the Tan family, an established merchant who migrated to Penang in the late eighteenth century, extended his business tentacles to Phuket in the early 1820s (Wang 1965, p. 29). With financial help from a Siamese tax officer called Naiyit, Tan Tam and his associate, Yong Ching Siew, expanded their business by establishing Hup Hin Kongsi, a tin mining and trading company in 1828.[12] During the 1850s–60s, Tan Tam's tin mining and trading business reached its peak. He ultimately owned 320 hectares of tin mining lands and obtained exclusive export rights in Phuket tin (Beattie 2003, p. 3). Besides the Tan family, there were also other prominent families, such as the Yeoh, the Lim, the Cheah, and the Ong, who also had enormous interests in the tin industry. The Yeo family owned five mining companies and employed about 700 coolies (Songprasert 1986, pp. 109–10). With the extensive involvement of the Big Five in tin mining activities, the average output of tin ore in Phuket reached 5,000 tons (84,000 piculs) per year in the 1880s, as compared to earlier period of 500 tons (Songprasert 1986, p. 90; Hamilton 1815, pp. 458–59).

Perak, a western Malay state, was another rich tin producing place for the Big Five families. To tap the mineral riches of this area, the Big Five collaborated with Che Ngah Ibrahim, an influential local Malay ruler, and Chung Keng Kwee, a Hakka mine owner and leader of the powerful Hai San, a Hakka *hui*. Chung Keng Kwee controlled 15,000 coolies and most of the tin mines in Larut, providing financial support for their mining activities (Khoo 1972, p. 209; Wong 1963, pp. 77, 78, 104). In one case,

Khoo Thean Teik and Koh Seang Thye supplied a sum of $60,000 Spanish dollars in goods, money and ammunition to Chung Keng Kwee and Tan Yit Hoon for their mining activities and for their violent actions against the arch-rival Ghee Hin, a Cantonese-dominated *hui*.[13] In return, Chung Keng Kwee and Tan Yit Hoon needed to repay the two creditors with 70 per cent of the tin produced by them at their mines.[14]

Capital invested by the Big Five and certain Siamese (in the case of Phuket) played the most important role in developing the tin mining business in the Siamese and Malay states, especially before the 1880s. The trading company involved, the Chop Chip Hock, was owned by members of the Khoo, Tan, Cheah, and Lim families. By late 1890s, they had made a loan of $135,000 to the tin miners and traders in Tongkah, Trang, Krabi, and Tavoy. Phraya Wichitsongkhram, the Governor of Phuket was also a keen financer. He managed state funds of up to 160,000 baht ($96,000) per year for the tin mining operations in Phuket (Songprasert 1986, p. 92). English and Armenian capital was also indispensable in financing those tin mining ventures. As John Drabble recognized, the English mainly invested in trade before the 1860s to 1870s, but their indirect funding for mining was considerable (Drabble 2000, p. 55). For instance, Captain Weber, a rich English merchant in Penang, provided $40,000 to Lim Teo Jong to open tin mines in Phuket (Songprasert 1986, p. 134). Michael Arratoon Anthony and Joseph Manook Anthony, two rich Armenian brothers in Penang, were close mining partners of the Cheah family of Penang. All together they became the partners of the mining companies in Perak during 1860s–90s.[15] With the involvement of the English and Armenians investors, it is clear that the capital of the Big Five invested in the mining operation was a mixed rather than purely Chinese or Siamese capital.

The ships or junks that berthed at the harbour or sailed up the rivers would take the tin mined in those states to Penang. Khoo Teong Poh had two steamers, the *Betsy* and the *Petrel*, to ship tin from Phuket, and the steamer *Hanoi* to carry tin from Perak; Cheah Chen Eok always chartered the steamer *Sri Sarawak* to convey tin from Perak.[16] Most of the tin was sold by the tin distribution agencies (which were mainly controlled by the Big Five) (see Image 1 in photo inserts) and their associates to the United Kingdom, the United States, Singapore, Calcutta, Hong Kong, and Amoy. From 1860 to 1869, for example, Penang exported about 350,000 piculs and 107,000 piculs of tin to Great Britain and the United States of America respectively.[17] The extraordinarily active involvement of the Big Five in the tin industry had transformed Penang into the most important tin-trading port in Southeast Asia.

RICE FROM SOUTHERN BURMA AND THE BIG FIVE

The rice that frequently appeared on the list of the imports and exports of Penang from 1850s to 1900s was brought from southern Burma. The rice cultivated in Penang itself was never sufficient to feed its growing population. Kedah, its immediate hinterland, became Penang's main supplier of rice. When rice from Kedah became scarce in Penang due to the political disturbances of 1838–39 in Kedah, the Hokkien merchants imported an abundance of Tavoy and Moulmein rice, which was obtained at Rs 26–30 (Sp $13–15) per coyan, into Penang.[18] This rice was then sold at Sp $40–48 per coyan, making it costlier than the Kedah rice. In 1839 alone, there were about 700 coyans and 560 coyans of rice shipped from Tavoy and Moulmein to Penang respectively.[19] In the 1860s, the main source of rice supplies for Penang began to shift to Rangoon. The vast, flat, Irrawaddy–Sittang delta plains, which came under British rule in 1852, was turned into a rice-producing powerhouse. The area under rice cultivation in lower Burma expanded three-fold: from 402,000 hectares in 1855 to 1,255,000 hectares in 1880 (Brown 2005, p. 2). Penang imported rice from lower Burma through Rangoon since at least 1855. It was not until the 1860s that the inflow of voluminous quantity of Burmese rice into Penang began. The import rose from 93,929 pikuls in 1868 to 2,538,129 pikuls in 1890,[20] a twenty-seven fold increase. In this regard, Burma became undoubtedly the largest rice supplier of Penang for the second half of the nineteenth century.

The imported Burmese rice was mainly re-exported. The top five market destinations were Melaka, Singapore, western Malay states, Sumatra, and western Siamese states. It is clear that the surrounding states were the major market for the Burmese rice exported from Penang. The great demand for rice in those surrounding states was due to the unprecedented influx of coolies. In the period of 1879–90, 549,084 Chinese coolies were imported into Penang, with most of them then redistributed to Perak, Deli and Phuket, when the labour intense tin mining and tobacco planting were in operation. It is interesting to note that although Phuket and Trang, the two main southwestern Siamese rice markets, are on the way between Burma and Penang, rice was always shipped from Burma to Penang first, before it was re-shipped from Penang up to Phuket and Trang.

North Sumatra was another good market for the rice of southern Burma. During the Dutch blockade along the coast of Sumatra in the mid-1870s, top quality Rangoon rice exported from Penang, could fetch over $100 per coyan while its market price in Penang ranged $90–$92 (Tagliacozzo 2005, p. 329). In his petition to the British in Penang on December 1879, Lim Leng Cheak, a prominent merchant of the Lim family, complained that the Dutch blockade had caused him to lose a profit of $10,000, which he could have made from the cargo of $3,000 worth of rice bound for the northern coast of Sumatra.[21] The Big Five partnering the merchants of the Lee families established Chong Moh & Co., the largest shipping and trading firm, controlled two-thirds of the rice import of Penang.[22] Despite Burma's rice business being predominantly managed by the Indian merchants and with rice being mainly shipped in other directions, the Big Five still carved out a portion of Burma's rice to southwestern Siamese states, North Sumatra, China, and Singapore.

Although these Penang Hokkien merchants did not own any paddy fields in southern Burma, they managed to form partnerships with the local merchants (Indian, English, Burmese, and Hokkien or Cantonese), who were rice brokers or financiers with direct connections with growers, to secure the supply of cheap paddy. For example, Khoo Jeow, an established trader in Penang, moved to Rangoon in 1869 in order to expand his business. He went into partnership with a Cantonese and took the lease of an opium farm, which lasted for twenty-one years (Wright, Cartwright and Breakspear 1910, p. 317). Later, he started rice trading and milling business with Khoo Kin, a local Hokkien rice broker and financier, under the name of Sin Joo Hin & Co., and generated an even greater fortune.[23] Rice mills were in fact an essential part of the Big Five rice trade network since they sourced and processed paddy from the farms and stored rice for export. Khoo Jew was just one of the many examples of the Penang Hokkiens that successfully gained a foothold in the Burmese rice trading and milling business.

COCONUT AND SUGAR AND THE BIG FIVE

Unlike rice, coconut oil and brown sugar were produced by the Big Five from crops grown in their own fields. In the 1830s, James Low noted that

TABLE 2.4
Coconut Estates of the Big Five and Their Associates

Name of Proprietor	Name of Estates
Khoo Thean Teik	Pyah Troobong (200 acres)
Khoo Chow Sew	Tanjong Tokong (130 acres)
Lim Kong Wah & Khoo Seck Chuan	Yew Hua
Khoo Eu Bee	Eu Bee
Cheah Chen Eok	Cham Boey Kong
Tan Kay Beng & Chew Koe Lip	Kean Ann (200 acres)
Oh Ean Heng	Scotland (400 acres)
Oh Chong Leng	Erskins (50 acres)
Koh Teng Choon	Pula Betong (600 acres) Teng Choon (400 acres)
Foo Tye Sin	Cannter Hall (130 acres) Ansondale (315 acres)
Koh Sin (Seang) Tat	Ayer Etam (225 acres) Edinburgh (400 acres)
Koh Teng Gwan	Bali Pulo (200 acres) Batu Lanchang (60 acres)
Yap Hap Keat	(50 acres)

Sources: *The Penang Directory for the year 1874 including that of Deli*, pp. 45–46; *The Penang Almanack and Directory for 1876*, p. 41; 张少宽 [Teoh Shiaw Kuan], 槟榔屿华人史话 *Binlangyu Huaren Shihua* [Historical Anecdotes of the Chinese in Penang] (Kuala Lumpur: Prometheus Enterprise Sdn. Bhd. 光燧人氏事业有限公司, 2002), pp. 246–47.

there were 50,000 coconut trees (about 6,000 to 7,000 acres) in Penang (Low 1972, pp. 44, 49; Newbold 1971, pp. 69, 103). By 1874, the cultivated area of coconut had increased to 17,000 acres[24] and most of these estates were owned by the Big Five and their associates. Table 2.4 shows some of the estate proprietors in Penang:

Besides Penang, the Big Five also held vast coconut estates in Kedah and Province Wellesley. Along with the coconut estates, the Big Five operated most of the oil mills, such as Khie Heng Bee Mill, one of the largest oil mills in northern Malaya (Wright and Cartwright 1908, pp. 824–28). This oil mill could produce one hundred piculs of oil in a working day of twelve hours (Wright and Cartwright 1908, p. 824). The high demand from Moulmein, Pungah, Tenasserim coast, Melaka, and Singapore chiefly drove such large-scale planting of this crop. From 1844–53, Penang exported about 4,352 piculs of coconut oil to Pungah; 1,300 piculs to Moulmein; and 3,048 piculs to Singapore and Melaka.[25] In terms of coconut fruit, Penang exported 88,600 to Pegu, 133,100 to Arracan, and 287,958 to Moulmein in the period of 1848–50.[26] According to James Low, coconut planting could afford ample remuneration to the planter in Penang. He estimated that a 100 orlong (or a 132 acre) coconut estate could annually produce 400,000 nuts which would generate an income of $4,000–$8,000 (Low 1972, p. 47). Given this, Khoo Thean Teik, for example, who owned about 200 acres of coconut estates, might have earned about $8,000–$16,000 annually. With their vast coconut estates, the Big Five monopolized the supply of coconut oil and fruits to the surrounding states.

Sugar was another profitable agricultural crop. The cultivated area of sugar, which was concentrated mainly in Province Wellesley, had increased from 900 acres in the 1830s to 10,000 acres by 1860 (Khoo 1972, p. 93). Although the amount of investment by the Big Five families in sugar estates is unknown, some family members had clearly built up their wealth on sugar. For example, Khoo Guek Chio, one of the founding members of Khoo Kongsi in 1835, possessed some sugar cane lands and engaged in the manufacturing of sugar in Bukit Tambun and Batu Kawan in Province Wellesley;[27] Cheah Eam, an established merchant who was one of the founders of Cheah Kongsi in 1820 and a good friend of the Sultan of Kedah, owned some estates in Province Wellesley;[28] Lee Ghe Ang, who owned a vast piece of land of 1,304 acres in Province Wellesley, had about 500 acres of land cultivated with sugar by 1861. The export of sugar from Penang had increased about seven-fold, from 9,713 piculs in 1837–38 to 70,945 piculs in 1855. From 1844 to 1853, sugar from Penang to Moulmein and Great Britain registered at about 11,796 piculs and 141,016 piculs respectively.[29] James Low estimated that in the mid-1830s, 100 orlongs or about 132 acres of sugar estate could yield about $3,770 in a year, after the expenses had been deducted (Low 1972, pp. 56–57). With his sugar estate alone, Lee Ghe Ang could thus have generated an annual income of about $16,000. Of course from the 1860s to the 1880s, his earnings soared when the export of sugar in Penang skyrocketed because of the growing demand for sugar in Hong Kong and Great Britain.[30]

PEPPER AND THE BIG FIVE

It is impossible to leave pepper off the list when we come to examine the major cash-crop cargos in Penang's entrepot trade. As pepper was the most valuable of the Sumatran imports into Penang, it contributed crucially to the port's prosperity and to the build-up of wealth of the mercantile elite of the Big Five. Aceh and Deli were the main exporters of pepper to Penang since the early nineteenth century (Reid 1969, pp. 14–15; Cummings 1994, pp. 98–99). In 1849–50, Penang imported 46,199 piculs of pepper from these two places. This quantity constituted about 80 per cent of the total pepper exported from Penang in the same period of time. It is clear that Penang was the main transhipment centre for the pepper of Aceh and Deli, most of which was re-exported to the adjacent states (Singapore, Aracan, and Rangoon) or India, Great Britain, and America (see Table 2.5).

From 1870s to 1890s, Sumatra continued to be the major exporter of pepper to Penang and the volume averaged 120,000–140,000 pikuls a year. Despite being separated by the Melaka Straits, the traders and merchants

TABLE 2.5
Import of Pepper from Sumatra (Aceh & Deli) and Export of Pepper from Penang (in piculs)

Years	Import from Sumatra	Export from Penang
1844–45	39,539	35,650
1845–46	39,403	39,978
1847–48	36,204	37,536
1848–49	24,709	25,773
1849–50	46,191	56,519
1852–53	30,384	25,108

Source: Tabular Statements of the Commerce and Shipping of Prince of Wales Island, Singapore and Malacca for the official year 1844–45, 1845–46, 1847–48, 1848–49, 1849–50, and 1852–53 (Calcutta: Military Orphan Press, various years).

of Penang's Big Five families became a vital part of the Aceh–Deli–Penang pepper business. Not only did they dominate the shipping and trading activities, they were also deeply involved in the production. In 1852 alone, there were at least fifteen square-rigged vessels[31] owned by these Hokkiens that frequented the west coast of Aceh and Deli and brought large quantities of pepper back to Penang. The leading merchants of the Lim family had eight vessels that sailed between Aceh and Penang and dealt in pepper. Lim Chee Boo's 227-ton brig the *Mariners' Hope* and 162-ton brig the *Hero*, for example, shipped 13,200 piculs of pepper from the west coast of Aceh to Penang in 1863.[32] Khoo Kong Mah of the Khoo family, who had some financial support from the German firm, partnered Ban Seng & Co., a Singapore-based firm, and operated a few junks carrying pepper from Achee to Penang in the 1870s.[33] Unlike the Chinese pepper planting in Siamese Chantaburi or Sumatran Bangka and Riau, the pepper planters of Aceh and Deli were local Acehnese and Batak people. By providing capital support to the Sultans, Syahbandars or Orang Kaya, the Hokkien merchants formed alliances with Acehnese or Batak chiefs who in turn enjoyed close connections with native pepper planters. Because of such connections the Sultan of Deli, an ally of the Batak chiefs, was able to make a huge advance of $30,000–$40,000 a year to the Batak people for clearing, planting and harvesting pepper gardens.[34] In return the Batak pepper planters sold the pepper at the fixed rate of approximately $3–$5 per picul.[35] Thanks to such an arrangement, the Penang Hokkiens secured a cheap supply of Acehnese and Deli pepper, which could be resold at $4–$12 per picul (for black pepper) and $7–$24 per picul (for white pepper) in the Penang market.[36] In this way, the Hokkien merchants of the Big Five cornered the pepper market in Aceh and Deli and channelled the supplies to Penang for higher prices. They acquired great wealth through this very profitable pepper trade.

One of the most prominent of these Hokkien traders was Khoo Thean Poh. Khoo was actively involved in the pepper trade, particularly along the western coast of Aceh in the 1860s. Together with Khoo Kay Chan, Lim Pet Lean, and Lim Tit, he formed a company that operated seven sailing vessels.[37] Khoo settled in Meulaboh for a few years and became acquainted with Teuku Imam Muda, the raja of Tenom and Teuku Yit, a prominent Acehnese trader. He provided loans to Teuku Imam to plant pepper. Besides, he also had his daughter married to Syed Mohemed Al-Atas, a wealthy Acehnese merchant of Arab descent based in Penang. Through such relations with the Acehnese, Khoo gained a monopoly on the pepper trade which the Europeans found difficult to break. The Katz Brothers, a German trading firm, tried to obtain pepper by offering higher price to Teuku Imam Muda in 1883. But the Acehnese chief turned it down. Eventually, the German firm was forced to enter into a joint venture with Khoo in order to obtain pepper.

OPIUM AND THE BIG FIVE

Opium was one of the essential items making up the shipping cargoes traded by the merchants of the Big Five families since the early nineteenth century. Penang was both a depot for the opium imported by the British from India as well as a centre for opium distribution to China and the surrounding states. The British merchants were the main importers of Indian opium into Penang, but the dissemination of this Indian opium to surrounding states was primarily in the hands of the Hokkien merchants of the Big Five. From 1844 to 1850, there were about 2,314 chests of opium imported annually into Penang from Calcutta and Bombay and about 2,112 chests were re-exported to Aceh, Moulmein, Pungah, Kedah, and Deli.[38] The native chiefs or lords and labourers were the main users of this opium (Trocki 1990, p. 55). Although the opium market of those surrounding states in the first half of the nineenth century was relatively small, the sale of opium proved to be profitable for the Hokkien merchants.[39]

With the growing presence of tin mining and plantation coolies in those states from the 1860s onwards, the economic value of opium became more significant. To establish a firm control over the opium business, the Big Five became deeply involved in opium revenue farming. Revenue farming was fiscal device whereby the state auctioned to private interests some of its sovereign rights in revenue raising. Where opium was concerned it allowed a private company to hold the monopoly on the distribution and sale of consumable opium for a fixed period in return for a rent paid to the government.[40] The opium revenue farm was often auctioned off to the highest bidder. If opium was a luxury for high ranking locals, it was a necessity for thousands of hardworking coolies in the interior especially. This massive number of consumers turned opium into a lucrative bulk commodity. Gaining a monopoly of opium production and distribution would mean having the exclusive right to deal in this valuable item, which made it easy to control coolies and promised to generate a high level of cash flow and thus create large pools of capital.[41] With more capital and coolies in hand, the Big Five would be able to open larger mines or plantations and employ more coolies, who in turn would consume more opium and provisions, whereupon the cycle would start again. Control of opium was thus undoubtedly the principal driving force behind a string of economic operations. Because of this, the competition for the opium revenue farms in the region was the most cut-throat business, so the

Big Five always organized themselves into syndicates that aimed to secure the farms of Penang and other states as well.

By this means, the Big Five was able to pool bigger capital from the merchants of the other prominent Hokkien families, such as the Gan, the Khaw, the Ong, the Koh, and the Lee, and of the Hakka and the Cantonese families and gained firm control of the opium revenue farm in Penang for much of the second half of the nineteenth century and for the first decade of the twentieth century. The Penang opium revenue farm, which was introduced by the British in 1791, became the most profitable and capital-intensive enterprise in the Big Five's business empire from 1860 onwards. This can be gauged from the progressive increase of the annual rental from 1860 to 1909, as shown in Table 2.6. More importantly, the annual rental of Penang's opium revenue farm constituted almost half of Penang's annual state revenue (see Table 2.7).

TABLE 2.6
The Annual Rental Rates of Penang Opium Farm 1860–1909

Farm Term (Years)	Annual Rental ($)
1860–62	72,120
1862–65	78,000
1865–67	78,600
1867–68	94,200
1868–70	90,000
1871–73	137,610
1874–76	230,350
1877–79	257,590
1880–82	440,640
1883–85	480,000
1886–88	600,000
1889–91	743,923
1892–94	852,000
1895–97	600,000
1898–1900	720,000
1901–3	1,140,000
1904–6	2,124,000
1907–9	1,620,000

Sources: Lena Cheng U Wen, "British Opium Policy in the Straits Settlements 1867–1910", Academic Exercise, University of Malaya, Singapore, 1960, pp. 80–84; *Straits Settlements Legislative Council Proceedings*, 21 April 1869.

TABLE 2.7
Penang's Opium Revenue Farm Annual Rent as a Percentage of Total Revenue of Penang, 1876–1900

Year	Rent ($)	Total Revenue ($)	Percentage (%)
1876	230,350	486,424	47.4
1877	257,590	616,392	42.0
1880	440,640	902,876	48.8
1883	480,000	982,595	48.8
1886	600,000	1,216,688	49.3
1889	743,923	1,643,714	45.3
1892	852,000	1,304,230	65.3
1895	600,000	1,418,511	42.3
1900	720,000	1,736,214	41.5

Source: Robert L. Jarman, *Annual Reports of the Straits Settlements* (Slough: Archive Editors Ltd., 1998), vol. 2 1868–83, pp. 158, 183, 215, 260, 289, 413–414, 463, 585; vol. 3 1884–91, pp. 54, 97, 206, 263, 341, 512, 539, 615; vol. 4 1892–1900, pp. 7, 83, 153, 215, 265, 321, 383, 467, 545.

The Penang farm was an important base for the Big Five to obtain the supply of opium from India to sell to the large local Chinese coolie population. More importantly, it served as a mechanism for the Big Five to build their capital and extend their investment arm to secure other opium monopolies in the surrounding states and beyond. Forming an alliance with Chung Keng Kwee, the Hakka *Kapitan* of Perak, the Big Five spent more than $2.8 million to dominate all the revenue farms spreading from upper Perak to lower Perak for seventeen years, from 1880 to 1897.[42] In Kedah, Lim Leng Cheak, a leading merchant of the Lim family, together with his Penang associates and the Cantonese *Kapitan* of Kedah, successfully controlled the most profitable opium farm in Kulim, the most important Chinese town in Kedah for six years, from 1886 to 1891 (Wu 2003, pp. 43–44). In the mid-1890s, the Big Five led by Lim Kek Chuan of the Lim family and a few prominent Hakkas, grouped under the Penang opium syndicate, formed an alliance with Kedah's Hokkien Choong family, a close friend of the Sultan of Kedah, and pumped in about $1.4 million to hold the lease of all the Kedah opium farms for fifteen years, from 1895 to 1909 (Wu 2003, pp. 87–89). In 1899, this Penang opium syndicate formed a partnership with Puck Chung, a Cantonese merchant of Rangoon, and paid Rs 480,000 ($240,000) to gain control of the Rangoon opium licence for three years.[43]

By forming a close alliance with the local Siamese rulers, the Big Five families were able to gain control of most of the opium monopolies in the southern Siamese provinces for decades. For example, the Tans (Tan Tam, Tan Chuan, and Tan Kae Yee) collaborated with Phraya Wichitsongkhram (1853–78), the governor of Phuket, to monopolize the wholesale and retail trade of opium on the island (Songprasert 1986, p. 117). Cheah Peck Yee, a leader of Cheah Kongsi[44] in Penang, who went to trade in Krabi in 1861 or 1862, was appointed by the governor of Nakhon Si Thammarat in 1866 to manage all tax farms in Krabi;[45] Khoo Bun Kiad, a wealthy merchant and a creditor of the Raja Satun, had a monopoly of the revenue farms in Satun until 1890 (Songprasert 1986, p. 63–64).

Turning to Sumatra, the Big Five's interests in revenue farming on the East Coast were already established before the Dutch extended their influence to this area in 1858–65. This was particularly the case in Asahan, where import and export duties, as well as the opium and gambling monopolies, had been entrusted to Ong Boon Keng, a Penang merchant and close associate of the Big Five (Reid 2005, p. 196). He was the partner of Khoo Kay Chan in the firm of Ching Hong in Penang.[46] He also headed the Penang Opium Farm of 1850s–70s in which Khoo Thean Teik, Lee Toh, Lee Kee and Ong Boon Eng were partners.[47] In the 1880s and 1890s, the Big Five also gained control of the opium farm in Deli.[48] Around the turn of the century, leading members of the Big Five cooperated with prominent Hakka figures of Medan like Tjong Jong Hian (Chang Yu Nan 張煜南), the Lieutenant of Chinese, and Tjong A Fee (Chang Hung Nan 張鴻南), the Chinese Captain, to obtain the opium monopoly for the entire region of Sumatra's east coasts in 1908–10 (Buiskool 2003, p. 3).

The Big Five did not confine their opium farming interests to the adjacent states of Penang; they also extended their control to Singapore, Johor, and even across the South China Sea to North Borneo (Sabah), Sarawak, and Hong Kong. Grouped under the Penang Opium-farming Syndicate, the Big Five, first led by Koh Seang Tat in 1879, and then by Chiu Sin Yong in 1883, by Gan Ngoh Bee in 1895, by Khoo Hun Yeang in 1901, by Khaw Joo Choe in 1907, took control of the Singapore and Johor opium farm for twenty-one years (Cheng 1960, pp. 85–86). At the same time, the Penang Opium-farming Syndicate went to Hong Kong and succeeded in gaining control of the Hong Kong opium farm for two terms, 1880–82 and 1889–91.[49] Under the leadership of Khoo Hun Yeang in 1901, the Penang Opium-farming Syndicate moved to North Borneo and Sarawak and dominated the opium farms there for several years from 1901 to 1906.[50] In view of this extensive involvement of the Big Five and their associates in the opium revenue farming of different states, it is clear that the ambitious Big Five aimed to control not only one or two but a ring of opium monopolies that could generate larger and faster capital accumulation. For example, Ban Cheng Bee syndicate which was formed in 1895, successfully gained control of Penang's opium revenue farm for the period of 1895–97 and made a profit of $700,000. Another syndicate, Ban Cheng Bee, made a profit of $1.9 million by controlling the Singapore opium revenue farm for three years.[51]

COOLIE TRADE: ANOTHER ARM OF THE BIG FIVE

As tin mining was labour intensive, a large number of coolies were recruited for Phuket and Perak. By the 1880s, Phuket had a workforce of 50,000 coolies (Songprasert 1986, p. 90; Brown 1988, p. 96). Since the members of the Tan, the Yeoh, the Lim, and the Ong families owned most of the tin mines in Phuket, they employed at least two-thirds of the coolies. With the discovery of rich tin deposit at Klian Pauh in 1848, Larut in Perak instantly became a magnet for thousands of Chinese coolies (Khoo 1972, p. 69; Wong 1965, p. 26). By 1862, the Chinese population in Larut stood at about 20,000 to 25,000 men; in the next ten years, the population increased to about 30,000 to 40,000 (Wong 1965, p. 27). The cultivation of cash crops also put a heavy demand on the coolie trade. By the 1860, there were about 8,000 coolies in the estates of Province Wellesley; by 1894, Perak had an estate coolie force of 7,500 (Purcell 1948, p. x; Lim 1976, p. 104). The largest coolie force, however, was to be found in the labour-intensive tobacco plantations of East Coast of Sumatra. By 1890, the number of Chinese coolies in the East Coast of Sumatra had reached 53,806 (Reid 2005, p. 223).

The presence of such a colossal number of coolies in the region clearly reflected the unprecedented expansion of cash-crop planting and tin mining activities, both stimulated by the spiralling demand for primary products in the industrial West. By the 1860s, the explosion of export-oriented agricultural and mining undertakings caused an acute labour shortage in the local area. As a result, the coolie trade became not only the main channel to provide the labour supply but also a very profitable business. By establishing a close-knit network of sourcing, transporting, and distributing coolies between Penang, Hong Kong, Swatow, and Amoy, the mercantile elite of the Big Five families were able to transform Penang into a major Chinese labour distribution centre and to monopolize the coolie trade at the northern end of the Straits of Melaka.

The coolie depots of Penang, the coolie *hongs* (recruitment centres) of Hong Kong, Swatow and Amoy, and a fleet of vessels constituted the essential mechanism of the coolie trade network that centred on Penang. Interestingly, all this was controlled by a handful of merchants of the Big Five and their associates. For example, Khoo Joo Chian, who was a depot keeper and coolie broker, operated a coolie depot, Chop Ban Tek Heng in Penang, and had two agents at Swatow, Chop Seng Huat and Hok Khi, to recruit coolies.[52] To transport the coolies from Swatow to Penang, he could commission his relative, Khoo Teong Poh, a steamship-owner, the shipping agent, Lim Yam Seng & Co. and a commission agent, Hock Cheong Yeung Hong, at Swatow to handle the traffic.[53] The biggest coolie depot was owned by Khoo Thean Teik, who had a virtual monopoly over the disposition of indebted coolies (Reid 2005, p. 203). His coolie depot, Chop Khun Ho, the largest in Penang, received coolies shipped by his fellow clansman, Khoo Teong Poh, from the coolie agents, Hock Cheong Chan at Amoy, or Tek Ge Hong at Swatow.[54] In the period of 1879–90, 549,084 coolies were imported into Penang, with most of them then redistributed to the surrounding states. Perak, Deli and Phuket received about 80 per cent of the coolies from Penang. Since the Big Five and their associates commanded the coolie trade network, it is no exaggeration to say that they were in charge of this massive flow of coolies in and out of Penang.

The trade in coolies was no different from the trade in other commodities. As a tradable "commodity", coolies were always intended to be disposed of at the place where highest prices could be made. Not all the coolies were sold at the same price, although they were recruited from China at the same cost of $17–$20 per head.[55] The market demand and the dialect-group background were the main determinants of price. Planters in Deli, Kedah, and Province Wellesley, for example, were willing to pay $70–$80 for a Teochew coolie but only $40–$50 for a Hakka during 1860s and 1870s.[56] With the increasing demand for plantation labour in the 1880s, the price of the Teochew coolies, who were regarded as the best agriculturalists, and of Hakka coolies could climb to $125–$140 and $70–$80 per head respectively.[57] This was particularly the case in Deli where the rapid expansion of tobacco estates was taking place during the mid-1880s. In order to gain maximum profit, the coolie brokers in Penang tried every means, including forcible abduction, to bring as many Teochew and Hakka coolies as possible to Deli.

Such acts of profiteering consequently caused a severe shortage of coolie supply in Perak and Province Wellesley. In 1887, the shortage of labour arising from the competition of the Dutch planters in Sumatra led the principle Perak miners to propose a scheme for importing coolies directly from Swatow and Hong Kong, under the joint supervision of British and Chinese authorities (Wong 1965, p. 68). Later, in 1890, some prominent planters of Province Wellesley petitioned the British authorities to rectify the situation. For example, Khaw Boo Ann, a rich Teochew sugar planter of Province Wellesley, not a member of the interest group of the Big Five, urged the Straits Government to establish government coolie depots in Penang and Swatow.[58] In this way Khaw Boo Ann hoped to bypass the Big Five's monopoly and obtain coolies from an alternative source. However, such depots were never established by the British colonial government due to the great risk involved in the coolie business or the lack of connections. By controlling an effective system of supply, transportation and distribution of coolies, the Big Five were able to dominate the coolie business in the region until the early twentieth century.

CONCLUSION

The Hokkien merchants and traders of the Big Five families, who formed the predominant group of the Chinese mercantile community in Penang, played a very preponderant role in the economic arena of the Penang-centric region. Their economic interests were manifold and spread well beyond Penang. The extraordinarily active involvement of the Big Five in regional shipping and entrepot trade centring on Penang and the surrounding states served as the fundamental motor of their capital accumulation and of Penang's nineteenth-century role as an entrepot. Besides, the Big Five also ventured into commercial agriculture, tin mining, coolie trading and opium farming for more profit-making and capital accumulation. All these economic activities of the Big Five helped make Penang both a trading centre and a regional base for the supply of capital and labour. By forming strategic alliances with a group of economically successful and politically influential elites of other dialect and ethnic groups in Penang and its neighbouring states, the Big Five successfully gained control over all the major economic sectors. It enabled the Big Five to establish a strong economic base as well as control a circle of enterprises whose operations were interconnected with each other. Plantations and tin fields were worked by coolies to produce exportable commodities that were taken to market by ships belonging to the Big Five; in turn, the coolies who produced the commodities became the consumers of opium, rice and China goods whose supply was controlled by the companies or enterprises directed by members of the Big Five families. The Big Five thus were in a position to handle almost every input and output in this circle of economic operations.

This chapter has demonstrated that the Big Five attained a genuine regional economic ascendancy, and discussed some of the business strategies that enabled their success. But there was more to it than that. As the next chapter shows a web of flexible and interlocking family networks wove together and helped to secure these extensive business alliances. How did the Big Five construct this familial web to secure their economic interests? The next chapter attempts to tease out the intricate family networks centring around the Big Five.

Notes

1. Kenneth McPherson, "Penang 1786–1832: A Promise Unfulfilled", in *Gateways of Asia: Port Cities of Asia in the 13th–20th centuries*, edited by Frank Broeze (London: Kegan Paul International, 1997), pp. 110–13. See also Anthony Webster, *Gentlemen Capitalists: British Imperialism in South East Asia 1770–1890* (London, New York: Tauris Academic Studies, 1998), pp. 27–48; and Dianne Lewis, *Jan Compagnie in the Straits of Melaka, 1641–1795* (Athens: Ohio University Center for International Studies, 1995), p. 110. Before the conquest of Riau by the Dutch, Riau was a centre for the British country trade in the Archipelago since 1761.
2. Wang Gung Wu, "Merchant Without Empire: The Hokkien Sojourning Communities", in *The Rise of Merchant Empires: Long-Distance Trade in The Early Modern World, 1350–1750*, edited by James D. Tracy (New York: Cambridge University Press, 1990), pp. 408–11; Yen Ching Hwang, *Community and Politics: The Chinese in Colonial Singapore* (Singapore: Time Academic Press, 1995), pp. 72–73; Li Tana, "The Water Frontier: An Introduction", in *Water Frontier: Commerce and the Chinese in Lower Mekong Region, 1750–1880*, edited by Nola Cooke and Li Tana (Lanham: Rowman & Littlefield, 2004), pp. 5–6; and James Chin Kong, "Merchants and Other Sojourners: The Hokkiens Overseas, 1570–1760", PhD thesis, University of Hong Kong, 1998, pp. 24–31, 169–200.
3. 世界谢氏宗亲第五届恳亲大会纪念特刊 *Shije Xieshe Zongqing Diwujie Kenqing Dahui Jinian Tekan* [Special Issue on the 5th World Cheah Clansmen Conference], 北马谢氏宗祠和槟城谢氏福侯公公司 *Beima Xieshe Zongci He Bincheng Xieshe Fuhougong Gongsi* [North Malaya Cheah Si Chong Soo & Penang Cheah Si Hock Hew Kong Kongsi] (Penang, 1989), p. 88.
4. *Pinang Gazette and Straits Chronicle*, 28 July 1882, p. 4.
5. *Prince of Wales Island Gazette*, 25 May 1825, p. 2.

6. *PGSC*, 23 February 1838, p. 3; 7 July 1838, p. 3; 2 February 1839, p. 4; 9 February 1839, p. 3.
7. *PGSC*, 7 April 1838, p. 4; 28 April 1838, p. 3; 7 July 1838, p. 3; 24 January 1863, p. 4.
8. *PGSC*, 23 February 1856, p. 4; 22 March 1856, p. 4; 21 June 1856, p. 4.
9. *PGSC*, 29 November 1856, p. 4.
10. *PGSC*, 30 April 1844, p. 3; 20 April 1850, p. 4; 29 June 1850, p. 4; 17 January 1852, p. 4; 14 February 17 July 1852, p. 3.
11. *PGSC*, 29 October 1892, p. 5.
12. *Taigao Pujishen Huaren Tuohuangshi*, p. 30.
13. *Cases Heard and Determined in Her Majesty's Supreme Court of the Straits Settlements*, vol. 4 (Somerset: Legal Library Publishing Services, 1885/90), pp. 136–40.
14. Ibid., pp. 136–40.
15. *PGSC*, 28 February 1879, p. 3. See also *The Penang Almanack and Directory for 1876*, p. 31; and Nadia H. Wright, *Respected Citizens: The History of Armenians in Singapore and Malaysia* (Australia: Amassia Publishing, 2003), p. 156.
16. *PGSC*, 14 and 17 January 1879, p. 4; 2 July 1886, p. 5.
17. "Penang Market Report", *The Penang Argus and Mercantile Advertiser*, 16 March 1870, p. 3.
18. *The Maulmain Chronicle*, 9 January 1839, p. 1. See also E.A. Blundell, "Letter dated 9 December 1839", *Selected Correspondence of Letters Issued From and Received in the Office of the Commissioner Tenasserim Division for the Years 1825–26 to 1842–43* (Rangoon, Burma: Office of the Superintendent, Government Printing and Stationary, 1928), p. 182. The rice was also obtained through barter system and most of the time, the Chinese bartered goods with the Burmese for rice. A coyan is equivalent to approximately 1,334.7 kilogrammes.
19. *The Maulmain Chronicle*, January–December 1839 (the total amount of rice from Maulamin to Penang is compiled from the record of the weekly exports list).
20. Straits Settlements Blue Book for the year 1868 and 1890.
21. *Annual Report — Penang Chamber of Commerce 1879*, pp. 12–13.
22. *PGSC*, 29 October 1892, p. 5.
23. *The Burma Gazette*, 26 January 1889, p. 73.
24. *The Penang Directory for the year 1874 including that of Deli*, pp. 45–46; Khoo Kay Kim, *The Western Malay States 1850–1873: The Effects of Commercial Development on Malay Politics* (Kuala Lumpur: Oxford University Press, 1972), p. 93.
25. Compiled from *Tabular Statements of the Commerce and Shipping of Prince of Wales Island, Singapore and Melaka for the official year 1844–45, 1845–46,*

1847–48, 1848–49, 1849–50, and 1852–53 (Calcutta: Military Orphan Press, various years).

26. Compiled from *Tabular Statements of the Commerce and Shipping of Prince of Wales Island, Singapore and Melaka for the official year 1848–49, 1849–50 and 1852–53*.
27. *PAMA*, 27 February 1868, p. 2.
28. Oral information provided by Cheah Jin Teong, Chairman of the Cheah Kongsi in July 2004.
29. The figures are compiled from *Tabular Statements of the Commerce and Shipping 1844–53*.
30. In 1868, Hong Kong and Great Britain imported 2,450 piculs and 52,101 piculs of sugar from Penang respectively. *Straits Settlements Blue Book for the year 1868*, p. 410. But, in 1884, Penang exported 84,176 piculs and 146,441 piculs to Hong Kong and Great Britain respectively. *Straits Settlements Blue Book for the year 1884*, p. U143.
31. This number of vessels owned by the Hokkien merchants of Penang is compiled from the various issues of *PGSC of 1852*.
32. *PGSC*, 23 May 1863, p. 5; 26 December 1863, p. 5.
33. *Straits Echo*, 1 January 1904, p. 12.
34. *PAMA*, 31 October 1867, p. 6. See also CO273/3, The Chairman of the Chamber of Commerce Prince of Wales Island to the Resident Councilor of Prince of Wales Island, 19 July. Most of the capital from the local chiefs to the native pepper planters were in fact provided by the Hokkien merchants and capitalists of Penang. For example Khoo Boey, Khoo Cheah, Khoo Seck Chuan, Lim Cheng Kar, and Cheah Yeah were the frequent creditors of the Acehnese and Malay rulers at the East Coast of Sumatra.
35. *PAMA*, 31 October 1867, p. 6.
36. *PGSC*, 30 March 1839, p. 4; 17 August 1844, p. 4.
37. 'Report on *Nisero* Incident' in Foreign Office Files (FO422), p. 61.
38. The figure is compiled from *Tabular Statements of the Commerce and Shipping of Prince of Wales Island, Singapore and Melaka for the official year 1844–45, 1845–46, 1847–48, 1848–49, and 1849–50* (Calcutta: Military Orphan Press, various years).
39. For instance, Khoo Sew, a merchant of the Big Five, shipped nine chests of Benares opium, priced at $550 per chest in Penang, to Aceh where it fetched $1,200 per chest. Altogether he made a profit of about $5850. *PGSC*, 18 August 1855, p. 5.
40. Howard Dick, "A Fresh Approach to Southeast Asian History", in *The Rise and Fall of Revenue Farming: Business Elites and the Emergence of the Modern State in Southeast Asia*, edited by John Butcher and Howard Dick (New York: St. Martin Press, 1993), p. 1.

41. Carl A. Trocki, "Opium and the Beginnings of the Chinese Capitalism in Southeast Asia", *Journal of Southeast Asian Studies* 33 (2002): 297. See also Howard Dick, "A Fresh Approach to Southeast Asian History", in *The Rise and Fall of Revenue Farming*, pp. 9–11.
42. *PGSC*, 31 October 1879, p. 4; 10 October 1891, p. 5; 30 October 1894, p. 3. This figure is only the total for 1880 to 1891. The amounts for the other years are not available.
43. *PGSC*, 22 March 1899, p. 5.
44. It was a clan organization set up by a group of merchants of the Cheah family.
45. *PGSC*, 9 and 16 August 1879, pp. 3–4; Phuwadol Songprasert, "The Development of Chinese Capital in Southern Siam, 1868–1932", PhD thesis, Monash University, 1986, p. 62.
46. *PAMA*, 16 September 1871, p. 3.
47. *PAMA*, 22 February 1872, pp. 2–3.
48. Khoo Oon Keong together with Lim Toh Seang, Ong Kim Ho Neoh and Cheah Geok Keat Neoh held the Ban Ho Lee Opium Farm at Deli in 1889–91. *Pinang Gazette and Straits Chronicle*, 1 May 1893, p. 2 and 17 September 1895, p. 2.
49. Carl Trocki, "The Internationalization of Chinese Revenue Farming Networks", in *Water Frontier,* p. 169. See also Elizabeth Sinn, "Preparing Opium for America: Hong Kong and Cultural Consumption in the Chinese Diaspora", *Journal of Chinese Overseas*, vol. 1, no. 1 (May 2005): 30 and *The Penang Herald*, 5 July 1888, p. 2. For the first term, Koh Seang Tat, Ong Beng Teck of Penang and Lee Keng Yeam of Singapore invested $885,600. Later Koh Cheng Sian, a son of Koh Seang Tat, led the Penang syndicate to take over the Hong Kong opium farm. They were backed by the Big Five in Penang.
50. *The Singapore & Straits Directory 1904*, pp. 376, 394. Khoo Hun Yeang's revenue farming company was called Ban Chin Lee & Co. based in Sandakan, capital city of North Borneo. His revenue farming company in Sarawak was Chop Chin Hok Bee.
51. *Straits Echo*, 3 November 1911, pp. 942, 945.
52. *PGSC*, 7 November 1890, p. 6. See also CO 275/41, evidence taken before the Labour Commission of 1890, p. 7.
53. *The Hong Kong Directory and Hong List for the Far East for 1891* (Hong Kong: Robert Fraser-Smith, 1891), p. 276; *The Chronicle and Directory for China, Japan, & the Philippines* (Hong Kong: Hong Kong Daily Press Office, 1884), p. 346.
54. "Reports of Protector of Chinese for 1879 and 1881", *Straits Settlements Legislative Council Proceedings*, 1880 and 1882, pp. 92, 175; "Report of

Committee appointed to consider and take evidence upon the condition of Chinese Labourers in the colony", *Straits Settlements Legislative Council Proceedings*, 1876, p. 10; *The Chronicle and Directory for China, Japan, & the Philippines* (Hong Kong: Hong Kong Daily Press Office, 1884), p. 352.
55. Chai Hon-Chan, *The Development of British Malaya 1896–1909* (London: Oxford University Press, 1964), p. 109; *PGSC*, 7 November 1890, p. 6.
56. *PGSC*, 7 November 1890, p. 6.
50. *PGSC*, 11 July 1890, p. 4 and 7 November 1890, p. 6; see also Anthony Reid, *An Indonesian Frontier: Acehnese and Other Histories of Sumatra* (Singapore: Singapore University Press, 2005), p. 217.
50. *PGSC*, 11 July 1890, p. 4 and 29 July 1890, p. 5.

3

KITH AND KIN
The Big Five Familial Web

The secret of how the Big Five could assert their dominance in the Penang region lies in the multiple alliances between them and other prominent families. However, different from the conventional beliefs that Chinese family networks were as closed as they could be, cross-dialect and cross-ethnic alliances played a major role in the Big Five's business partnerships. Yet this cluster of five families was able to form all these alliances and attain their economic predominance in the face of the fluid and plural socio-economic environment of the region. This chapter explores how and why this situation came about.

The family network of the Big Five, which was composed of a web of kinship ties based on extended consanguineal lineages[1] and strategic intermarriages, inextricably bound the five families together and while also connecting them to other prominent Hokkien and Hakka families. Further a field, Indo-Malay families in Penang, Kedah, Perak and North Sumatra as well as Siamese and Chinese families in southern Siam and southern Burma were all woven into the net of marriage alliance. Extensive criss-crossing of kinship ties clearly served as an important foundation for the forging of inter-family and inter-ethnic alliances and partnerships between business families in the promising, yet potentially hostile and insecure, environment of competing colonial and indigenous powers. Through this web of kinship ties the Big Five families were able to establish their business concerns in Penang and the surrounding states.

Clan association in Penang is more popularly known as *kongsi* and here it refers to an autonomous organization of shared interests based upon blood ties and geographical affinity among its members.² Each of the Big Five was grouped within and represented by its own *kongsi*: the Seh Khoo Kongsi, the Seh Cheah Kongsi, the Seh Yeoh Kongsi, the Seh Lim Kongsi, and the Seh Tan Kongsi (Yen 1995, pp. 81–86). Both Cheah Kongsi and Tan Kongsi were established in 1810; it was then followed by the Yeoh in 1834, the Khoo in 1835, the Tan in 1851, and the Lim in 1863.³ With such groupings each of the five families was able to develop extended consanguineal lineages which in turn led to the formation of a substantial agnatic or blood-related kinship group. This lineage organization was not invented by the Big Five families in Penang but taken from the kinship system practised in their ancestral Fujian province. The lineage assembly had played an influential role in Fujianese society since at least Song times, and it became a key element in advancing economic endeavours during the Ming–Qing period. As Ng Chin Keong commented on the role of lineages in southern Fujian:

> Lineage organizations had close relations with the development of maritime trade during the turbulent years of the sixteenth and seventeenth centuries. Large lineages were able to organize voyages and provide manpower and capital. The great profits from trade, in turn, consolidated the lineage power (Ng 1983, p. 216).

The Penang *kongsis* of the Big Five were also different from the *kongsis* in West Borneo and Johore. The Lan Fang Kongsi of West Borneo was organized for gold mining (Wang 1994) and the Ngee Heng Kongsi of Johore for the cultivation of gambier and pepper (Trocki 1979, p. 6). The Big Five's *kongsis*, however, were established for shipping and maritime trade, and later to provide education, welfare, and religious and judicial services to the clan members.

AGNATIC KINSHIP OF THE BIG FIVE FAMILIES

With their pool of agnatic kin, the prominent figures of the respective five families could conveniently rely upon their sons, brothers, cousins, uncles and other kinfolk to manage and advance not only maritime trade, but also other business, such as revenue farming, cash-crop planting and tin mining. For example, Khoo Guek Chio 邱月照, a trader and landholder as well as a founder-member of Seh Khoo Kongsi, had nine sons.[4] Most of them assisted their father in the business, but Khoo Thean Teik 邱天德, the third son, became the most prominent. Thean Teik later took over his father's business and recruited his two younger brothers, Khoo Thean Poh 邱天保 and Khoo Thean Lye 邱天来, and his own sons, Khoo Hun Kung 邱汉江, Khoo Hun Chin 邱汉津, and Khoo Hun Yeang 邱汉阳 to help manage opium farms, pawn-broking shops, coconut and sugar estates, tin trading and general merchandise businesses over Penang, Province Wellesley, Kedah and Perak from the 1860s to the 1880s.[5] In the 1890s, Khoo Hun Yeang inherited the business interests of his father and expanded the business tentacles from Penang to Singapore and Borneo (Sabah and Sarawak). In Sarawak, for example, Hun Yeang was involved in construction and revenue farms. He was the principal partner in the Messrs. Chin Hock Bee, which held the opium, arrack and gambling farms from 1899 to 1909.[6] In 1902, his son, Khoo Siew Jin, moved on to manage the opium, arrack and gambling farms in Sarawak. He also appointed one of his kinfolk, Khoo Sian Tan 邱仙旦, to hold the power of attorney for his revenue farms in Sarawak during 1904 to 1906 (Lee and Chow 1997, p. 68). Sian Tan, an influential businessman, was a close friend of Sir Charles Vyner Brooke, the third White Raja of Sarawak (Chen 1946, p. 93). Another eminent figure of the Khoo family, Khoo Teong Poh 邱忠波, a well-known merchant in the East because of his revenue farm and shipping, which went from the 1840s to the 1890s, recruited his sons, Khoo Ghin Choe, Khoo Mah Lek and Khoo Phee Soon and brother, Khoo Teong Pan, as partners in his shipping company. It became the Bun Hin & Co., with extensive branches in Singapore, Penang, Phuket, Hong Kong and Amoy.[7]

Now let us turn to the Cheah family of the Big Five, Cheah Teah or Cheah Kim Ting 谢金锭, who migrated to Penang in the early 1780s and founded Eng Huat & Co. 永发号 to trade in pepper and cloth and venture in planting in Aceh.[8] In the 1860s, his eldest son, Cheah Boon Hean 谢文贤 joined Hock Leong & Company at Larut and became involved in mining and planting.[9] Later he extended his business interests into construction and a Chinese medicine shop in Taiping. In running all these businesses, Boon Hean had at least three of his six sons as assistants. Around the 1900s, Cheah Cheang Lim 谢昌霖, the youngest son of Boon Hean, worked closely with his father's business associates and expanded the business by investing more in tin mining and rubber planting in

Perak.[10] He had his elder brother, Cheah Cheang Hee 谢昌禧 and the only son, Cheah Ghim Leng 谢锦铃 as business partners and assistants. It was the same story with the Yeoh family. The two brothers, Yeoh Paik Tatt 杨碧达 and Yeoh Paik Keat 杨碧吉 together with a kinsman, Yeoh Tay Thor, formed the Tiang Lee & Co. 长利公司, and dealt in Straits produce (rice, pepper, and tapioca), and Western goods (hardware, flour wines & beer), and held rubber and coconut plantations in Province Wellesley (Lee and Chow 1997, pp. 193–94).

Moving to the Lim family, we find Lim Leng Cheak 林宁绰, one of the most important Hokkien towkays with large business concerns ranging from revenue farms to plantations. He had his brother, Lim Phee Cheak 林丕绰, and his sons, Lim Eow Hong 林耀煌 and Lim Eow Thoon 林耀椿, to manage the family business. Lim Eow Hong, the eldest son who succeeded his father's business in 1900s, expanded it by forming partnerships with a few kinsmen, such as Lim Kek Chuan 林克全, Lim Mah Chye 林妈栽, Lim Soo Chee 林士志, and Lim Seng Hooi 林成辉 in the Penang opium and spirit farms of 1907–9, the Eastern Shipping Co., the Criterion Press, and Great Eastern Insurance (Wu 2003, p. 108; Lee and Chow 1997, p. 108). Lim Mah Chye 林妈栽, another prominent merchant together with his brothers commenced a company under the name of Chin Huat & Co. 振发 to trade in rice in Penang and Moulmein.[11] Later, he branched out into tin trading under the firm of Chin Guan & Co. 振源 and revenue farms in Penang, Kedah, Perak, Selangor, Negri Sembilan, Setul and Perlis.[12]

Coming to the last case, that of the Tan family, the same story goes on. Tan Cheng (Geok) Tam/Tan Tam 陈清淡, the Chinese Capitan of Phuket, had his kinsmen, Tan Neo Yee 陈威仪 and Tan Ky Wan 陈开运, and two sons, Tan Lean Kee 陈莲枝 and Tan Lean Chung 陈莲从 as assistants in running the tin-mining and trading in Phuket and Thalang from the 1850s to 1860s (Wang 1965, p. 31; Teoh 2002, pp. 34–36). On the death of Tan Gaik Tham, Lean Kee, the eldest son, took over the business. Working closely with his kinsmen, brothers and sons, Lean Kee was able to expand the business from tin-mining and trading to shipping, tax farming and pawn-broking (Beattie 2003, p. 6). Tan Hup Swee 陈合水, a merchant and shipper, recruited his two sons, Tan Kim Kheng 陈锦庆 and Tan Kim Leong 陈锦隆 to work in his firm, Kim Keng Leong & Co. (Chop Kim Chang 锦昌号) in the 1860s, which not only dealt in hardware (steel & iron bars), but also held the agency for several lines of steamers, notably the Seang Line owned by Lim Chin

Tsong 林振宗, the richest businessman of Rangoon. This line mainly carried China produce and Chinese coolies from Singapore, Hong Kong, Swatow and Amoy to Burma via Penang (Feldwick 1917, pp. 867–68).

In view of this pattern of staffing and partnerships, it is clear that the pool of agnatic kin was not only a good source of manpower but also an immediate and ready sphere for the leading members of the respective families to derive trustworthy assistants or partners to serve the purpose of their business pursuits. The agnatic kinship ties were undoubtedly one of the reliable bonds utilized by the Big Five to supplement structural deficiencies in the colonial and indigenous states at the time, like legal uncertainty and the ambivalent attitudes of the ruling elite towards safeguarding and advancing their business interests.

AFFINAL KINSHIP OF THE BIG FIVE

The kinship ties were not confined only to agnatic relations and within the boundaries of each of the five families. To begin with, extensive intermarriage took place between the Big Five. Moreover, the intermarriages extended far beyond Penang and bound them to the other western Malay states (Kedah, Perak, Melaka), northern Sumatra (Aceh, Deli, Asahan, Medan), southwestern Siam (Phuket, Ranong, Trang), and southern Burma (Rangoon). As a result, the five families were not only heavily interrelated by multiple marriages between themselves but also with other prominent regional families. With these integrating, cross-family, cross-ethnic marriages, the five families constructed a complex web of matrimonial interrelationships (see Diagram 3.1).

INTERMARRIAGES AMONG THE BIG FIVE

It is difficult to pinpoint when the five families started to practise intermarriage. While some family genealogies claim that the intermarriages between the five families had been going on since the period of the Ming dynasty in China,[13] it is certain that it started quite early, and was done in a deliberate way, when the Big Five settled in Penang. As we can see from Diagram 3.1, Khoo Seck Chuan 邱石泉, Khoo Beng San 邱明山, Khoo Sim Bee 邱心美, Khoo Chow Siew 邱昭脩 and Khoo Ban Seng 邱万盛, the leading members and merchants of the Khoo family, took their wives from the other four families, the Cheah, the Tan, the Lim, and the Yeoh. The daughters of the leading members of the Khoo family

DIAGRAM 3.1
The Intermarriages of the Five Families and Other Families in Penang

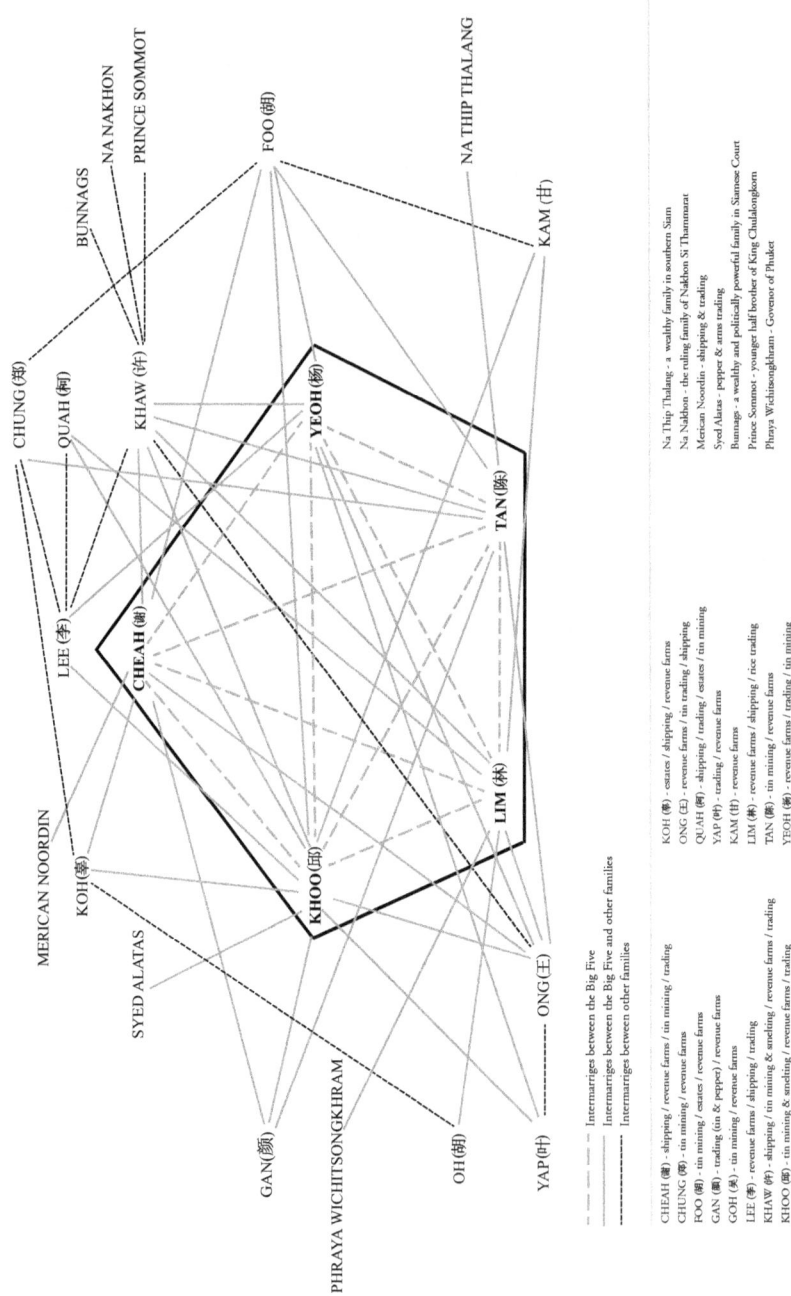

--- Intermarriges between the Big Five
--- Intermarriges between the Big Five and other families
——— Intermarriges between other families

CHEAH (谢) - shipping / revenue farms / tin mining / trading
CHUNG (郑) - tin mining / revenue farms
FOO (胡) - tin mining / estates / revenue farms
GAN (颜) - trading (tin & pepper) / revenue farms
GOH (吴) - tin mining / revenue farms
LEE (李) - revenue farms / shipping / trading
KHAW (许) - shipping / tin mining & smelting / revenue farms / trading
KHOO (邱) - tin mining & smelting / revenue farms / trading

KOH (辜) - estates / shipping / revenue farms
ONG (王) - revenue farms / tin trading / shipping
QUAH (柯) - shipping / trading / estates / tin mining
YAP (叶) - trading / revenue farms
KAM (甘) - revenue farms
LIM (林) - revenue farms / shipping / rice trading
TAN (陈) - tin mining / revenue farms
YEOH (杨) - revenue farms / trading / tin mining

Na Thip Thalang - a wealthy family in southern Siam
Na Nakhon - the ruling family of Nakhon Si Thammarat
Merican Noordin - shipping & arms trading
Syed Alatas - pepper & arms trading
Bunnags - a wealthy and politically powerful family in Siamese Court
Prince Sommot - younger half brother of King Chulalongkorn
Phraya Wichitsongkhram - Governor of Phuket

Sources: Appendix 2 and Appendix 3.

Kith and Kin: The Big Five Familial Web

also married into the other four families. For instance, Khoo Siew Kun 邱绣巾 and Khoo Siew Soon 邱绣顺, the second and the fourth daughters of Khoo Seck Chuan 邱石泉, married Yeoh Cheng Tek 杨清德, a leading tin and pepper merchant and a headman of the Seh Yeoh Kongsi, whose three younger sisters also married into the Khoo family and one married into the Lim family (Teoh 1997, pp. 187–88).

Lim Mah Chye 林妈栽 of the Lim family, a revenue farmer and tin trader and a trustee of Seh Lim Kongsi, wed Cheah Geok Kee, a daughter of Cheah Eok (Lee and Chow 1997, p. 114). His eldest son, Lim Chin Guan 林振源 married Yeoh Saw Heang, a daughter of Yeoh Cheang Chye 杨章才, a director of Seh Yeoh Kongsi; the youngest son, Lim Ang Kee 林红柿 took his wife from the Cheah family (Lee and Chow 1997, p. 107). Lim Eu Toh 林有道, a senior partner of Messrs. Tiang Lee & Co. and a member of the Penang Municipal Commission, whose mother was from the Tan family, contracted two marriages with the daughters of Khoo family. His first marriage was with Khoo Soon Neoh 邱顺娘, the second daughter of Khoo Thean Poh 邱天保, a director of Seh Khoo Kongsi, a leader of Kian Teik Tong, and a prominent revenue farmer and trader who had business interests stretching from Penang to Kedah, Aceh, Phuket and Singapore (Lee and Chow 1997, p. 109). With the demise of his first wife, Eu Toh married Khoo Kuat Siew, the eldest daughter of a merchant of Rangoon.

INTERMARRIAGES BETWEEN THE BIG FIVE AND OTHER FAMILIES

As noted above, the Big Five's networks also extended to the other prominent Hokkien and Hakka families in Penang and the adjacent states. The affinal linkage between the five families and the other eight significant Hokkien families (the Koh, the Khaw, the Lee, the Gan, the Ong, the Oh, the Yap, and the Kam) was manifest clearly in the constant marriages of sons and daughters into each other's families. Khoo Cheng Lim 邱清临, the eldest son of Khoo Wat Seng 邱悦成, who was the principal donor and one of the founders of Seh Khoo Kongsi, married Koh Keng Yean 辜轻烟, the second daughter of Koh Kee Jin 辜雨水 and granddaughter of Koh Lay Huan.[14] A daughter of the Khoo family, Khoo Sim Neoh, was wed to Koh Teng Choon 辜登春, the eldest son of Koh Kok Chye and grandson of Koh Lay Huan.[15] Khoo Guat San 邱月山 had his son, Khoo Being Hock, marry Khaw Swee Ee, a daughter of Khaw Sim Kong, the Governor of Ranong.[16] Lim Soo Chee 林士志, the eldest son of Lim Kek Chuan 林克全, a prominent revenue farmer and tin trader, married a granddaughter of Khaw Sim Chua, the Raja of Luan Suan, who married Yeoh Siew Chee of the Yeoh family (Lee and Chow 1997, p. 109).

Cheah Kim Suet 谢琴雪, the eldest daughter of Cheah Chen Eok 谢增煜, a wealthy revenue farmer and a highly respected community leader, became a wife of Gan Keng Yeang 颜庆阳,[17] the second son of Gan Kim Swee 颜金水, a prominent revenue farmer and trader, whose family members, such as brothers and nephews, were actively involved in trading Straits produce, such as gambier, rice and tin in Calcutta, Rangoon and Saigon. Cheah Joo Si 谢如丝, a daughter of Cheah Eu Ghee 谢有义, a trader and landowner, was wed to Ong Hun Teng 王汉鼎, the eldest son of Ong Guan Cheng 王元清, a rich tin trader;[18] Cheah Sun Phek 谢纯璧, another daughter of the Cheah family, married Lee Phee Yeow 李丕耀, a shipping magnate and owner of vast sugar estates;[19] Tan Hup Swee, a shipping agent and import and export merchant, contracted a marriage with Kam Kian Neo 甘捷娘, the second daughter of Kam Su Kau 甘四教, a wealthy merchant of Penang.[20] Khoo Sek Chuan, a shipper and financier, married Yeap Kheng Bee 叶匡美, who was the eldest daughter of Yeap Guan Seng 叶源成 and the younger sister of Yeap Hup Keat 叶合吉, a prominent Hokkien community leader and revenue farmer.[21]

The Hakka families with which the five families had contracted marriages were the Foo and the Chung families, with the former being Yongding 永定 Hakka and the latter Zengcheng 增城 Hakka.[22] Foo Tye Sin 胡泰兴, who was a prominent planter and merchant community leader had one of his wives from the Lim family, Lim Cheok Bee; two of his daughters married Cheah Chen Eok of the Cheah family and Tan Kheam Hock of the Tan family, a revenue farmer, coolie agent and municipal commissioner, who migrated to Singapore in 1889.[23] Foo Choo Choon 胡子春, the "Tin King", who held extensive mining interests in Perlis, Perak, Selangor and Phuket, had a cousin married to Cheah Boon Hean 谢文贤 of the Cheah family;[24] his second daughter married to Yeoh Boon Tean, the fifth son of Yeoh Cheang Chye.[25] Chung Keng Kwee 郑景贵, a tin mining magnate and Kapitan Cina of Perak, took one of his wives from the Tan family, Tan Gaik Im Neoh 陈玉荫娘.[26] She was a daughter of Tan Kim Jao or Tan Jao 陈锦灶, the leader of Ho Seng *hui* 和胜会 in Phuket. Chung Thye Phin 郑大平, the fourth son of Keng Kwee, married a daughter of the Khoo family and a daughter of the Tan family.[27]

Apart from all these matrimonial ties with the Hokkien and Hakka families, the Big Five also extended marriage connections to the rich and powerful families of other ethnic groups, for example, Siamese and Acehnese. Khoo Thean Poh 邱天保 of the Khoo family, a pepper trader and revenue farmer and deputy headman of Kian Teik Tong 建德堂 or Toa Peh Kong 大伯公 *hui*, was affinally related to Syed Mohamed Alatas, an Acehnese merchant of Arab descent, who was a leader of the Muhammaden Red Flag society. Syed Mohamed Alatas, who married the daughter of Khoo Thean Poh and possessed close trade connections with Aceh, was a key figure in helping the Acehnese resistance against the Dutch siege of the 1870s by smuggling arms from British India to Aceh via Penang (Khoo 1993, p. 35).

A daughter of Cheah Tek Swee of the Cheah family married the only son of Nina Merican Noordin,[28] who was a prominent and wealthy Merican or Kling merchant and proprietor in Penang. Nina Merican Noordin was the second son of Mohamed Merican Noordin, a leading Merican merchant who started trading in Penang in about 1820.[29] By 1830, Mohamed Merican Noordin had built up an extensive trading business and had already become one of the most influential merchants in Penang. His company was one of the largest consigners in Penang and he consigned vessels trading across a wide area stretching from Penang to Chittagong, Arakan, Deli, Aceh, Bombay, Calcutta, and Singapore (Fujimoto 1988, p. 60). Besides, he also held considerable house and shop property and a large estate in Province Wellesley, known as Noordin Estate (Wright and Cartwright 1908, p. 752). Outside of business, he was also a well-known social and political figure, being appointed several times as Municipal Commissioner and Justice of the Peace (Fujimoto 1988, p. 205). Nina Merican Noordin, the second son of Mohamed Noordin, together with his brothers, took over the family business in 1870. Nina Merican Noordin, and his eldest brother, Vappoo Merican Noordin, were not only actively engaged in trade and shipping, but also deeply involved in the Red Flag secret society. As ironical as it may sound, both of them were appointed as special Jurors for Penang in 1876 (Fujimoto 1988, pp. 204–5).

Through their nephew's (Khaw Joo Ley 许如利) marriage to Klub Bunnag (Cushman 1991, p. 138). Cheah Tek Thye 谢德泰 and Cheah Tek Soon 谢德顺 of the Cheah family became affinally connected to the ruling class in Bangkok. Klub Bunnag was a daughter of Won Bunnag, the Minister of the South from 1869 to 1888 (Cushman 1991, p. 25). The Bunnag family was a very powerful family that had dominated the Siamese court since the 1820s. The Bunnags controlled two of the three most powerful ministries — the ministry controlling the administration of the Southern provinces (Krom Kalahom) and the ministry which dealt with foreign trade and foreign affairs (Krom Phrakhlang) and administered much of the revenue system and governed the Gulf provinces (Wyatt 1994, pp. 128–29). In addition, the Ministry of Lands (Krom Na) was controlled by affinal relatives of the Bunnags for all but thirty years of the period 1832–74 (Wyatt 1994, p. 130). Besides the Bunnag family, Khaw Joo Ley also established matrimonial ties with the Siamese royal family. One of his granddaughters married Mom Chao Vibul Sawatwong, a son of Prince Sommot.[30] Another nephew, Khaw Joo Ghee 许如义 and brother-in-law, Khaw Sim Bee 许心美 of these two Cheah brothers took their wives from the west coast branch of the Na Nakhon family which dominated politics and revenue collection in the states along the southwestern coast — Takuapa, Takuathung, Phangnga and Krabi (Cushman 1991, p. 23). Khaw Joo Ghee married Prem, who was a daughter of Phra Borisutlohaphumintharathibodi, the Governor of Takuathung, and Khaw Sim Bee wed Nuan, whose father was Phraya Senanuchit, the Governor of Takuapa (Cushman 1991, p. 23). Lim Ang Kee 林红柿 of the Lim family had his daughter, Lim Meh Beow, married to the son of Phraya Wichitsongkhram, the Governor of Phuket.[31]

This pattern of extensive and intersecting marriage ties of the Big Five families revealed several interesting phenomena. First, the five families were affinally related to each other as well as to the other prominent Hokkien families not only in Penang, but also in Rangoon, Phuket, Ranong, Kedah, Perak, and Deli. Those Hokkien families were the established capitalists and leading figures who commanded substantial business concerns and a degree of political influence in the realm of colonial and indigenous authorities. The Koh and the Khaw families, for instance, are the best examples. However, the affinal alliances of the five families were not exclusively Hokkien-oriented. The five families had in fact constructed a web of cross-dialect and cross-ethnic marriage networks. Through this web of networks, the five families became closely linked to the Hakka Foo and Chung families, the Siamese Bunnag, Na Nakhon and Na Thip Thalang families, the Merican Noordin family, and the Acehnese Syed Alatas family, who were powerful and influential in their own business and socio-political spheres. For example, Chung Keng Kwee 郑景贵 of the Chung family, the headman of Hai San society, controlled the largest number of coolies in Larut and dominated the tin mines and revenue farms in Perak; Vappoo Merican Noordin and Nina Merican Noordin of Merican Noordin family, the leaders of the Red Flag society, commanded close business and family connections with Aceh and Calcutta.

Second, the Big Five families and the other Hokkien and Hakka families managed to perpetuate their affinal connections with each other by renewing intermarriages between families over successive generations. This marriage renewal was clearly exhibited in the Yeoh, the Lim, the Tan, the Khoo, the Cheah, the Khaw, the Koh, and the Chung families. For example, Yeoh Cheng Teik 杨清德 of the Yeoh family, who took two Khoo sisters as wives, had his three sisters married into the Khoo family and in the next generation Cheng Teik's eldest son and second daughter also wed into the Khoo family; Khaw Sim Khim 许心钦, who himself married a daughter of the Lim family, had his son, Khaw Joo Tok 许如琢, marrying a daughter of the Lim family and two granddaughters, Khaw Phaik Saik and Khaw Phaik Boey, marrying into the Lim family; Koh Kok Chye 辜国彩, whose wife was Cheah Thoe Neoh, had two great-grand sons, Koh Leap Teng 辜立亭 and Koh Cheng Sian 辜禎善, both married to the daughters of the Cheah family; Tan Lean Kee 陈莲枝 had his two daughters and one granddaughter wed into the Chung family. These are but few of many instances of the repeated generational intermarriages between families. These marriage practices were certainly more than a reflection of wealthy families' customs.

This leads to my third point, the intermarriages between the Big Five and other families were judicious and strategic, rather than spontaneous and coincidental. The marital partners of the Big Five were largely drawn from the politically influential and economically successful families in Penang and the surrounding states. Having members of those prominent families as affines, the Big Five families gained status and at the same time converted a potential competitor into an ally. Put in another way, these marital bonds created a dynamic and inclusive economic relationship between two or more families. In so doing, the Big Five were able to extend corporate bonds between families for business expansion and monopolization. The Penang Opium Syndicate is a case in point. Through a combination of marriage links and business partnerships, the Big Five families grouped together with affinal relatives in that syndicate to control the opium farms in Penang for many years. Using this solid base, the Big Five were able to secure the farms in Kedah, Perak, Johor, Riau, Melaka, Singapore, Bangkok, Rangoon and Hong Kong in various years in the late nineteenth century. The intermarriages, intentionally arranged for the purposes of business alliance, were surprisingly stable in nearly all cases. There were some conflicts but these were not of any particular weight.

It is clear that the family network of the Big Five Hokkien families comprised two layers of relationships — agnatic and affinal kinship. These two layers of kinship systems served as the ready and trustworthy resources which the mercantile elite of the Big Five heavily relied on for capital, manpower and partners in their business pursuits. In view of this, the family network was indubitably an essential and inseparable component of the Big Five families' trade networks. Putting their extensive family networks to work, the Big Five were able to incorporate the wealthy and powerful elites of their own, of other dialect groups, and indeed of other ethnic groups, to forge a formidable interest group to advance their enterprises from Penang to the surrounding states. It is important to note, however, that despite this closely-knit and extensive family network, the Big Five were not invulnerable. In time, the mercantile leadership of each of the Big Five families and other families became embroiled in unresolved conflicts of interest which eroded the interest group at the turn of the century. The Big Five's conflicts of interest are discussed in Chapter 7.

CONCLUSION

By establishing a matrix of business alliances, which was complemented and sealed with family networks, the Big Five had an edge over their rivals. The family network of the Big Five, based on blood and matrimonial ties, not only cut across state, dialect, and ethnic boundaries, but also across the generations. The family network was indeed instrumental in facilitating socio-economic cooperation among the Big Five on a remarkable scale, especially in the process of expanding the pool of reliable local and regional partners and of mobilizing and channelling capital, manpower, and military resources collectively and efficiently for common economic ventures. What is more, they were able to perpetuate their family network over time, consolidating wealth and power over more than one generation. In other words, this extensive family network constituted a subtle and unwritten "infrastructure", thanks to which the Big Five were able to form an integrated ring of regional trade networks which became a driving economic force in this Penang-centred region for most of the nineteenth century. Among their enterprises, opium farming emerged as the nucleus in the mid-nineteenth century. It became the most effective vehicle for capital accumulation by developing and perpetuating the systems of consumption and commodity production. In this regard, opium revenue farms became the most contested business in the second half of the nineteenth century. How did the closely knit Big Five ward off competition to maintain their dominance in the opium-farming business? The answer to this question is the subject of discussion in the next chapter.

Notes

1. Consanguineal lineages mean a group of people related by descent from a common ancestor through known links.
2. Yen Ching Hwang, *A Social History of the Chinese in Singapore and Malaya 1800–1911* (Singapore: Oxford University Press, 1986), p. 75. See also 槟城龙山堂邱公司: 历史与建筑材料 *Bincheng Longshantang Qiugongsi: Lishi Yu Jianzhu Cailiao* [Leong San Tong Khoo Kongsi: The History and Architecture] (Penang: Bincheng Longsantang Qiugongsi Chuban Xiaozu 槟城龙山堂邱公司出版小组 [Leong San Tong Khoo Kongsi Publication Committee], 2003), p. 14.
3. Tan Kim Hong, "Organizational Structure and Development of Hokkien Kongsi, Penang", in *The Story of Hokkien Kongsi, Penang* (Penang: Hokkien Kongsi, 2014), pp. 50, 57, 66, 79. See also 陈耀威 [Tan Yeow Wooi], "殖民城市的血缘聚落: 槟城五大姓公司" *Zhimin Chengshi De Xueyan Juluo: Bincheng Wudaxin Gongsi* [Blood-related Kin Congregation in a Colonial City: Penang's Big Five *Kongsis*], a paper presented at Workshop on Southeast Asian Hokkien Studies 东南亚福建学研讨会, Selangor, Malaysia, 2005, p. 12.
4. *Xinjiang Qiuzengshe Zupu* [The Genealogy of the Sin Kang Khoo and Chan Clans], vol. 21, p. 12.
5. *The Penang Argus and Merchantile Advertisers*, 4 August 1870, pp. 3–4 and 10 November 1870, p. 4.
6. *The Singapore & Straits Directory 1904*, p. 394.
7. *Pinang Gazette and Straits Chronicle*, 1 October 1891, p. 3; see also *The Chronicle and Directory for China, Japan, & the Philippines* (Hong Kong: Hong Kong Daily Press Office, 1884), p. 599.
8. 世界谢氏宗亲第五届恳亲大会纪念特刊 *Shijie Xieshe Zongqing Diwujie Kenqin Dahui Jinian Tekan* [Special Issue on the 5th World Cheah Clansmen Conference] (Penang: North Malaya Cheah Si Chong Soo & Penang Cheah Si Hock Hew Kong Kongsi 北马谢氏宗祠和槟城谢氏福侯公公司, 1989), p. 89.
9. *Shijie Xieshe Zongqing Diwujie Kenqin Dahui Jinian Tekan*, p. 90.
10. Ibid. See also Lee Kam Hing and Chow Mun Seong, *Biographical Dictionary of the Chinese in Malaysia* (Kuala Lumpur: Pelanduk Publications, 1997), pp. 12–13.
11. Lee and Chow, *Biographical Dictionary of the Chinese in Malaysia*, p. 114. See also *Straits Echo*, 24 August 1927, p. 684.
12. The eldest son, Lim Chin Guan (林振源) later took over his father's business. Lee and Chow, *Biographical Dictionary of the Chinese in Malaysia*, p. 107.
13. The intermarriages between the Khoo family and the other four families since the Ming dynasty could be traced in volume 6 of 新江邱曾氏族谱 *Xinjiang Qiuzengshe Zupu* [The Genealogy of the Sin Kang Khoo and Chan Clans].

14. Wong Choon San, *A Gallery of Chinese Kapitans* (Singapore: Ministry of Culture, 1963), p. 14; see also *Binlangyu Fujian Gongzhong Ji Jiazhong Beimingji*, p. 79.
15. *PGSC*, 29 May 1888, p. 5. The couple had five sons and two of them were famous figures in Penang — Koh Seang Tat and Koh Seang Tek.
16. *PGSC*, 15 November 1894, p. 2.
17. *PGSC*, 27 April 1893, p. 2; see also 泉州譜牒華僑史料與研究上冊 *Quanzhou Pudie Huaqiao Shiliao Yu Yanjiu Shangce* [Quanzhou Genealogy: Overseas Chinese Historical Materials and Studies vol. 1] (Beijing: Zhongguo Huaqiao Press 中国华桥出版社, 1998), p. 369.
18. *Binlangyu Fujian Gongzhong Ji Jiazhong Beimingji*, pp. 18, 220.
19. Ibid., p. 60.
20. 颖川堂陈公司: 神主簿 *Yinchuantang Chengongsi: Shenzu Bu* [Tan Kongsi's Record Book of Spirit Tablet], compiled in 1969, p. 7. See also *Binlangyu Fujian Gongzhong Ji Jiazhong Beimingji*, p. 85.
21. *Binlangyu Fujian Gongzhong Ji Jiazhong Beimingji*, pp. 39, 200–3. See also MISC 1420/92. Yeap Hup Keat served as a director of all the Hokkien public cemeteries for thirteen years and owned about ten brick shop houses and 38 sq. orlongs (about 50 acres) of coconut estates. Around 1892, he was heavily in debt and became bankrupt. All his properties were put on auction by P.A.L.S.V. Shedambaram Chetty and the Government of Perak.
22. The Yongding Hakka was also known as Hokkien Hakka and originated from the Ding Zhou prefecture in Fujian province while the Zengcheng Hakka originated from the Zengcheng district in Guangdong province.
23. Lee and Chow, *Biographical Dictionary of the Chinese in Malaysia*, pp. 44, 159. Tan Kheam Hock's father was Tan Teng Pong, who was an established trader in Penang from the early to the mid-nineteenth century. Together with Cheah Eu Beng and Chew Chu In, he operated a shop in Beach Street.
24. 檳州華人大會堂慶祝成立一百週年新廈落成開幕紀念特刊 *Binzhou Huaren Dahuitang Qingzu Chengli Yibai Zhounian Xinxia Luocheng Jinian Tekan* [Commemorative Publication of Centenary Celebrations and Inauguration of New Building, Penang Chinese Town Hall] (Penang: Binzhou Huaren Dahuitang, 1983), p. 173.
25. *Straits Echo*, 3 June 1904, p. 12.
26. 陈耀威 [Tan Yeow Wooi], 慎之家塾: 室内可移动文物普查 *Shenzhi Jiashu: Shinei Ke Yidong Wenwu Pucha* [Inventory of Movable Artifacts for Private School of Chung Keng Kwee] (Penang: Tan Yeow Wooi Culture & Heritage Research Studio, 2004), p. 22. Also see *Straits Echo*, 3 December 1919, p. 2011.
27. 南洋名人集传 *Nanyang Mingren Jizhuan* [South Sea Chinese Biography], no. 1 vol. 2, p. 18. Chung Thye Phin, in fact, had five more wives, namely Lee Sau Yeng, Chan Kwai Chee, Oh Jit Kwai, Wong Yoon Hoe, and

Ho Foon Kaee. See Jeffrey Seow, "Chung Thye Phin", in *Biographical Dictionary of Mercantile Personalities of Penang*, edited by Loh Wei Leng et al. (Penang and Kuala Lumpur: Think City and MBRAS, 2013), p. 130.
28. *PGSC*, 6 October 1892, p. 2. Mericans or Klings were also known as Chulians. They belonged to the Marakayar group originating from the Coromandel Coast of India. The Mericans were mainly maritime people. See Ragayah Eusoff, *The Merican Clan: A Story of Courage and Destiny* (Singapore: Times Books International, 1997), pp. 29–30.
29. Helen Fujimoto, *The South Indian Muslim Community and the Evolution of the Jawi Peranakan in Penang up to 1948* (Tokyo: Institute for the Study of Languages and Cultures of Asia and Africa, 1988), p. 59. Merican was the Marakayar group of Indian Muslims in India and they were also one of the first batches of migrants who settled in Penang.
30. *Straits Echo*, 11 August 1910.
31. *PGSC*, 14 May 1895, p. 2.

4

OPIUM FARM RIVALRY

The Penang-centred region of the 1860s to the 1880s witnessed not only dynamic commercial and intensifying business competition. Opium revenue farming generated the most intense competition among the mercantile and political elite groups in the region. The Ghee Hin, a sworn brotherhood *hui* controlled by the Cantonese, Teochew, Hakka (mainly Fui Chew) business elite, was the arch-rival of the Big Five. Besides, the Big Five also faced challenges from the Siamese local chiefs and British officials who attempted to break their monopolistic control of opium farms. This chapter investigates this competition. It begins by introducing the Cantonese, Teochew, and Hakka that clustered around the Ghee Hin before considering the challenges posed by the Ghee Hin, the Siamese, the British, and the Singapore Hokkien mercantile elite to the Big Five's opium and tin business. It then examines the strategies the Big Five adopted to deal with these challenges, showing how the Big Five weakened the challengers and achieved their opium farming hegemony in the region.

SWORN BROTHERHOOD *HUI*: THE GHEE HIN AND KIAN TEIK TONG

The sworn brotherhood *hui*, more commonly known in Western sources as secret societies, were an inseparable element of the nineteenth-century Chinese society in the region. Carl Trocki has defined the sworn brotherhood *hui* as organized agencies of social control and avenues of economic progress.[1] As Francis Light wrote in January 1794 to the Governor-General of Bengal, the Chinese in Penang were a "valuable acquisition, but speaking a language which no other people understand, they are able to form parties and combinations in the most secret manner against any regulation of government" (Purcell 1948, p. 40). Light's statement indicated the existence of the sworn brotherhood *hui*, or the so-called secret societies in 1790s Penang. The Ghee Hin, founded in about 1790, was most probably the first and dominant *hui* there (Wong 1964/65, p. 120; Teoh 2002, p. 232). At the time it was jointly controlled by a group of influential Hokkien and Cantonese merchants.

In the early nineteenth century, however, as the Hokkien faction emerged as a dominant force in the business of revenue farming and played an active role in shipping and trading, the growing economic wealth of its main families enabled them to become more powerful in the *hui*. This may have caused great uneasiness among the Cantonese leaders who feared being swallowed up. Whatever the case, in 1844 some Hokkiens, mainly the members of the Big Five families and their associates, left the Ghee Hin and established their own sworn brotherhood *hui* — the Kian Teik Tong, more commonly known as Toa Peh Kong.[2] Very likely, their departure arose from a power struggle or infighting within the Ghee Hin. After that, the mercantile elite of the San Neng Cantonese, the Teochew, and Huizhou Hakka were firmly in control of the Ghee Hin.[3] Lee Coyin or Lee Gou Yen 李国英, Ho Ghi Siew 何义寿, and Chin Ah Yam 陈亚炎 were the leaders of the Cantonese faction; Soo Ah Chiang 苏亚昌 was the leader of Huizhou 惠州 Hakka faction; Khaw Boo Aun 许武安 was the leader of the Teochew faction. Obviously, the leadership of the Ghee Hin was made up of prominent figures from four different dialect groups (see Table 4.1).

The leaders of the Ghee Hin were some established and well-off merchants and proprietors in Penang, Province Wellesley and Perak. Lee Coyin, the president of the Ghee Hin from 1859 to 1865, for example, owned a jewellery and goldsmiths shop at Bishop Street of Penang. Oh Wee Kee, the vice-president of the Ghee Hin from 1859 to 1880s, operated the Oh Wee Kee & Co. at 67 Penang Street, Penang, which dealt in baked goods, butchery and provisions. Ho Ghi Siew, who served as the president from 1865 to 1873, ran bakeries, confectionery stores, soda-water manufacturing, and hotels (Victoria & Albert on Penang Street), as well as two ships, the steamer *Holyrood* sailing between Penang, Rangoon and Karrikal (Karaikal), and the steamer *Perse* plying between Penang and Aceh. Chin Ah Yam, who succeeded Ho Ghi Siew as the president from 1873 to 1899, owned a construction company in Penang. Khaw Boo Aun, who became the Sin Seh or secretary of the Ghee Hin in the 1860s, was an established sugar planter and merchant, with vast sugar estates in Province Wellesley and Perak as well as two steamers, the *Rajah* and *Fair Penang*, operating between Penang, Perak, and Langkat (see Table 4.2).

TABLE 4.1
Dialect Factions and Leaders of the Ghee Hin, 1860s–90s

Cantonese	Hokkien	Teochew	Hakka (Huizhou/Fui Chiew)
Lee Coyn or Lee Gou Yen 李国英/遇贤	Oh Wee Kee 胡维期/围棋	Khaw Boo Aun 许武安	Soo Ah Cheong[1] 苏亚昌/亚松
Ho Ghi Siew 何义壽			
Chin Ah Yam 陈亚炎			
Boey Yoo Kong 梅耀广			
Wong Ah Chong 黄进聪			

Note: [1] According to Tan Kim Hong, his Chinese name should be 苏正祥安 and he was probably a Cantonese. See 陈剑虹 Tan Kim Hong, 走近义兴公司 *Zoujin Yixing* Gongsi [The Story of Ghee Hin Kongsi in Penang] (Penang: Tan Kim Hong, 2015), pp. 140–41.

Sources: Mervyn Llwellyn Wynne, *Triad and Tabut: A Survey of the Origin and Diffusion of Chinese and Mohamedan Secret Societies in the Malay Peninsula 1800–1935* (Singapore: Government Printing Office, 1941), p. 268; 陈剑虹 Tan Kim Hong, 走近义兴公司 *Zoujin Yixin* Gongsi [The Story of Ghee Hin Kongsi in Penang] (Penang: Tan Kim Hong, 2015), pp. 116–17, 124–25; Wong Choon San, *A Gallery of Chinese Kapitans* (Singapore: Ministry of Culture, 1963), pp. 70–77 and 81–83.

The Ghee Hin of Penang, which functioned as the society's headquarters, had its branches in southern Burma, southwestern Siam, the western Malay states and the East Coast of Sumatra. As in Penang, the branches in those states were also controlled by the local mercantile elite. Lee Nie Hee, for example, a Sin Neng Cantonese and a jade trader and revenue farmer in Rangoon, became the chief leader of Rangoon's Ghee Hin branch from the 1870s to 1890s. Sit San, a Hokkien, who held extensive business in bird's nests, opium farming and tin mining in Maliwun, the

TABLE 4.2
Business Involvement of the Ghee Hin Leaders, 1860s–90s

Name of Leaders	Name and Address of Company	Type of Business
Lee Coyin	Unknown (Bishop Street of Penang)	Operated a jewellery and goldsmiths
Oh Wee Kee	Oh Wee Kee & Co. (No. 67 Penang Street of Penang)	Bakery, Butchery and Provisions
Ho Ghi Siew	Victoria & Albert (Penang Street)	Hotel
	Son Tuk Seng Bakery (Chulia Street)	Bakery, Confectionery and soda-water manufacturing
		Shipping (Steamer Holyrood and Steamer Perse)
Chin Ah Yam	Unknown	Construction
Khaw Boo Aun	Chop Kau Heng 高兴号 Chop Kau Huat 高发号 Feng Yu Hang 豐裕行	Sugar Planting Sugar Factory Sugar Mill Shipping (Steamer Rajah and Steamer Fair Penang)

Sources: The Penang Almanack and Directory for 1876, p. 34; *The Penang Argus and Mercantile Advertiser*, 15 April 1869, p. 4; *Pinang Gazette and Straits Chronicle*, 7 January 1879, p. 5; 24 January and 14 May 1879, pp. 4, 6; Lee Kam Hing and Chow Mun Seong, *Biographical Dictionary of the Chinese in Malaysia* (Kuala Lumpur: Pelanduk Publications, 1997), pp. 25, 57.

southernmost township of Mergui, was the head of the Ghee Hin branch in Maliwun from the 1860s to 1890s. Chiu Ah Cheoh, a San Neng Cantonese, who was a carpenter closely involved in revenue farming, led the branch of Ghee Hin in Kulim of Kedah; Tan Chuan, a Hokkien tin miner, was the leader of Ghee Hin in Phuket from the 1820s to 1870s (see Table 4.3).

TABLE 4.3
Ghee Hin's Branches and Leaders in the Region, 1870s–90s

Name of Leaders	Branch's Location	Business
Lee Nie Hee 李乃喜 Xinning (San Neng) Cantonese	Rangoon	Jade trader and revenue farmer
Sit San 薛山 Hokkien	Maliwun	Bird's nests, opium farm and tin mining
Chiu Ah Cheoh 趙亜爵 Xinning (San Neng) Cantonese	Kedah	Carpenter and revenue farmer
Tan Chuan 陈大川 Hokkien	Phuket	Tin mining

Sources: 方雄普 Fang Xiong Pu, 朱波散记 — 缅甸华人社会掠影 *Zhubo Sanji — Miandian Huaren Shehui Lueying* [Short Essays on the Burma's Chinese Society] (Hong Kong: Nandao Chubanshe 南岛出版社, 2000年), p. 268; Arnold Wright, H.A. Cartwright and Oliver Breakspear, *Twentieth Century Impressions of Burma: Its History, People, Commerce, Industries and Resources* (London: Lloyd's Greater Britain Pub. Co., 1910), p. 326; W.T. Hall, "Report on Tin Mining in Perak and in Burma", *Supplement to the Burma Gazette*, no. 23 (8 June 1889): 414–15; Wong Choon San, *A Gallery of Chinese Kapitans* (Singapore: Ministry of Culture, 1963), pp. 56–57; 王重阳 Wang Zhong Yang, "泰国普吉省华人拓荒史" *Taiguo Pujishen Huaren Tuohuangshi* [History of Chinese Pioneers in Phuket], 南洋文摘 *Nanyang Digest* vol. 6, no. 5 (1965): 36.

With their sound economic background and influential position in the *hui*, these leaders of the Ghee Hin were able to channel capital through the society's extensive network of the *hui* into the more lucrative business of revenue farming in the region. Their involvement in this business inevitably brought the leaders of the Ghee Hin into direct competition with the Big Five families, making the Ghee Hin the arch-rival of the Big Five in the revenue farming businesses in the southern Siamese states, the western Malay states, and the East Coast of Sumatra.

As noted before, Kian Teik Tong or Toa Peh Kong was the sworn brotherhood *hui* closely associated with the Big Five. It was an instrument used by the members of the Big Five to achieve or secure their own economic interests and progress. Since its inception in 1844, the core of the *hui* was always dominated by the Big Five, the mercantile elite (see Table 4.4).

Thanks to this entrenched domination, the Big Five were able to operate Kian Teik Tong side by side with their businesses, as a sort of auxiliary. This was why Kian Teik Tong branches were so spread out over wide distances, extending to Satun, Trang, Krabi, and Phuket on the southwestern coast of Siam, Moulmein, Mergui, Tavoy, Pegu, and Rangoon in southern Burma, Aceh, Deli, Langkat, and Asahan in the North and the East coast of Sumatra, and the western Malay states of Kedah and Perak.[4] These branches were controlled by close associates of the Big Five who were also well-established local merchants and community leaders. Tan Lwee 陈雷, for instance, a committee member of Kian Teik Tong of Rangoon, owned shipping and rice-milling businesses and served as a member of the Municipal Committee for nine years.[5] Around 1865, the Burmese King Mindon sought his assistance to establish a bank in Mandalay (Wright, Cartwright and Breakspear, eds. 1910, p. 314). In Phuket, the branch was led by Tan Gaik Tam, a Chinese Captain who operated tin mines and monopolized the tin exports of Phuket.[6]

Apart from having family members as leaders of the overseas branches, the Kian Teik Tong of the Big Five also formed alliances with other *hui*, such as the Ho Seng which included Hokkien, Malay, Indian, and Jawi Peranakan members; the Hakka-dominated Hai San, and the Indo-Malay Red Flag. These *hui* or societies also had their branches spread over other states, such as Perak, Kedah, Phuket, and Deli. With such cross-state, cross-ethnic, and cross-dialect allies, the Big Five effectively and conveniently mobilized the Kian Teik Tong, most of the time as private militia to guard their business monopolies or to pursue their business opportunities such as the control of opium revenue farms. As a result, the on-going competition between the Big Five on one side, and the Ghee Hin, the Siamese and the British on the other, for the control of opium revenue farms inevitably spawned a series of bloody inter-*hui* or inter-coalition battles in Penang and the surrounding states. The 1867 Penang riot, the Krabi riot of 1878, the Taiping coolie riot of 1879, and the Deli plantation coolie revolts of 1884 are all cases in point. By unravelling these so-called riots or revolts, we will see how the leading elements of the Big Five families incorporated other forces, such as the economic elite and non-elite of different ethnic and dialect groups, into their network and manipulated them to monopolize opium farms in Penang and beyond.

TABLE 4.4
The Leaders of the Kian Teik Tong or Toa Peh Kong, 1850s–60s

President	Khoo Thean Teik
Vice President	Khoo Thean Poh *alias* Khoo Poh
Vice President	Neo Oo Teoh
Master, the Secretary (teacher)	Lim Beng Kwa
Clerk	Khoo Mah Pean
Councilors	Lim Hwa Chum / Lim Toa Sew / Lim Kim Sae / Lim Pick Tek / Lim Gin / Lim Chong Lay / Cheah Oon Hoot / Cheah Phuan / Cheah Kong Soo / Cheah Pick Siew / Cheah Chew Huan / Khoo Cheng Seng / Teoh Hong / Teoh Ching Yen / Chew Kow / Yeoh Teo / Yeoh Whey Siew / Yeoh Yeong / Yeoh Hong Hin / Yeoh Pang / Yeh Chong Leh / Tan Hong Cheam / Lee Seng Toh / Lee Boon Thean / Lee Mah Yeok / Lee Pean Peh / Ong Boon Keng / Ong Boon Teik / Neoh Lam Yeong / Neoh Hong Toon / Neoh Kom Pang / Neoh Chow Chong

Sources: Compiled from Mervyn Llwellyn Wynne, *Triad and Tabut: A Survey of the Origins and Diffusion of Chinese and Mohammedan Secret Societies in the Malay Peninsular 1800–1935* (Singapore: Government Printing Office, 1941), pp. 252, 258; Wilfred L. Blythe, *The Impact of Chinese Secret Societies in Malaya: A Historical Study* (London: Oxford University Press, 1969), pp. 138, 142; 张少宽 Teoh Shiaw Kuan, 槟榔屿华人史话 *Binlangyu Huaren Shihua* [Historical Anecdotes of the Chinese in Penang] (Kuala Lumpur: Prometheus Enterprise Sdn. Bhd. 光燧人氏事业有限公司), 2002, pp. 43, 48, 244; 张少宽 Teoh Shiaw Kuan, 槟榔屿福建公冢暨家冢碑铭集 *Binlangyu Fujian Gongzhong Ji Jiazhang Beimingji* [Epigraphic Inscriptions of Penang Hokkien Cemeteries] (Singapore: Society of Asian Studies, 1997), p. 185; Khoo Kay Kim, *The Western Malay States 1850–1873: The Effects of Commercial Development on Malay Politics* (London: Oxford University Press, 1972), pp. 205, 222; *Report of the Commissioners Appointed Under Act XXI of 1867 to Enquire into the Penang Riots; Together with Proceedings of the Committee, Minutes of Evidence and Appendix* (Penang: Ludwig Theodore Demello, 1868), pp. 6, 31.

THE 1867 PENANG RIOT

On 3 August 1867, George Town, the business centre of Penang, was engulfed by dreadful scenes of killing and violence. The Indo-Malay secret societies, the Red Flag, siding with the Kian Teik Tong, had come into open conflict with the White Flag group that supported the Ghee Hin. The riots involved 30,000 Chinese and 4,000 Indo-Malays and paralysed George Town for ten days (Pieris 2002, p. 9; Cowan 1981, pp. 52–53; Yen 1986, p. 198). There were 450 to 500 killed and 1,000 houses burned.[7] According to the colonial authority, the rioting was primarily due to long accumulation of quarrels between the *hui* members since 1857.[8] This official explanation of the Penang riots of 1867 is, however, shallow and simplistic. By claiming ideological differences and struggles as the main cause of the riots, neither M.L. Wynne nor W.L. Blythe gave a satisfactory historical explanation (Wynne 1941, pp. 67–90; Blythe 1969, pp. 129–48). Mak Lau Fong's contentious linking of the cause of the riots with the competition between *hui* over occupational monopolization is only partly convincing. While he correctly noted that the source of the conflict lay in an inter-secret society struggle for the exclusive control of certain economic rights and occupations, such as excise farming in the case of Penang (Mak 1981, pp. 48, 51), he did not explain why this monopoly was so significant to the sworn brotherhood *hui*. In order to grasp the root cause of the riots, we need to contextualize the conflicts into the Penang socio-economic setting, which was characterized by a close relationship between revenue farming and the system of export commodity production, and in particular to consider how the opium farm was inseparably tied to the production of tin, sugar, and coconut, and tobacco.

As discussed in the previous chapter, the mid-nineteenth century saw the growing production of agricultural and mineral commodities in Phuket and Perak, sugar in Province Wellesley and coconut in Penang. For example, while in 1843–44, 12,800 pikuls of locally-produced sugar were exported, by 1850–51 this doubled to 44,700 pikuls, and tripled to 69,352 pikuls in 1854–55 (Jackson 1968, p. 142). Tin, exported to England and the United States of America, increased five-fold from 23,842 pikuls in 1860 to 124,907 pikuls in 1866.[9] An increasing number of coolies also pointed to an expansion of production, since tin mining and cash-crop agriculture were labour-intensive enterprises. By 1860, the Chinese population of Penang numbered 28,018, with 8,204 in Province Wellesley, 20,000 in Perak, and 25,000 in Phuket (Purcell 1948, p. x; Wong 1965, p. 27; Gerini 1986, p. 169). With such a large number of Chinese who were mainly coolies, opium was in high demand as it was considered an absolute necessity by the coolies in tin mines and plantations. To the mercantile elite of Penang, therefore, opium was not only a profitable and easily saleable commodity, but also a means of controlling coolies and sustaining their productivity. The significant role of opium as an economic *modus operandi* could also be found in Singapore. As Carl Trocki observes in his work, *Opium and Empire*:

> Opium, the preparation, distribution, and consumption of which was the other integral part of the Chinese economy of Singapore, was not only a system of labor exploitation but actually made the system work to the profit of the shopkeepers, the secret societies, revenue farmers, and the colonial government … it became the main device whereby economic, political, and administrative control was extended over the Chinese population of Singapore. If the plantation owners and the advancers of capital were to recapture the coolies' wages and the surplus value produced by the labours, they needed a share in the farming system. If they were to reap the rewards of their investments, they needed to control both the production and the consumption of the labor force (Trocki 1990, pp. 67, 69, 70).

Taken together, opium, coolies, and the production of exportable agricultural and mineral commodities were closely intertwined and formed the foundation of the commercial system which the mercantile elite of the Big Five families depended on for profit-making and wealth-building.

In April 1867, a Penang opium farm which had been leased out from 1 May 1867 to 3 April 1869 in Penang appreciated to $94,200 per year from $78,000 per year of the last lease and scored the highest rent since the introduction of opium farming in Penang.[10] By bidding so much, the leaders of Ghee Hin and their associates successfully wrested control of the opium farm from the leaders of the Kian Teik Tong in May 1867. As the Penang opium farm served as the distribution centre, losing control of it came as a severe blow to the Kian Teik Tong, whose mercantile-elite leaders were the owners and financiers of tin mines and cash-crop plantations in Penang and the surrounding states. Without the monopoly they could no longer profit from opium sales. Worst of all, they had to either procure expensive opium from their rivals to supply their coolies, or face shortages of opium supply that might lead to their coolies' refusing to work or deserting, jeopardizing mining and cash-crop production, and badly impacting on trade.

This well-founded economic fear was what prompted the Kian Teik Tong and its ally, the Red Flag, to seek to destroy the Ghee Hin's control of the newly-gained opium business through organized violence. Mahani Musa, the author of *Malaya Secret Societies in the Northern Malay States 1821–1940s*, asserts that the close association of the Red Flag and White Flag with the Kian Teik Tong and the Ghee Hin respectively was because the leaders of the two Indo-Malay societies wanted to strengthen their influence in the society (Musa 2003, p. 79). She is partly right. Their alliance, to be more precise, was based on the entrenched business interests of the mercantile elite leaders. Thus we see that Cheah Pek Ee, leader of Kian Teik Tong, and Abdul Kader Merican, leader of the Red Flag Society, had been partners in the revenue farming business in Penang since the 1850s;[11] while Khoo Thean Poh, the vice-president of Kian Teik Tong and Syed Mohamed Alatas, another leader of the Red Flag, were close partners in the pepper and firearms trade between Aceh and Penang (Khoo 1993, pp. 35, 63). It also seems likely that Syed Mohamed Alatas had an interest in the opium business. Likewise, the leaders of the White Flag and the Ghee Hin came together on the same business grounds.

The battle that flared up in the commercial hub of George Town, in the area enclosed by Beach Street, Church Street, Pitt Street and Acheen Street, was thus no accident (see Map 4.1). The area next to the waterfront that included Acheen, Armenian, Chulia, and Beach Streets housed not only the major *kongsis* and *hui* but also numerous shops, godowns, and wharves, and was thus strategically and commercially important to the mercantile elite of Penang (Hussin 2002, p. 90). It was this area that became the locus of all the major trade and business transactions, including the preparation, distribution and sale of retail opium in Penang. In order to disrupt the opium business operations of the Ghee Hin, the leaders of the Kian Teik Tong and the Red Flag mobilized thousands of fighting men of different ethnic and dialect groups — Indians, Malays, Acehnese, Javanese, Hokkiens and Hakkas from Phuket, Kedah and Perak to launch attacks on the shops, godowns and wharves operated by the Ghee Hin and the White Flag (Blythe 1969, pp. 130–32; Wynne 1941, pp. 245–59; Musa 1999, pp. 163–64). In the face of this offensive, the Ghee Hin and the White Flag mustered their fighting men of Indians, Malays, Cantonese, Teochews and Hakkas (mainly from Huizhou) from Phuket, Province Wellesley, Kedah, and Perak to make counter-attacks on the Kian Teik Tong and the Red Flag.[12] In order to defeat their rival, the leaders of the Ghee Hin rewarded $12–20 to its fighting men to have a member of the Kian Teik Tong killed, while the leaders of the Kian Teik Tong offered $30 to get a member of the Ghee Hin slaughtered.[13]

MAP 4.1
Areas in George Town (Penang) Affected by the 1867 Riots

SYMBOLS:
1. Kian Teik Tong (Toa Pek Kong)
2. Khoo Kongsi
3. Acheen Street Mosque
4. Cheah Kongsi
5. Ghee Hin
6. Government Office
7. Supreme Court
8. Chinese Temple (Kong Hock Keong)
9. Kapitan Kling Mosque

Source: This map is drawn according to the map which appears in the *Penang Gazette* on 4 April 1867 (Courtesy of Tan Yeow Wooi).

The Kian Teik Tong was well supplied with powerful firearms (muskets and small canons) from the mercantile leadership of the Big Five and their associates. This was why, despite the numerical strength of the Ghee Hin camp, the Kian Teik Tong was able to gain the upper hand in the battle. Exploiting the chaos, the leaders of the Kian Teik Tong, namely Khoo Thean Teik and Lee Toh, were able to smuggle a huge quantity of opium in and out of Penang.[14] A maze-like network of gateways and passages, big and small, traversing and connecting the shops, *kongsis*, godowns and wharves of the Big Five families became secret strategic channels by which the leaders of the Kian Teik Tong and the Red Flag were able to convey illicit opium, firearms and fighting men between Penang and the surrounding states. Khoo Thean Teik owned two shops located next to a wharf and opposite a gateway of the Khoo *Kongsi* house on Beach Street (see map in photo inserts).[15] The arrangement of the wharf, shops and *kongsi* house easily allowed for the secret passage of smuggled goods like opium and firearms. After being unloaded at the wharf and brought to the shops contraband only needed to be carried across the street to the *kongsi* house whose five strategic gateways would have functioned as the distribution centre. The five gateways linked the Khoo *Kongsi* house to four different streets or directions: one to Cannon Street in the south, one to Acheen Street in the west, one to Beach Street in the north, and two to Armenian Street in the east.[16] Using these gateways, Thean Teik and his clansmen easily gained access to the Kian Teik Tong, other *kongsis* (the Cheah, the Lim, and the Tan), and the Red Flag's headquarters and delivered firearms, fighting men and opium to them in no time during the riot.

The combination of militant attacks and smuggling by the Kian Teik Tong camp was highly detrimental to the opium business of the Ghee Hin camp. The leaders-cum-opium farmers of the Ghee Hin suffered a great loss of revenue in the first year of the lease.[17] When they failed to pay the rent owing, the British authority revoked the Ghee Hin's opium farm lease and re-let the farm in June 1868. Lee Toh and Ong Boon Keng, the two leaders of the Kian Teik Tong successfully bid for the farm at $90,000 per year for the period of July 1868–March 1870 (see Table 4.5).[18]

Taking all this into consideration, it is clear that the underlying cause of the Penang riots was the rivalry for the control of opium farming in Penang. Using the petty quarrels between *hui* members as a pretext and a justification in their action against the rival *hui*, the Big Five kept their true agenda carefully concealed in the background. The battles were fought to protect or secure the monied interests of the mercantile leaders at the top rather than for the welfare of the masses on the bottom of the sworn

TABLE 4.5
Penang Opium Farm Annual Rent, 1855–70

Year	Rent($)	Farmer
1855–56	57,000	Kian Teik Tong
1856–57	67,560	Kian Teik Tong
1857–58	N/A	N/A
1858–59	N/A	N/A
1859–60	N/A	N/A
1860–61	72,120	Kian Teik Tong
1861–62	72,120	Kian Teik Tong
1862–63	78,000	Kian Teik Tong
1863–64	78,000	Kian Teik Tong
1864–65	78,000	Kian Teik Tong
1865–66	78,000	Kian Teik Tong
1866–67	78,000	Kian Teik Tong
1867–68	94,200	Ghee Hin
1868–69	90,000	Kian Teik Tong
1869–70	90,000	Kian Teik Tong

Note: N/A = Not Available
Sources: Papers laid before the Legislative Council by Command of His Excellency the Governor, *Straits Settlement Legislative Council Proceedings 1869*, p. 2; *Annual Reports of the Straits Settlement 1856–57*, p. 84.

brotherhood *hui*. Strictly speaking, the struggle was a form of leverage operated by the leaders of the Big Five families to reclaim the opium farming network which constituted the linchpin of their profitable commercial system in Penang and the region.

THE KRABI RIOT OF 1878

In 1878, the leaders of the Kian Teik Tong went into action again to wield their political and economic might to secure their revenue farms in the neighbouring Siamese province of Krabi. By forming a close alliance with Phraya Nakhon Si Thammarat, Cheah Pek Ee 谢伯夷, a leader of the Kian Teik Tong in Krabi, had kept control of all the revenue farms in Krabi since 1866 (Songprasert 1986, p. 62). In 1876, Phra Itsarathichai, the younger half-brother of Phraya Nakhon Si Thammarat, who was appointed as the first governor of Krabi, took over the rights to tax collection himself.[19] This unexpected change caused not only a political setback for Phraya Nakhhon Si Thammarat, but also a huge business loss to Cheah Pek Ee. Losing his revenue farms, Pek Ee complained to Phraya Nakhon Si Thammarat and demanded compensation. But instead of paying compensation, Phraya Nakhon Si Thammarat persuaded Pek Ee to assassinate the new governor.[20] With a supply of firearms and fighting men from his counterparts, Tan Neo Yee and Tan Pai Wun, the two leaders of Kian Teik Tong in Phuket, Pek Ee decided to carry out the assassination. On 21 January 1878, Pek Ee mobilized about 175 fighting men and launched an attack on the governor's house at midnight.[21] Although they successfully killed the governor, Pek Ee and eighty followers were apprehended by the government forces from the adjacent provinces within a few days (Songprasert 1986, pp. 173–74). The Siamese government was able to punish all except the leader, Pek Ee, who claimed to be a British subject and demanded the protection of the Straits government.

The arrest of Pek Ee immediately caused a huge stir in Penang. Not only was he a leader of the Krabi's Kian Teik Tong, he was also a community leader of the Cheah Kongsi of Penang. It was not surprising then, that the counterparts of Pek Ee in Penang — the mercantile leaders of the Big Five who were also the chiefs of Penang's Kian Teik Tong — went to Pek Ee's rescue. In 1879, the case of Pek Ee became the subject of public discussion in the *Pinang Gazette and Straits Chronicle*, a popular local newspaper. On 6 August 1879, an article was published to defend Pek Ee that argued any British subject, who sojourned or resided for a time in Kedah, Patani, Kuala Muda, Perlis, Songkhla, Kelantan, Trang, Tongkah or any other dependency of Siam in the Malayan Peninsula, was still entitled to British protection.[22] It also maintained that the Bowring Treaty of 1855 between England and Siam did not require a British subject to register with the British Consulate outside Bangkok in order to receive British protection.[23]

On 16 August 1879, another article appeared in the *Pinang Gazette and Straits Chronicle* not only to echo the argument in the article of 6 August, but also to firmly uphold the status of Pek Ee as a British subject. It stated:

Pek Ee never declared that he intended to remain in Ghirbee for ever or until death. The honor given to him as "Luang Pachim Nakhon" was an honorary given to him as a token of respect for his good conduct in improving the revenue of Ghirbee and not because he was naturalized or Siamese subject. The fact that his wife and children reside in his home in Penang and have kept up a regular trade between Ghirbee and this place in conjunction with his 3 sons during the last 10 to 12 years proves that the business he was carrying on there was a branch of the trade here and that he has done nothing to forfeit his rights as a British subject.[24]

The appearance of these two articles clearly shows that the Big Five, who had a close connection with James Young Kennedy, the proprietor of the *Pinang Gazette and Straits Chronicle* and a member of the Legislative Council (Wu 2003, p. 75), used their ally's press to publicize the case of Pek Ee in order to rally support and put pressure on the Straits government to intervene. Around the end of August 1879, the Straits government did press the Siamese government to send Pek Ee back to Penang for trial. But the Siamese government refused the Straits government's demand on the grounds that Pek Ee, who had resided in the Siamese territory for nearly twenty years and held the title of Luang Prachim Nakhon, was a Siamese subject and subject to Siamese law. Nevertheless, the Straits government ignored the Siamese argument and responded by claiming that Phraya Nakhon Si Thammarat was the prime mover, and asking for him to be arrested and punished (Songprasert 1986, p. 174). Under the mounting pressure from the British, the Siamese eventually permitted Pek Ee to be brought back to Penang for further investigation and trial.

In the case of Phraya Nakhon Si Thammarat, the Siamese government found that it was almost impossible to prosecute this powerful governor, whose family's influence prevailed throughout the south. In the early 1890s, the Siamese government abandoned the case and allowed him to regain the governorship of Nakhon Si Thammarat. It is interesting to note that Cheah Boon Ean, the son of Cheah Pek Ee, took over his father's business in Krabi in 1882, and most probably went into partnership with his father's old ally, Phraya Nakhon Si Tammarat, who was back into power.[25]

THE 1879 COOLIE RIOT OF TAIPING

In September 1879, just about a month before the commencement of a new tender, Sir Hugh Low (see Image 2 in photo inserts), the British Resident of Perak, decided to combine all the revenue farms in Perak into one comprehensive unit, which included opium, spirits, gaming, pawnbroking, tobacco, atap (roofing thatch), and the collection of the duty on tin.[26] The background to this surprise move lay in the cost of the Perak War, which was launched by the Straits government to arrest the Malay rulers who had assassinated the first Resident of Perak, J.W.W. Birch, in Perak in 1875. In other words, through this "all-in-one" revenue farm plan, the Straits government intended to recoup its Perak war expenses which amounted to $550,000.[27] This plan, which allowed one party to have monopolistic rights over all the farms, was very disruptive to the existing regional-based revenue farming system, especially the opium farms. Under the regional-based system, the mine owners or *hui* leaders had control of a number of their own opium farms that imported raw opium and manufactured and sold cooked opium at their own price to the coolies, who worked in the mines at different regions in Perak (Gullick 1953, p. 48). However, a single opium farm for the whole of Perak would mean a centralization of importation and distribution of opium as well as a controlled price.

By introducing such a revenue farming plan, Low hoped to increase the state revenue with a rent at $42,000 a month when the new lease began in 1880.[28] In other words, the one-year rent for all the revenue farms would be $504,000. However, Low's grand plan was not without opposition. The financiers of the mines (the leaders of the *hui*), who were primarily from the Big Five, protested that the "one revenue farm" would entail a monopolization by outsiders and unreasonably push up the retail price of cooked opium, which would be unacceptable to the mining coolies (Sadka 1968, p. 193). They suggested that Low should impose higher import duty on raw opium to raise state revenue. However, Low paid no heed to the grievance and proceeded to invite tenders.

Low had never thought that his intransigence would spawn a series of coolie riots, closure of shops and mining strikes that would paralyse Taiping, the biggest town in Larut, for three days. On 3 October 1879, a mob of 300 to 400 miners (coolies) surrounded Low's residency in the morning and demanded that he drop his proposed opium farm.[29] Calling troops from the barracks, Low succeeded in driving the mobs into the town where they ran amok, breaking into shops and looting the gambling farm. The chief of the Perak Armed Police led a detachment to dispel the mobs, they resisted fiercely by throwing metal pieces, and in one case firing a revolver at the police. Amidst this commotion, the police opened fire, killing twenty-seven and wounding twenty-three rioters.[30] Immediately after the mob was dispersed, all the shops were closed and the mines stopped operation. The shopkeepers refused to sell a single article of food to any

Europeans and even threatened to poison every European in the place.[31] On 4 October, a group of towkays, headed by Khoo Thean Teik and Chung Keng Kwee (see Images 3 and 4 in photo inserts), went to see Low and promised to induce the shopkeepers to reopen their shops. Low agreed to discuss their grievances in a meeting fixed on 6 October.[32] The following day, 5 October, another riot broke out at the Kamunting Gambling Shop.[33] After a two-hour discussion in the meeting of 6 October, Low bowed to the demands of the miners, abandoning the scheme of one farm and adopting the proposal to increase the import duty on raw opium from $2 to $5 a ball.[34]

Given this sequence of events, it is clear that the leaders-cum-financiers of the *hui* (like Khoo Thean Teik and Chung Keng Kwee) were the masterminds behind the agitation. What really concerned these two leaders, as we have explained, was the loss of control over the preparation and retail sale of opium, which had been the main means to exercise a hold over their labour force and to increase their profit margin. By controlling its preparation and sale, the leaders could minimize the production cost and maximize the prices of opium. More often than not opium was also adulterated to reduce production cost.[35] Then the adulterated opium was supplied to the coolies at exorbitant prices (200 per cent to 300 per cent above market prices) under what was called the "truck system" (Drabble 2000, p. 55; Wong 1965, p. 75). This was the system for supplying of provisions (rice, opium, liquor, tobacco, oil) by the mine owners or advancers to coolies at mark-ups of as much as 200 per cent to 300 per cent. It was one of the crucial ways by which the leaders of the *hui* accumulated their wealth. For them, the introduction of a single farm system posed a threat to their entrenched profit-making system in Larut. To defend the system, the *hui* leaders instigated organized riots and strikes designed to force the British to terms. Their withdrawal of the comprehensive revenue farm and the continuation of the regional farm system in Larut was undoubtedly a concession to the economic power of the Big Five and their associates, who controlled a well-knit network of revenue farms, tin mines and coolie force.

THE 1884 PLANTATION COOLIES REVOLT OF DELI

During the last four months of 1884, Deli on the East Coast of Sumatra witnessed a sequence of coolie riots flaring up across the tobacco estates. The coolies, belonging to two different brotherhood *hui*, Ho Seng and Ghee Hin, took up arms ranging from sticks and parangs to revolvers to fight against each other.³⁶ Binjei, Medan and Labuan were the hardest hit by these riots. Mobs of coolies, especially Ho Seng members, charged the towns and raided brothels and houses to kill the members of the Ghee Hin.³⁷ By December 1884, the riots engulfed more estates and spread to Serdang.³⁸ In one estate, all of the 300 coolies rose to attack the manager and three assistants with stones. Many Chinese were killed or injured as well as members of other ethnic groups such as Bataks, Malays and Dutch officers.³⁹ By stationing more military forces there and arresting the ringleaders, the Dutch eventually suppressed the riots.

To the Dutch authority, these estate riots were simply criminal acts committed by coolies who were influenced by secret societies. However, as with the other cases discussed in this chapter, the riots were something more than that. On available evidence, it seems that they were part of a plot by wealthy businessmen, who were also government officers and leaders of the brotherhood *hui*, to weaken their rivals in the competition for the Deli revenue farming business, bidding for which opened at the end of 1884.⁴⁰ Their success in gaining control of the revenue farms here gave them a highly profitable business since Deli was one of the most important tobacco producing regions in the world, and housed about 20,000 coolies by 1884 (Reid 2005, p. 223). Khoo Teng Ko 邱登果, the Lieutenant of Chinese in Laboean, Lim Tek Swee 林德水, the Kapitan China of Deli, and Lim Tjing Keh 林清溪, the Lieutenant of Chinese in Bindjey,⁴¹ were most probably the leaders of Ho Seng; certainly they were closely connected to the Big Five in Penang. Khoo Teng Ko, for example, was an active patron in Penang. From 1882 to 1890, he had made donations of 2,000 *yuan* (dollars) to most of the temples and public cemeteries managed by the Big Five (Teoh 2003, p. 235). He also partnered Khoo Soo Ghee and Khoo Eow Chaw of Penang to establish a general trading store, Chop Ee Seng, at No. 144 Beach Street in Penang.⁴² Through this intricate association with the leaders of Ho Seng in the East Coast of Sumatra, the Kian Teik Tong of the Big Five became an ally of Ho Seng, and could have played a part in organizing the coolie riots, which as elsewhere, are best understood as a form of economic leverage.

THE DOMINANCE OF THE BIG FIVE AND THE DECLINE OF THE GHEE HIN

Taking account of the prominent and influential position of the Kian Teik Tong–Hai San camp in Larut, it was not surprising that Sir Hugh Low leased all the major revenue farms (opium, spirits, pawn-broking and gambling) to Khoo Thean Teik's syndicate for the years 1880, 1881 and 1882 (see Table 4.6).

By being granted all these revenue farms, the allied Kian Tek Tong–Hai San financial group represented by Khoo Thean Teik and Chung Keng Kwee had in fact gained the revenue farm monopoly in Perak. As absurd as it may sound, the syndicate led by Khoo and Chung only paid an annual rent of $122,120, which was about $380,000 less than the original amount ($504,000) Low had hoped to realize from the consolidated revenue farm scheme. From then on, the Big Five and their associates continued to dominate revenue farming throughout Perak until at least the early 1900s, while the Ghee Hin could only gain control of the Larut gaming and pawnbroking farm for 1883–85. Their loss of control of the opium farms signalled the declining influence of the Ghee Hin in Larut.

Having crowded out the Ghee Hin from the revenue farming business, the Big Five became the dominant economic force. This was particularly obvious in opium farming. The Big Five and their associates controlled the opium farms not only in Penang, but also in Phuket, Krabi, Kedah, Perak and Deli. In the face of such a formidable opponent, the commercial leadership of the Ghee Hin was eventually reduced to a subordinate position. By the late 1880s, the Ghee Hin of Penang was in a deep financial crisis, with internal disputes among the leaders. Choo Ah Wat, Wong Ting Tong and

TABLE 4.6
Perak's Major Revenue Farms and Farmers, 1880–82

Farms	Farmers	Annual Rent ($)
Krean and Kurow General Farm	Khoo Thean Teik	42,000
Larut Gambling, Pawnbroking, Spirit and Tobacco Farms	Chung Keng Kwee	56,720
Perak River Farm of Opium Duties	Khoo Thean Teik	19,200
Perak River Farm of Tobacco Duties	Khoo Thean Teik	2,640
Perak River Attap Farm	Low Kim	1,560
Total		**122,120**

Source: *Pinang Gazette and Straits Chronicle*, 7 October 1879, p. 4.

Chin Ah Yok, who were the headmen of the Ghee Hin, had mismanaged the business of the *hui* and incurred heavy debts. In one case, these headmen started a sugar cane plantation and mill at Balik Pulau in Penang in 1889 with *hui* money and a loan of $9,500 from Tan Kim Keng,[43] a Big Five family member, but it ended in a loss. By 1890, the debts and liabilities of the Ghee Hin amounted to $30,000.[44] Such financial difficulties ignited a legal conflict between the leaders of the Ghee Hin, with Chin Ah Yok suing Choo Ah Wat and Wong Ting Tong for misappropriation of $21,523 in *kongsi* funds.[45]

Furthermore, the headmen were also under pressure from the British authorities, following the Societies Ordinance 1889, to dissolve their *hui*. On 12 May 1890, forty-six trustees of the property of the Ghee Hin authorized a committee of eleven headmen to sell the lands owned by the *hui* via public auction to settle all debts and liabilities and to pay gratuities to the headmen and the general body of members.[46] On 21 August 1890, an order was made by the Governor in Council, under Section 11 of the Ordinance, declaring the Ghee Hin would be dissolved on 24 November 1890.[47] Although the Kian Teik Tong controlled by the Big Five was also dissolved around the same time, the mercantile elite of the Big Five were able to form a Chinese Traders Society, which was also known as Hock Teik Cheng Sin 福德正神庙, to take over the business and properties (Tan 2007, p. 39). The dissolution of the Ghee Hin thus marked not only the collapse of a formerly powerful economic force but also the eventual supremacy of another economic force — the Big Five.

CONCLUSION

The 1860s–80s period in this Penang-centred region can best be described as the era in which business expansion and competition were intense, particularly in opium revenue farming. The series of conflicts throughout the region clearly indicated that the Big Five were pursuing their opium farming in an economic arena containing a number of competing forces. Among them, the Ghee Hin was the most aggressive. By commanding a large troop of coolies and forming alliances with the mercantile or political elite of different dialect and ethnic groups, both the Big Five and the Ghee Hin could mobilize armed power and financial resources to compete with each other for economic dominance. With their strategic alliance and shrewd manipulation, the Big Five leaders, who also dominated the leadership of the Kian Teik Tong, were able to gain the upper hand in all these rivalries. When facing competition from the numerically powerful Ghee Hin, the Big Five amalgamated the Kian Teik Tong with the Hai San, the Ho Seng and the Red Flag. Confronting indigenous powers, such as the Siamese chiefs, the Big Five resorted to force and then turned to the British for protection, playing the card of their status as British subject. But the Big Five would not hesitate to challenge the British by instigating coolie disturbances when their interests conflicted. The sworn-brotherhood *hui* of Kian Teik Tong was an effective tool used by the Big Five not only to create cross-dialect and cross-ethnic alliances within mercantile and political elite, but also to mobilize the non-elite class of coolies to attain dominance in opium farming.

Opium revenue farms were not the only economic monopoly the Big Five competitively pursued and jealously guarded. The tin mining business was another important money-maker. Over this the Big Five also actively sought to establish a monopoly that encountered stiff competition from the Ghee Hin and the powerful Singapore Hokkien business clique. The next chapter tells the story of the Big Five's contest for the control of this lucrative mineral enterprise.

Notes

1. Carl A. Trocki, "The Rise and Fall of the Ngee Heng Kongsi in Singapore", in *Secret Societies Reconsidered*, edited by David Ownby and Mary Somers Heidhues (New York: M.E. Sharpe, 1993), p. 91.
2. Khoo Kay Kim, *The Western Malay States 1850–1873: The effects of commercial development on Malay politics* (Kuala Lumpur: Oxford University Press, 1972), p. 112. See also *Binlangyu Huaren Shihua*, p. 239.
3. Some Hokkiens still remained in the Ghee Hin, with Oh Wee Kee (胡维期/围棋) as the leader of its remaining Hokkien faction.
4. Jennifer Cushman, "Revenue Farms and Secret Society Uprisings in Nineteenth Century Siam and the Malay States", *RIMA (Review of Indonesian and Malaysian Affairs)* 23 (1989): 6–11; Phuwadol Songprasert, "The Development of Chinese Capital in Southern Siam, 1868–1932", PhD thesis, Monash University, 1986, pp. 140–52; 方雄普 [Fang Xiong Pu], 朱波散记 — 缅甸华人社会掠影 *Zhubo Sanji — Miandian Huaren Shehui Lueying* [Short Essays on the Burma's Chinese Society] (Hong Kong: Nandao Chubanshe 南岛出版社, 2000年), pp. 268, 338–40; Mervyn Llewelyn Wynne, *Triad and Tabut: A Survey of the Origin and Diffusion of Chinese and Mohamedan Secret Societies in the Malay Peninsula A.D. 1800–1935* (Singapore: Government Printing Office, 1941), pp. 403–17. The first branch of Kian Teik Tong in Burma was established in Moulmein in 1843. By the late nineteenth century, there were about seventy branches spreading over Burma.

The branches in North Sumatra were most probably affiliated with the Ho Seng.
5. Arnold Wright, H.A. Cartwright, and Oliver T. Breakspear, eds., *Twentieth Century Impressions of Burma: Its History, People, Commerce, Industries and Resources* (London: Lloyd's Greater Britain Pub Co., 1910), p. 314. The Municipal Committee was vested with the authority to take care of the construction and maintenance of roads, streets, drains, and bridges in a colonial city.
6. Songprasert, "Chinese Capital in Southern Siam", p. 142. He donated $2 to the opening of the first Hokkien cemetery in Penang at Batu Lancang in 1805 and $34 to the restoration of Penang's oldest temple, the Kong Hock Keong (广福宫 Guang Fu Gong) in 1862/63. Wolfgang Franke and Chen Tie Fan, *Chinese Epigraphic Materials in Malaysia, vol. II* (Kuala Lumpur: University of Malaya Press, 1982–87), pp. 538, 715.
7. *The Penang Argus and Mercantile Advertiser*, 12 March 1868, p. 2.
8. *The Penang Argus and Mercantile Advertiser*, 31 October 1867, p. 5. See also Mervyn Llwellyn Wynne, *Triad and Tabut: A Survey of the Origin and Diffusion of Chinese and Mohamedan Secret Societies in the Malay Peninsula 1800–1935* (Singapore: Government Printing Office, 1941), pp. 249–50.
9. "Penang Market Report", *The Penang Argus and Mercantile Advertiser*, 16 March 1870, p. 2.
10. Opium revenue farming was introduced into Penang in 1791 and the rent for the year of 1791–92 was $3,499. See Wong Lin Ken, "The Revenue Farms of Prince of Wales Island 1805–1830", *Journal of South Seas Society*, vol. 19, nos. 1 and 2 (1965): Appendix I.
11. *Pinang Gazette and Straits Chronicle*, 9 June 1855, p. 4.
12. Wilfred L. Blythe, *The Impact of Chinese Secret Societies in Malaya: A Historical Study* (London: Oxford University Press, 1969), pp. 130–32; see also F.S. Brown, "Report upon the secret societies — Papers laid before the Legislative Council by His Excellency the Governor, 28th August 1869", in *Straits Settlements Legislative Council Proceedings 1867–68*, p. LXXVI.
13. "Minutes of Evidence taken before the Commissioners under the Penang Riots Enquiry Act of 1867", *Straits Settlements Legislative Council Proceedings 1867–68*, p. 120.
14. Ibid., pp. 57 and 62. See also Blythe, *The Impact of Chinese Secret Societies in Malaya*, pp. 130–32.
15. *The Penang Argus and Mercantile Advertiser*, 15 December 1870, p. 3.
16. Chen Kuo-Wei and Huang Lan Shiang, "Meaning in Architectural and Urban Space of the Penang Kongsi Enclave", paper presented at the Penang Story International Conference 2002, p. 10. Also see 槟城龙山堂邱公司: 历史与建筑材料 *Bincheng Longshantang Qiugongsi: Lishi Yu Jianzhu Cailiao* [Leong San Tong Khoo Kongsi: The History and Architecture] (Penang: Leong San Tong Khoo Kongsi Publication Committee 槟城龙山堂邱公司

出版小组, 2003), p. 57 and Tan Lye Ho, ed., *Bestowing Luck and Prosperity on All: Hock Teik Cheng Sin Temple* (Penang: Hock Teik Cheng Sin Temple, 2007), pp. 88–89. There was a secret passage connecting Khoo Kongsi to Kian Teik Tong which has its main entrance facing Armenian Street.
17. *Annual Report of the Straits Settlements 1868*, p. 38.
18. *The Penang Argus and Mercantile Advertiser*, 13 October 1870, p. 3. Lee Toh or Lee Seng Toh (李成都), who was the Gee Ko (vice-president) and Ong Boon Keng (王文慶) who was a councilor, took charge of the *hui* business while Khoo Thean Teik and others were taken into custody by the British authority.
19. *PGSC*, 9 July 1879, p. 3. See also Songprasert, "Chinese Capital in Southern Siam", pp. 172–73.
20. *PGSC*, 9 July 1879, p. 3. See also Songprasert, "Chinese Capital in Southern Siam", p. 173.
21. *PGSC*, 9 July 1879, p. 3.
22. *PGSC*, 6 August 1879, p. 4.
23. *PGSC*, 16 August 1879, p. 3. The Bowring Treaty was signed on Britain's behalf by Sir John Bowring, governor of Hong Kong, with the Siamese King Mongkut (Rama IV, 1851–68). Under the terms of the treaty, British merchants were permitted to buy and sell in Siam without intermediaries, a consulate was established, and British subjects were granted extraterritorial rights.
24. *PGSC*, 16 August 1879, p. 3.
25. *PGSC*, 26 September 1879, p. 3. See also Songprasert, "Chinese Capital in Southern Siam", pp. 174–75.
26. CO 273/100, The Late Riot at Larut, 9 September 1879, pp. 6, 11, 12. See also Philip Loh, "Social Policy in Perak", *Peninjau Sejarah*, vol. 1, no. 1 (July 1966): 37; Blythe, *The Impact of Chinese Secret Societies in Malaya*, p. 251; and Emily Sadka, *The Protected Malay States 1874–1895* (Kuala Lumpur: University of Malaya Press, 1968), p. 192.
27. CO 275/24, Paper laid before the Legislative Council by command of His Excellency the Governor: Perak War expenses, 20 May 1880, p. 201 and 24 August 1880, p. 347.
28. CO 273/100, The Late Riot at Larut, 9 September 1879, p. 6. See also Loh, "Social Policy in Perak", p. 37; Blythe, *The Impact of Chinese Secret Societies in Malaya*, p. 251.
29. *PGSC*, 7 October 1879, p. 3. See also CO 273/100, The Late Riot at Larut, 18 October 1879, pp. 1–2; and Blythe, *The Impact of Chinese Secret Societies in Malaya*, p. 251. According to Hugh Low's report, the number of miners was 1,500 to 2,000, four to five times larger than the number reported in *PGSC*.
30. *PGSC*, 7 October 1879, p. 4.
31. *PGSC*, 7 October 1879, p. 3.
32. *PGSC*, 7 October 1879, p. 4. See also Loh, "Social Policy in Perak", p. 38.

33. CO 273/100, The Late Riot at Larut, 9 September 1879. See also Loh, "Social Policy in Perak", p. 38.
34. *PGSC*, 10 October 1879, p. 3. See also Loh, "Social Policy in Perak", p. 38.
35. *PGSC*, 7 October 1879, p. 3.
36. *The Penang Times*, 3 and 10 September 1884, p. 2.
37. *The Penang Times*, 20 September 1884, p. 2.
38. *The Penang Times*, 3 December 1884, p. 2.
39. *The Penang Times*, 21 January 1885, pp. 2–3.
40. *The Penang Times*, 27 September 1884, p. 1. The advertisement for the bidding of the revenue farms in the East Coast had frequently appeared on the first page of the *Penang Times* since early September.
41. Arnold Wright and Oliver T. Breakspear, *Twentieth Century Impressions of Netherlands India: Its History, People, Commerce, Industries, and Resources* (London: Lloyd's Greater Britain Publishing Company Ltd., 1910), p. 581. Lim Tek Swee (林德水) was the top donor who contributed 1,000 *yuan* (dollars) for the reconstruction of Lim Kongsi of Penang in 1893. In 1866–91, he also contributed a substantial amount of donation to the public cemeteries and temples managed by the members of the Big Five families.
42. *PGSC*, 2 August 1879, p. 6.
43. *PGSC*, 2 August 1891, p. 6.
44. *PGSC*, 3 February 1891, p. 5.
45. *PGSC*, 15 January 1891, p. 6.
46. *PGSC*, 3 February 1891, p. 5.
47. *PGSC*, 3 February 1891, p. 5.

5

THE CONTEST FOR "WHITE GOLD"

Tin had been mined and traded in Southeast Asia since at least the tenth century. Although the production and trade in the early period was limited in scale, tin was no doubt a valuable and popular commodity.[1] The mountain ranges in peninsular Burma, Thailand and Malaya share the same geological structure of granite masses forming and contain rich tin reserves (Courtenay 1972, pp. 47–52; Ooi 1963, pp. 295–97). This tin belt, centred in Malaya and extending for hundred of miles northwards into southern Thailand and lower Burma, and southwards to the islands of Singkep, Bangka and Billiton, was the richest and most extensive in the world. It was not until the Industrial Revolution spurred the demand for tin and motivated Chinese merchants and miners, however, that this tin belt was turned into a production powerhouse. As mentioned in Chapter 2, the tin mining business in Phuket and Perak, the two richest tin producing states in the nineteenth century, was in the hands of the Big Five. But this does not mean that the Big Five faced no challenges. In fact, the competition for "White Gold" (tin) was no less than for "Black Gold" (opium). It is not surprising that the Ghee Hin was one of the most aggressive competitors, since tin mining was a very profitable enterprise and was also inextricably tied to the opium farming business. Besides Ghee Hin, the Singapore Hokkien mercantile elite also made attempts to break into the Big Five's tin mining domain in Larut of Perak. This chapter will examine the competition from the various sides and how the Big Five responded.

LARUT AND THE BIG FIVE'S TIN MINING INTERESTS

With the discovery of tin fields in late 1840s, Larut quickly became the magnet for coolies and capitalists from Penang.[2] This phenomenon was due to the expansion of the U.K. tinplate industry which in turn led to an increasing demand for Straits tin. The Hakka from Zengcheng 增城 district of Guangdong province, who formed the majority of the members of the Hai San *hui*, were the first miners who went to Larut. In the early 1860s, they emerged as the largest group of miners in Larut and outnumbered the miners of the Ghee Hin, who were mainly the Hakka from Huizhou 惠州 district of Guangdong province with a small number of Cantonese from Xinning 新寧 district of Guangdong province, in the proportion of nearly two to one (Khoo 1972, pp. 69–70). These two factions made up nearly four-fifths of the total population of Larut. The tin fields and the miners who worked at them were financed by the mercantile elite, who were also the leaders of the *hui*, in Penang. For example, Oh Wee Kee, a merchant and the vice-president of the Ghee Hin, personally made an advance of $5,000 to finance the miners in Klian Bahru of Larut in 1865 (Khoo 1972, p. 70).

Khoo Thean Teik, the headman of the Kian Teik Tong, and his associate, Koh Seang Thye (most probably Koh Seang Tat) outperformed their Ghee Hin rival. In 1873 and 1874, they provided money and goods worth $60,000 to Chung Keng Kwee, the chief of the Hai San *hui*, who controlled about 10,000 coolies and most of the mines in Larut.[3] With the combination of Kian Teik Tong's financial power and Hai San's control of manpower, the leaders of the Kian Teik Tong obtained valuable tin for trade; conversely, with Kian Teik Tong's capital and provisions Hai San recruited more coolies and therefore expanded their mining.

What was more, Hai San and Kian Teik Tong had the strong backing of a local Malay chief, Che Ngah Ibrahim. Since 1862, Che Ngah Ibrahim had followed in his father's (Che Long Ja'afar) footsteps and sided with the Hai San, which commanded the largest number of mining coolies and emerged as the strongest *hui* in Larut.[4] Che Ngah Ibrahim held absolute administrative authority over Larut: he levied taxes, collected revenue, farmed out duty-collecting rights, and granted land on his own free will. (Winstedt and Wilkinson 1974, p. 81; Sadka 1968, pp. 26–27). Thanks to this relationship, the leaders of the Kian Teik Tong were awarded the right to collect tin duty in Larut. Foo Tye Sin, for instance, collected 850 slabs of tin as duty from Larut in 1874 alone (Burns 1976, p. 22). In return,

Che Ngah Ibrahim received generous financial loans from Khoo Thean Teik, Foo Tye Sin, Ong Boon Teik, and Koh Seang Tat. In one case, he received a loan of $4,000 from Foo Tye Sin and Ong Boon Keng (Khoo 1972, p. 209).

THE OUTBREAK OF LARUT WARS: TUSSLE OVER TIN MINES

The Ghee Hin was naturally uneasy and jealous of the Hai San's acquisition of the favour of Che Long Ja'afar and later, Che Ngah Ibrahim. The tension between the two eventually led to three major conflicts in Larut, almost all of them fought between the Cantonese from Xinning and the Hakkas from Huizhou and Zengcheng. In the first and second Larut "wars" of 1861 and 1865, the antagonists were the Ghee Hin led by Soo Ah Chiang and the Zengcheng Hakka of the Hai San headed by Chung Keng Kwee, who in turn was backed by the Mentri Larut and the Kian Teik Tong of Penang. The Ghee Hin were beaten in the first two conflicts. They lost their tin mines and their leader, Soo Ah Chiang, was captured and executed.[5] After that, the Ghee Hin began to experience a shift in its leadership. After the death of Soo Ah Chiang, the Huizhou Hakka members slowly migrated out of Larut and headed to the lower part of Perak (Kinta), Selangor or Negeri Sembilan.[6] The growing number of Xinning 新寧 Cantonese of the Ho Hup Seah 和合社, an affiliated *hui* of the Ghee Hin, quickly filled in the vacuum left by the Huizhou Hakka.

In 1872–73, the Xinning Cantonese, who became the majority in the Ghee Hin-Ho Hap Seah league, fought against the Zengcheng Hakka. Hokkiens, Teochews, and the British were also involved. In February 1872, the Ghee Hin, under the leadership of Ho Ghi Siew, marshalled more fighting men and weapons from Penang to launch a month-long ferocious attack on the Hai San that drove the Hai San out of their stronghold, Klian Pauh, in March 1872 (Wong 1963, pp. 72–73; Winstedt and Wilkinson 1974, p. 83; Khoo 1972, pp. 166–67). The Ghee Hin recaptured all their lost mines and took possession of all the mines belonging to the Hai San. Things went so badly for the Hai San that the leaders of the Kian Teik Tong of Penang, who had been the financial supporter and provisions supplier of the Hai San and had crucial stake in their business, had to enter the scene directly to help the Hai San to turn the tables on the Ghee Hin. They zealously marshalled munitions, fighting men and a battle fleet to launch a counter attack on the Ghee Hin. In one instance,

Khoo Hong Chooi used his junk to ship 100 fighting men, 200 muskets and bayonets, 8 pieces of small ordinance with shot, and 400 spearheads to Larut in October 1872. Within four days, the leaders of the Kian Teik Tong secretly brought 2,000 muskets, over 10,000 pounds of gun powder, and 1,000 fighting men to join the Hai San.[7]

The Kian Teik Tong also actively invoked the support of the Penang British government against the Ghee Hin. In December 1872, Khoo Thean Teik complained to the British authority that his vessel *Fair Malacca*, which was sailing with trade goods to Larut, had been fired on by the Ghee Hin junks, which were blockading the coast of Larut. By emphasizing that his vessel was a British steamer of Straits registration, and piloted by a British captain, Khoo Thean Teik primed the British authority to regard the Ghee Hin's attack as a challenge to British power. As a result, Governor Sir Harry Ord treated the incident as a case of piracy and sent off Captain Denison, the senior naval officer, to seize the two Ghee Hin junks involved.[8] What is important to note in this is that the so-called incident was in fact a ploy of Khoo Thean Teik to obtain the aid of the British navy to break the Ghee Hin's coastal blockade.

By July 1873, the leaders of the Kian Teik Tong and Ngah Ibrahim decided to make another move to obtain the full support of the British in fighting against the Ghee Hin. Offering a monthly salary of $5,000 and one third of the revenues of Larut, Ngah Ibrahim successfully persuaded Captain Speedy, the superintendent of police in Penang, who had earned but a monthly salary of $200, to relinquish his position and work for him.[9] The Ghee Hin suffered a decisive setback in September 1873, when Sir Harry Ord, infuriated by the Ghee Hin's refusal to cease fire, decided to throw the whole weight of British support on the side of the Kian Teik Tong–Han San–Ngah Ibrahim alliance (Gullick 1953, p. 34; Cowan 1981, pp. 119–20). Recognizing Ngah Ibrahim as an autonomous ruler, Ord permitted firearms to reach him and the Han San, while also authorizing Speedy to recruit sepoys from India.[10] Having the British on their side, the Kian Teik Tong camp believed that the expulsion of the Ghee Hin from Larut was imminent and the monopolization of the tin mines in Larut would soon be in their hands. However, the ambition of the Kian Teik Tong camp was thwarted by a certain turn of events in November 1873.

THE INVOLVEMENT OF TAN KIM CHING

The Ghee Hin's hope now rested on another Malay chief, Raja Abdullah, who had sided with the Ghee Hin since 1872 in the hope of getting support to expel Ngah Ibrahim from Larut and claim the succession to the Sultanate. Seeing the Ghee Hin camp in a greatly disadvantageous position he turned for help to Tan Kim Ching 陈金钟, a prominent Hokkien merchant and Singapore leader, by promising to lease him the Perak river revenue farm for ten years at $26,000 a year.[11] With the arrival of Sir Andrew Clarke, the new governor of the Straits Settlement, Tan Kim Ching and his business associate, W.H. Read, who was also a member of the Legislative Council, successfully lobbied the British authority to recognize Raja Abdullah as the legitimate Sultan of Perak.[12] By inducing the leaders of the Ghee Hin and Hai San as well as the Malay chiefs to sign the Treaty of Pangkor in 1874, the British authority seemed to have appeased everyone — Raja Abdullah was installed as the Sultan; other Malay chiefs were given some perks and maintained their status quo (except Sultan Ismail who was deposed, but was to be given a title and a pension); the Hai San was allocated the tin mines in Klian Pauh, while the Ghee Hin was given the tin mines in Klian Bahru — and peace was restored in Larut (Winstedt and Wilkinson 1974, p. 99; Barlow 1995, pp. 45–49; Wynne 1941, pp. 282–98; Parkinson 1960, pp. 323–24).

In reality, the British authority and Tan Kim Ching were the biggest winners in the settlement of the Larut Wars. A British Resident was introduced to assist the Sultan. With the presence of a Resident in the Malay court, the British extended their direct intervention into the Malay politics, especially to the collection of import–export duties and revenues. When the first Resident of Perak, J.W.W. Birch (see Image 5 in photo inserts) assumed office in November 1874, the Malay chiefs had to surrender their rights to collect revenue or duties to the Resident (Blythe 1969, p. 190; Sadka 1968, pp. 83–84). In order to facilitate the collection of duties and revenues in the state, Birch wanted to centralize the local revenue farming system by creating a single opium revenue farm for the whole of Perak (Burns 1976, p. 191; Blythe 1969, p. 191). This "one-and-all" Perak opium farm system, which sold one party the monopolistic right to import raw opium, and to manufacture and retail *chandu* (cooked opium), would replace the existing system whereby the mine owners or *hui* leaders had imported their own raw opium, paid opium duty to the tax-collector, and then manufactured and retailed the cooked opium to their mine coolies at considerable profit (Gullick 1953, p. 48). Being a close advisor of Sir Andrew Clarke on the Larut affair, Tan Kim Ching undoubtedly stood to benefit from this centralized farming system introduced by the Resident of Perak. His brother-in-law and the business representative Lee Cheng Tee 李清池 was granted a duty-collecting farm at the mouth of the Perak River for five years by Birch at an annual rental of $84,000.[13] In early 1875, Lee Cheng Tee was again awarded the opium farm for three years at $96,000 (Blythe 1969, p. 191).

Gaining control of the money-spinning duty and opium farms was no doubt important. But more importantly, the two revenue farms were the leverage used by Tan Kim Ching to tap into the rich tin reserves in Larut. Having the Perak river duty farm, Tan could collect export duty in the form of tin slabs from the tin miners or traders who intended to export their tin from Perak. With the "one-and-all" Perak opium farm, Tan could supply opium at exorbitant price to the tin miners in exchange for cheap tin slabs. In other words, Tan secured a good supply of tin from Larut without the need to own or finance a single tin mine. The drive for Tan to gain control of the tin in Larut must have come from the growing demand of tin in Singapore for export to meet the unprecedented expansion of tin-plate production in the United Kingdom, in order to feed the American canning industry. In the 1870s, the United States took 75 per cent of the outputs of the South Wales tin-plate industry (Cowan 1981, p. 140). Such spiralling demand had definitely pushed up the price of tin in the London Metal Market and in 1872, it reached £7 per hundredweight, the highest since 1823.[14] In order to maximize his profit, Tan decided to obtain tin directly from Perak instead of Penang, which had been the main source of Singapore tin import since the 1860s. In so doing, Tan was able to bypass the middlemen, namely the Big Five, who monopolized the tin trade in Penang. He was also deeply involved in the acquisition of revenue farms and tin mining in Chumphon, a southeastern Siamese coastal state, as well as in Selangor, Negri Sembilan, and Pahang, the other three Malay states, in the 1860s and 1870s.[15] This ambitious man seemed to have aimed at building his own revenue farming and tin empire which would run from the southern Siamese Peninsula down to the west coast of the Malay Peninsula.

The success of the Singapore Hokkien mercantile elite in winning the control of the revenue farms in Perak was not accidental. It was a result of the subtle relationship between Tan Kim Ching and Birch, the Resident of Perak. Before Birch took up the post in Perak, he had served as Colonial Secretary in Singapore from May 1870 and was probably a friend of Tan and Lee (Burns 1976, p. 7). During his time in office, Birch, who worked closely with Governor Sir Harry Ord, was heavily involved in the administration of the opium and spirit farms in Singapore. In 1873, he granted extension of the farm contract to the Seng Poh Syndicate for a period of three years without public competition (Khoo 1955/56, p. 43; Burns 1976, pp. 8–9).

The Seng Poh Syndicate, the Great Syndicate controlling the opium and spirit farms of Singapore, Johor, Riau and Melaka since November 1870, comprised Tan Seng Poh, Cheang Hong Lim, Tan Hiok Nee (Trocki 1990, p. 119) and most probably Tan Kim Ching and Lee Cheng Tee as well. In return for such favour, Birch was given loans from those farmers. By the time of his appointment to the post in Perak, Birch was improperly indebted to the opium and spirits farmers to the tune of $9,500–$10,500 (Barlow 1995, p. 97; Khoo 1955/56, p. 40). It is clear from the very start that Birch's grant of the right to collect duties on the Perak River and the opium farm to Lee Cheng Tee was more than a business deal. It could have been a scheme contrived by Birch to relieve himself of his desperate financial position, but more importantly, in the name of the settlement of Larut disturbances, the Pangkor Treaty of 1874 introduced not only British political power, but also Singapore's financial interests into Perak where the tin fields and revenue farms had been a preserve of Penang financiers.

The encroachment on the rights of revenue farming by the British Resident and Singapore's mercantile elite encountered strong opposition and resentment from the Malay chiefs and the Penang mercantile elite. In response to the monopoly of Cheng Tee Syndicate over the revenue farms, the leading members of the Big Five and their associates withdrew their capital and forced 3,000 to 5,000 coolies to leave Larut for Klang and other states.[16] This exodus of coolies caused not only a loss of consumers, but also a decline in tin production in Larut (Gullick 1953, p. 49). Both problems contributed to a sharp drop in the British revenue in Perak and left Birch no choice but to restore the old opium farming system, although the Cheng Tee Syndicate was still leased with the right to collect the export duty on tin and import duty on opium. Under the auspices of Birch, the Cheng Tee Syndicate was able to marginalize the interest of the Big Five in revenue farming and made inroads into the tin mining business in Larut.

The ineptness of the British authority in dealing with such intense competition between the Chinese towkays entangled with an intra-Malay power struggle led eventually to the murder of Birch in November 1875. His death shortened the operation of the Cheng Tee Syndicate in Perak. To defend their interests and drive the British out of Perak, the Malay chiefs, including the Sultan, plotted the killing of the Resident in July 1875 (Winstedt and Wilkinson 1974, p. 110; Musa 2003, p. 126). Birch was murdered in November 1875, prompting the furious British to launch a series of military offensives against the involved Malay chiefs (Wynne 1941, p. 329; Winstedt and Wilkinson 1974, pp. 115–16; Barlow 1995, pp. 157–67; Parkinson 1960, pp. 240–93). Ironically, it was the Pangkor

Treaty of 1874, which was supposed to resolve conflicts and bring peace that had sparked the disastrous Perak War which raged from November 1875 to March 1876. The Malay chiefs who were involved in the assassination of Birch were eventually captured and punished by the British (Wynne 1941, pp. 329–32; Gullick 1953, p. 61; Winstedt and Wilkinson 1974, pp. 99–100).

THE RESURGENCE OF THE BIG FIVE'S INTERESTS IN LARUT

While the death of Birch failed to curb the British economic and political influence in Perak, it did put an end to Tan Kim Ching's economic ambition. With the end of the Cheng Tee Syndicate, the leaders of the Kian Teik Tong–Hai San camp and the Ghee Hin–Ho Hup Seah camp were able to re-engage more actively in tin mining activities in Larut from the second half of 1876.

This situation might have forced the Kian Teik Tong to decide to reconcile with the Ghee Hin. Certainly, the relationship between them in the period was more cooperative than competitive. The evidence is that Khoo Thean Teik, the paramount leader of the Kian Teik Tong, went into partnership with Loke Yew 陆佑 (see Image 6 in photo inserts), one of the headmen of Ghee Hin, to operate tin mines in the Klian Bahru (Kamunting) area of Larut in 1876.[17] Around 1885, when the tin mines controlled by the Ghee Hin in Klian Bahru began to be exhausted, many members and coolies of the Ghee Hin left Larut to seek new tin fields in Kinta valley, which was located further inland.[18] Facing the paramountcy of the Kian Teik–Hai San alliance, the Ghee Hin eventually moved out of Larut and went to Kinta.

ANOTHER FRONT OF THE "WHITE GOLD": PHUKET AND THE BIG FIVE

While the Perak War was drawing to an end in March 1876, another event, a serious coolie uprising in the same month of the year, was about to take place in Phuket or Junk Ceylon, an island located on the southwestern coast of southern Siam. Once more this was related to the Chinese of Penang, and their interests in the "white gold". In this case, a band of about 300 coolies belonging to the Kian Teik Tong and the Ho Seng marched to the government offices to demand the release of two *hui* brothers, who had been arrested for assaulting some Thai sailors. Despite the release of the two, the gang which had grown to 2,000 men, refused to disband and began to rampage through the town (Cushman 1989, p. 6). The rioters burnt most government offices and officials' houses. Phraya Wichitsongkhram, the governor of Phuket, was unable to stop the rioting and took refuge. The riot was obviously targeted at the governor, who had announced the suspension of credit to all the Chinese mines in February 1876. Such a decision made by the governor was intended to use the state revenue to pay back the long overdue debt to the central government. There was also a rumour that the governor would advance credit to the Ghee Hin-affiliated miners. However, the sudden withdrawal of the fund agitated the miners, especially the allies of the governor, who had been promised credit for the operation and expansion of their tin mining enterprise. Moreover, the six-fold increase of Chinese poll-tax caused even more grievances and frustration among the miners (Songprasert 1986, pp. 168–69). The increase of Chinese poll-tax was another method used by the governor to raise money to settle his debts. Exploiting the arrest of the two *hui* members, the mine owners, who were also the leaders of the Kian Teik Tong and Ho Seng, initiated revolts and crippled Phuket for almost a month. In so doing, the mine owners-cum-*hui* leaders succeeded in forcing the government to the negotiating table. In order to contain the disturbance, Chun Bunnag (Chaomun Samoechairat), the Special Commissioner of Phuket, held a meeting with the leaders of Kian Teik Tong and Ho Seng (Cushman 1989, p. 6).

Before we turn to the negotiating table on 20 March 1876, it should be noted that Kian Teik Tong, the most powerful *hui* in Phuket, was primarily controlled by the leaders of the Tan, the Ong and the Yeoh families (see Table 5.1).

TABLE 5.1

Leaders of Phuket's Kian Teik Tong

Name of Leaders	Positions		Business
Tan Neo Yee / Tan Wee Ghee 陈威仪	President	大哥	Tin mining (Chop Lian Bee/莲美号)
Ong Boon Kiw 王文玖	Master of Lodge	军师	Tin mining
Ong Boon Thian 王本添	Red Cudgel	红棍	Tin mining
Ong Boon Eng 王文营	Black Cudgel	乌棍	Tin mining
Yeoh Boon Swee 杨文水	Executioner	刑堂	Tin mining

Source: 王重阳 Wang Zhong Yang, "泰国普吉省华人拓荒史" *Taiguo Pujishen Huaren Tuohuangshi* [History of Chinese Pioneers in Phuket], 南洋文摘 [Nanyang Digest], vol. 6, no. 5 (1965): 37.

For example, Tan Neo Yee or Tan Wee Ghee 陈威仪 (see Image 7 in photo inserts), a mine owner, operated at least three mines and controlled about 1,000 coolies (Songprasert 1986, p. 169). Being a leader of the Kian Teik Tong in Phuket, Neo Yee was also closely connected to the leaders of the Penang Kian Teik Tong and the Tan Kongsi. In 1878, he donated 600 dollars to the restoration of the Tan Kongsi's temple (Wolfgang and Chen 1982–87, p. 884). The Ho Seng, which was a close ally of the Kian Teik Tong, was led by Tan Kim Jao or Tan Jao 陈锦灶 of the Tan family. When he first arrived at Phuket, Tan Jao worked in a tin mining and trading company, Chop Hap Hin 合兴号 owned by Tan Tam, the first kapitan and leader of the Kian Teik Tong.[19] With the support of Tan Tam, Tan Jao was able to set up his own mining company, Chop Jin Seng 振盛号 in the 1860s.[20] He also donated 600 dollars to the restoration of the Tan Kongsi's temple in 1878 (Wolfgang and Chen 1982–87, p. 884).

The Tan family members were the major beneficiaries at the negotiating table in 1876. To save Phuket's tin production, Chun Bunnag, promised to promote new businesses, enhance the living conditions of the coolies, and grant amnesty to the rioters (Cushman 1991, p. 41). At the same time, the *hui* leaders would also be given the monopoly of tin mining business and revenue farms in Phuket. Tan Jao and his son, Tan Pheck Kiad, together with two kinsmen, Tan Lian Ky and Tan Yang Sin, were appointed as wholesale distributors of opium throughout the island; Tan Neo Yee and Yeoh An Yian were permitted to cooperate with the governor in running farms for gambling, tin, spirits, pawnshops and timber (Songprasert 1986, pp. 171–72). On top of this, the *hui* leaders successfully negotiated with the government to abolish the Chinese poll tax and to reduce the levy of the mining royalty.

The compromising attitude of the Siamese authorities did not mean they were powerless in dealing with the *hui* leaders and their coolies. Instead, it was a strategy they adopted to maintain the status quo of *hui* leaders and to develop the economy of Phuket. In particular they wanted to fend off a British intrusion into Siam's southern-west frontier. Put another way, they wanted the *hui* leaders and their coolies to act as guardians of Siamese economic and political sovereignty in the southwestern territory, where their own political control was limited. With their local influence, the Kian Teik Tong *hui* leaders were able to marginalize the Ghee Hin and the local Siamese ruling family and conclude an agreement with the central government to monopolize the tin mining business to the rest of the nineteenth century.

"WHITE GOLD" FROM SOUTHERN BURMA: THE BIG FIVE AND THE GHEE HIN

Rapid growth in the international tin market saw not only Perak and Phuket, but also Mergui, the southernmost part of Burma which had the richest tin deposits, brought into contact with the Penang Chinese mercantile elite. Tin had been mined in Mergui since at least the early nineteenth century, but production in the mid-to-late nineteenth century remained relatively small when compared with Perak and Phuket.[21] Nevertheless, Mergui, especially the Maliwun Township, became a magnet for the Big Five and the Ghee Hin when a tin boom started in the mid-nineteenth century. Having cultivated a good relationship with Colonel Hopkinson, the Commissioner of the Tenasserim Division, Sit San 薛山, a Hokkien, who led the Ghee Hin in Maliwun, successfully gained the monopoly of tin mining concessions in the whole Maliwun Township area from 1860.[22] Being a leader of the only *hui* in Maliwun, Sit San was also invested with the powers of a *Myook*, or Extra Assistant Commissioner (Butler 1884, p. 28). With this position, Sit San was able to expand his monopoly rights over the manufacture of liquor, collection of edible bird's nests, and distribution of opium in Maliwun.

Beyond Maliwun, the influence of Sit San also extended to the Lenya Township at the north. His family members were in control of almost all the most productive mines there (see Table 5.2).

TABLE 5.2
List of Tin Mines Controlled by Sit San's Family in Lenya Township

Locality of the Mine	Owner's Name	Number of Coolies
Bokpyin Creek	Sit Sin & Sit Hauk	41
	Sit Kein	14
	Sit Sein	12
Lelan Hill	Sit Bok	28
Karathuri	Sit Pu Shein	90
Kyaukkyi Creek	Sit Pu Shein	25

Source: Supplement to the *Burma Gazette*, no. 33 (17 August 1889): 603.

It is important to note that Sit San constructed a family network to manage his businesses. Besides clan kinsmen, indigenous women were also incorporated through marriages to help in running the business. For instance, Sit San himself took a Malay-Burmese, Ma Mei, as wife and put her in charge of the smelting business.[23] Sit Pu Shein married a Burmese girl, Ma Chit Thu, who became a chief assistant in supervising tin mining operation.[24] Although the Ghee Hin under the leadership of Sit San dominated the tin mining and revenue farming business in Mergui, the import–export trade and shipping were in the hands of the Big Five.

Since at least the 1820s, the sea-borne trade of this part of southern Burma stretching from Moulmein to Mergui was orientated towards Penang. It is not surprising that the Big Five, who commanded a large fleet of ships, dominated this coastal trade. With their supreme maritime power, the Big Five were in a position to secure all the tin supply from the Ghee Hin in Mergui. With little or no access to sea transportation and tin market in Penang, the Ghee Hin had to rely on the Big Five to export their tin. Furthermore, the Big Five was the only source from which the Ghee Hin could obtain coolies from Penang to work in the mines and provisions to feed the coolies. A 278-ton *S.S. Zephyr*, for example, was jointly operated by the Big Five and the Khaw family to sail between Penang, Ranong, and Maliwun. It took tin from Ranong and Maliwun down to Penang and brought back coolies for the mines and Rangoon rice for the coolies. In each voyage, the *Zephyr* carried 30 to 40 slabs of tin; each slab of tin was bought at about $16–$17, a price $5–$15 lower than the market price in Penang.[25] Unlike in Perak and Phuket, the Big Five needed the Ghee Hin to engage in the tin business of Mergui. In a way, the Big Five formed an informal partnership with the Ghee Hin: the Ghee Hin mined the tin and the Big Five marketed it. It was not until 1895 that the Ghee Hin's mining monopoly in Mergui was broken. Dissatisfied with Ghee Hin's effort in improving the tin mining industry, the British government of India granted the mining concession to Captain Menzell who was financially backed by the Jelebu Mining and Trading Company in Malaya.[26] As an associate of Menzell, Chung Keng Kwee, the Perak tin tycoon and the Big Five's business partner, was encouraged and promised huge capital support to embark on tin mining in Mergui.[27]

CONCLUSION

In the nineteenth century, tin mining became the centre of attention among the mercantile elite as the rapid industrialization of Britain and the United States brought about an unprecedented demand generated by the tinplate industry. This sudden and substantial rise in the price of tin turned mining in the region into a very profitable enterprise. In order to gain the lion's share or monopolization of the tin mining business in Perak, Phuket and Mergui, the Big Five had to scramble and manoeuvre along with other interest groups, such as the Ghee Hin and the Singapore Hokkien mercantile elite. In Larut, the Big Five's attempt to establish a monopoly encountered stiff competition from the Ghee Hin and the powerful Singapore Hokkien business clique. By allying with the Zengcheng Hakka and the Malay chiefs and shrewdly winning the support of the Straits government, the Big Five were able to marginalize the Ghee Hin. When the Singapore Hokkien came to control the Larut tin business, the Big Five used their *hui* and coolie network to cripple their rival's influence. In Phuket, the Big Five mobilized their *hui* and coolies to challenge the local Siamese chiefs who intended to stop funding the tin mining operation and expansion. In so doing, the Big Five succeeded not only in weakening the power of the local Siamese ruling family, but were also able to negotiate with the Bangkok's central government to monopolize the tin business in Phuket. In Mergui, the Big Five collaborated with the Ghee Hin, who dominated the tin mining operation, and gained control of the tin trade.

The economic dominance of the Big Five did not, however, mark the end of all competition. Towards the end of the nineteenth century, the Big Five faced threatening competition from Westerners, who had access to large and stable capital as well as new forms of corporate organizations. These new threats now moved in from the European metropoles were most dangerous of all, protected by a colonial government that was rapidly changing from the phase of liberalism to management. We will examine these factors in the following chapter.

Notes

1. In fourteen century, tin was widely found and mined in various parts of the continental territories of the Malay Peninsula such as Tambralinga (Ligor), Kelantan, Pahang, and Trengganu. 苏继庼 [Su Jiqing], 岛夷志略校释 *Daoyi*

Zhilue Xiaoyi [Translation of the Records of Archipelago] (Beijing: Zhonghua Shuju 中华书局, 1981), pp.79, 96, 99, 102.
2. J.M. Gullick, "Captain Speedy of Larut," *The Malayan Branch of the Royal Asiatic Society*, vol. 26, pt. 3, (November 1953), p. 19. See also W.E. Everitt, *A History of Mining in Perak*, Johore Bahru, p. 12.
3. *Cases Heard and Determined in Her Majesty's Supreme Court of the Straits Settlements* (Somerset: Legal Library Publishing Services, vol. 4, 1885/1890), pp. 136–40.
4. "Report on the proceedings of Government relating to the Native States in the Malayan Peninsula" in *Proceedings of the Straits Settlements Legislative Council 1874*, p. 3. See also Khoo, *The Western Malay States*, pp. 130–31. See also R.O. Winstedt and R.J. Wilkinson, *A History of Perak* (Kuala Lumpur: The Malaysian Branch of the Royal Asiatic Society, 1974), pp. 81–82.
5. "Report of the Commissioners under Clause XIII of the Perak Engagement dated 20 January 1874" in *Straits Settlements Legislative Council Proceedings 1874*, p. 18. See also Wong Choon San, *A Gallery of Chinese Kapitans* (Singapore: Ministry of Culture, Singapore, 1963), pp. 70–72.
6. 李永球 Lee Eng Kew, *移国: 太平华裔历史人物集 Yiguo: Taiping Huayi Lishi Renwuji* [The Chinese Historical Figures of Taiping] (Penang: Nanyang Mijian Wenhua 南洋民间文化, 2003), p. 192.
7. *Parliamentary Paper on the Malay Peninsula*, vol. 1, 1872–79, p. 11; Wilfred Blythe, *The Impact of Chinese Secret Societies in Malaya: A Historical Study* (London: Oxford University Press, 1969), p. 178. See also C. Northcote Parkinson, *British Intervention in Malaya 1867–1877* (Singapore: University of Malaya Press: 1960), pp. 75, 76.
8. "Precis of Perak Affairs" in *Proceedings of the Straits Settlements Legislative Council 1874*, pp. 8–9. See also Cowan, *Nineteenth-Century Malaya*, pp. 117–18.
9. CO 273/85, Letter from William J. Jervois to Earl Carnavon, 18 October 1876. See also "Precis of Perak Affairs" in *Straits Settlements Legislative Council Proceedings 1874*, p. 10.
10. CO 273/85, Letter from William Francis Drummond Jervois to Earl Carnarvon, 18 October 1876. See also "Precis of Perak Affairs" in *Straits Settlements Legislative Council Proceedings 1874*, pp. 9–10.
11. "Enquiry as to Complicity of Chiefs in the Perak Outrages" in *Straits Settlements Legislative Council Proceedings 1877*, p. 5. See also Sadka, *The Protected Malay States 1874–1895*, p. 83, Parkinson, *British Intervention in Malaya 1867–1877*, p. 210 and Cowan, *Nineteenth-Century Malaya*, p. 219. Sultan Abdullah received $13,000 in advance from Tan Kim Ching.
12. "Enquiry as to Complicity of Chiefs in the Perak Outrages" in *Straits Settlements Legislative Council Proceedings 1877*, p. 3. See also Burns, *The Journals of J.W.W. Birch*, pp. 17–18.
13. *Straits Times Overland Journal*, 5 April 1877, p. 3.

14. Cowan, *Nineteenth-century Malaya*, p. 141. One hundred weight equals to 112 pounds (50.802 kg).
15. Phuwadol Songprasert, "The Development of Chinese Capital in Southern Siam, 1868–1932," Ph.D. thesis, Monash University, 1986, p. 88. See also Khoo, *The Western Malay States 1850–1873*, pp. 221–25 and Singapore and Straits Directory for 1888, p. 247. In 1888, Tan Kim Ching partnerd Syed Mahomed Bin A. Alsagoff, Syed Junied Bin O. Al Junied, C.C.N. Glass, C.M. Allan, and Lee Keng Yong and established Malay Peninsula Prospecting Co. to carry out tin mining in Pahang. Besides, Tan also involved in coolie trading and arms trading. He supplied 1,000 coolies to the British government for construction works in Bassein in 1855. He exported 220 muskets to Makassar on 24 March 1858. See also *The Singapore and Straits Directory for 1888*, p. 247; *Pinang Gazette and Straits Chronicle*, 14 July 1855, p. 1; "Home Department-Public Letters No. 37 of 1859" in *Straits Settlements Miscellaneous papers and original correspondence.*
16. "Memorandum on the financial condition of the Native States of Perak, Selangor, and Sungai Ujong" in *Straits Settlements Legislative Council Proceedings*, 9 March 1878, p. xiv. See also Gullick, "Captain Speedy of Larut," p. 49.
17. Lee Kam Heng & Chow Mun Seong, *Biographical Dictionary of the Chinese in Malaysia* (Kuala Lumpur: Pelanduk Publications, 1997), p. 123. See also *Yiguo: Taiping Huayi Lishi Renwuji*, p. 27. Loke Yew or Lok Yau went to Larut to start a trading business in around 1870. In 1875, he won a contract to supply provisions to British troops and became a good friend of Sir Hugh Low. In about 1886, he returned to Selangor and ventured into tin mining business and became a tin tycoon.
18. Wong, *A Gallery of Chinese Kapitans*, pp. 76–77. See also *Yiguo: Taiping Huayi Lishi Renwuji*, p. 236.
19. 王重阳 [Wang Zhong Yang], "泰国普吉省华人拓荒史 *Taiguo Pujishen Huaren Tuohuangshi* [History of Chinese Pioneers in Phuket]," 南洋文摘 [Nanyang Digest], vol. 6, no. 5, 1965, p. 30.
20. *Taiguo Pujishen Huaren Tuohuangshi*, p. 31.
21. *Pinang Gazette and Straits Chronicle*, 16 March 1895, p. 3. See also Teruko Saito and Lee Kin Kiong, *Statistics on the Burmese Economy: The 19th and 20th Centuries* (Singapore: Institute of Southeast Asian Studies, 1999), p. 148. During the British rule, there were two districts — Tavoy and Mergui in Tenasserim Division. The Mergui district was divided into four townships — Tenasserim, Mergui, Lenya, and Maliwun. In 1880s, Mergui district produced only a few hundred piculs of tin while Perak and Phuket produced thousands of piculs of tin.
22. Captain J. Butler, *Gazetter of the Mergui District, Tenasserim Division, British Burma* (Rangoon: the Government Press, 1884), p. 28. See *also PGSC*,

16 March 1895, p. 3. Sit San is also spelled as Sit Tshan. He was also known as Chet Syang.
23. *PGSC*, 16 March 1895, p. 3.
24. *Supplement to the Burma Gazette*, no. 33, 17 August 1889, p. 596.
25. *Supplement to the Burma Gazette*, no. 23, 8 June 1889, pp. 391, 393.
26. *PGSC*, 25 October 1895, p. 2.
27. *PGSC*, 16 March 1895, p. 3.

6

WESTERN MERCANTILE ELITE AND THEIR CHALLENGE TO THE PENANG CHINESE

Before the 1880s, direct competition from Westerners was insignificant since they had only a peripheral interest in the region and played an auxiliary role as providers of capital. However, the Western mercantile elite began to pose a competitive threat to the Big Five from the mid-1880s, a period which saw a shift from liberalism to management characterized by increasingly powerful colonial governments and rapid expansion of Western interests in trade, shipping, and insurance. This chapter explores the Western competition in this Penang-centred region and the countermeasures taken by the Big Five. It first examines the shipping and trading intrusions made by the large-scale and financially-powerful Western business concerns. It then turns to the response of the Big Five towards the Western challenge.

FROM LIBERALISM TO MANAGEMENT

The unprecedented Western penetration into the commercial orbit of Penang in the late nineteenth century was not simply a response to its profitable trade and commerce. It was also a result of intensifying international economic expansion and political rivalry. The last decades of the nineteenth century witnessed the change in the global economy from commercial to industrial capitalism.[1] As such industrial production became the engine of growth and the key to wealth and power in the West. From this period, Britain, until then the leading industrial power in the world economy, faced fierce competition from new Western industrial powers like Germany, France,

Holland, and America.² The challenge to Britain from these Western powers heralded an intense scramble for resources. Hence, Southeast Asia became more fully open to the impact of the Industrial Revolution and more Western states showed increasing interest in the region. In order to consolidate their control of economic resources and opportunities, the British and the Dutch, who had firmly established themselves in Southeast Asia, began to delineate their respective business spheres. To achieve this, corporate enterprises were organized to penetrate into all the major business sectors while state power was centralized to support this business thrust and, at the same time, to annex territories in contention and solidify colonial boundaries.

These new Western corporate enterprises were different from the Penang-based Western trading and entrepreneurial interests which had been established in the early-to- mid nineteenth century. They were incorporated companies, representing large capital resources and business interests centred mainly in the Western metropolitan cities. The Penang-based Western business interests, in contrast, were small-scale proprietary or partnership-based enterprises and their link to the Western commercial world was only through trade. Most importantly, the corporate enterprises became the dominant force in the Western business arena and worked hand-in-hand with the colonial governments for their business pursuits.

Prior to the late nineteenth century, the colonial governments, which adhered to liberalism, were too weak to manage their economies and enforce their authority over their subjects. The diffuse and decentralized administrative system in place at the time hindered state development. However, by the late nineteenth century, the state was strengthened through political centralization and administrative rationalization.³ The strengthening of state power hence raised its ability to exercise more effective and direct control over politics and economy. Thanks to this centralized political power and administration, the state was increasingly able to act as a patron by giving economic concessions while its developing Western-style bureaucratic and commercial frameworks favoured the corporate enterprises. All these changes were set to affect the manner in which business was conducted in the region and the framework in which the Big Five had to operate, in a way that fundamentally limited their mercantile interests.

WESTERN MERCHANTS PRIOR TO 1880s

Although Western merchants had formed part of the Penang business community since the beginning of the nineteenth century, before the

1880s they remained mainly as merchant-capitalists and proprietary-enterprise-based entrepreneurs. The businesses in which Westerners engaged revolved around trade, agricultural estates and some professions, such as solicitors, auctioneers, and chartered accountant firms. For example, David Brown, who came to Penang as a lawyer in 1801, became a pioneer planter and acquired a 380-hectare (950 acre) estate at Glugor in Penang (Tate 1996, p. 49); Edward Horseman, a British member of Parliament and Privy Counsellor, emerged as the biggest sugar plantation owner in 1856 with a planted area of more than 2,700 acres (Jackson 1968, p. 143); the Logan brothers, James and Abraham, who arrived at Penang in 1839, first set up a legal firm, (Daniel Logan, Barrister at Law, Solicitor General), and later moved into plantation agriculture, with 16,000 acres of paddy and coconut estates in Province Wellesley and 2,000 acres of fruit in Penang.[4] It is important to note that these Western proprietors primarily depended on the labourers or coolies supplied by the Big Five, who dominated the coolie trade in the region, to work their estates. Since indigenous labour was considered unsuitable for work on the estates, and Indian labour was not yet available in sufficient number, the Chinese coolies were highly in demand in plantation agriculture during this period.

Besides coolie supply, the European proprietors also relied on the Big Five for processing and transporting their agricultural commodities, especially coconut and tobacco. The Logan Brothers, for instance, contracted out coconut harvesting and manufacturing of coconut oil to the Big Five, who controlled not only a large workforce but also most of the oil mills in Penang and Province Wellesley. The Dutch entrepreneurs who owned most of the tobacco estates on the East Coast of Sumatra equally sourced their Chinese coolies from the Big Five and relied on the Big Five's shipping network to export their tobacco via Penang. As noted in the earlier chapters, the Big Five and their associates controlled an extensive maritime and riverine transportation network between Penang and Sumatra's East Coast. The sea-going ships of the Big Five brought coolies, provisions, opium, and firearms from Penang to the local ports of Sumatra's East Coast and sailed back with tobacco that had been shipped down river and stored at floating godowns.[5] The riverboats of the Big Five or their associates (the local Chinese agents) returned upstream with the goods from Penang.

Apart from agricultural enterprises, the Western mercantile elite also worked closely with the Big Five to trade Straits produce and Indian and Chinese goods. For instance, Victor Capel, a commissioner, general agent and auctioneer, partnered Khoo Cheng Neow, Cheah Hay Seang and Lim Goey to found Chop Chin Saing to trade tin, pepper and western manufactured goods.[6] Another example is A.A. Anthony. He chartered ships carrying Indian goods (opium, grain and cotton from Calcutta and Madras) to connect with ships owned by Chong Moh & Co., which sailed between Penang, southern Burma, Sumatra, the western Malay states, and China.[7] On the voyage back to India, A.A. Anthony's ships took on cargos of Straits produce (coconut, tin, betel nut, and pepper) and Chinese goods (China crockery, China tobacco and tea), which were supplied by Chong Moh & Co (Pongsupath 1990, pp. 244–47). It is clear that the business pursuits of a number of Western businessmen active in the region prior to 1880 were tied closely to the Big Five's various well-developed enterprises. This is not surprising since these enterprises in fact constituted the economic and commercial framework of the region. It is not an exaggeration to say that the survival and success of Westerner-owned enterprises here depended on the essential factors of production and distribution controlled by the Big Five. At the same time, the Big Five found Western merchants, who possessed considerable capital and political influence, extremely useful for expanding their business and increasing their own wealth accumulation. In sum, the business relationship between the Western merchants and the Big Five prior to 1880s was complementary rather than competitive.

By the mid-1880s, this complementary relationship between the Western merchants and the Big Five began to change when certain large-scale and financially-powerful Western trading and shipping interests began expanding aggressively into Penang's business orbit. Unlike the earlier, Penang-based Western businessmen, these concerns had their headquarters outside Penang, either in Europe or in the emerging primary cities like Singapore and Batavia (Allen and Donnithorne 1957, pp. 212–21; Pongsupath 1990, pp. 241–44). Furthermore, these organizations, which pursued extra-Penang and extra-Malayan business interests, were skilfully managed by well-connected and experienced financiers and merchants. The Big Five's regional shipping and trading, which together formed one of their main business pillars, were first to be challenged. Both the Straits Steamship Company and the Royal Dutch Packet Company, or Koninklyke Paketvaart Maatschappij (K.P.M.), sought to gain greater control of the regional shipping lines. Attracted to the regional shipping domain by the booming trade in agricultural and mineral commodities (rice, tobacco and tin) and labourers between the 1880s and the First World War, the new Western merchants became increasingly adversarial competitors of the Big Five, as the next sections show.

STRAITS STEAMSHIP COMPANY AND STRAITS TRADING COMPANY

Armed with a capital base of $421,000, in 1890 Theodore Cornelius Bogaardt, the Dutch manager of W. Mansfield & Company, a British trading and shipping agency based in Singapore, founded the Straits Steamship Company. Bogaardt hoped to exploit the increasing value of tin ore and the importance of regional shipping services as feeders for ocean going ships carrying high-demand Straits tin back to Europe (Tregonning 1967, p. 17; Wright and Cartwright 1908, p. 174). It is important to point out, however, that the Straits Steamship Company was not a purely Western enterprise, since there were three prominent Singapore Hokkien businessmen on the seven-man Board of Directors. They were Tan Keong Saik, Tan Jiak Kim and Lee Cheng Yan (Tregonning 1967, p. 17), all rich merchants and influential Straits community leaders. Moreover, they were experienced shippers whose own vessels sailed extensively between Singapore, Penang, Rangoon, Siam, and the Netherland Indies (see Table 6.1).

The joint forces of the Dutch and the three Singapore Hokkien towkays, with their extensive shipping experience and networks, formed a formidable threat to the regional shipping, so far dominated by the Big Five. Until then none of these Western and Hokkien merchants had been competitors of the Big Five before they went into partnership, but had only acted as agents of other business concerns or operated their shipping and trading businesses through agents in the region. W. Mansfield & Company had a branch in Penang serving as agents for the Ocean Steamship Company Ltd. and China Navigation Company Ltd. (Wright and Cartwright 1908, p. 177); Kim Seng & Co. had the Big Five's Bun Hin & Co. and Kay Tye as shipping and trading agents in Singapore and Penang respectively.[8]

The Singapore Hokkien formed the main force of the Straits Steamship Company. Among the five ships that made up the fleet, Kim Seng & Company contributed three.[9] This fleet was then put into operation along the west coast of the Malay Peninsula. To the directors of the Straits Steamship Company, especially the Hokkiens, navigating ships through the waters of the west coast was nothing new. The schooner *Malacca*, for example, had been cruising between Penang, Melaka and Singapore since 1885.[10] But by having its ships ply the Straits, the new company entered a head-to-head competition with the Big Five, whose vessels were

TABLE 6.1
The Business Backgrounds and Family Relationship of the Singapore Hokkien Merchants

Name	Family Relationship	Business	Social Leadership
Tan Keong Saik 陈恭锡 (1850–1909)	— Great-grandfather Tan Hay Kwan settled in Melaka around 1770s and then moved to Singapore. — Father, Tan Choon Sian, together with his brother Tan Choon Bock expanded the family shipping business. — Wife, daughter of Ang Kim Cheak, the proprietor of Ang Kim Cheak & Co.	— General Trading — Director of Singapore Slipway Company and Tanjong Pagar Dock Company — Property — Manager of Chop Sin Heng Tye, a tin trading firm, owned by Kapitan Yap Kwan Seng of Selangor	— Member of the Chinese Advisory Board and the Po Leung Kuk — Municipal Commissioner for 1886 — Justice of Peace
Tan Jiak Kim 陈若锦 (1859–1917)	— Great-grandfather, Tan Kim Seng, founder of Kim Seng & Co., migrated from Melaka to Singapore in 1819. — Father, Tan Beng Swee took over Kim Seng & Co. around 1865.	— Shipping and Trading — Owned steamer *Japan*, *Sharpshooter* and *Fair Singapore*, which plied between Penang, Melaka and Singapore	— Member of Legislative — Justice of Peace — Received Companion of the most Distinguished Order of St. Michael and St. George (C.M.G)

TABLE 6.1 (Cont'd)

Name	Family Relationship	Business	Social Leadership
Lee Cheng Yan 李清渊 (1841–1911)	— Born in Melaka in 1841. Migrated to Singapore in 1858 and started Lee Cheng Yan & Co. (Chop Chin Joo) together with brother Lee Cheng Gum)	— Lee Cheng Yan & Co. (Chop Chin Joo) engaged in import and export trade and later diversified into banking and real estate.	— Member of the Committee of the Tan Tock Seng Hospital — Member of the Chinese Advisory Board and the Po Leung Kuk — Justice of Peace — Founder of the Hong Joo Chinese Free School

Sources: K.G. Tregonning, *Home Port Singapore: A History of Straits Steamship Company Limited, 1890–1965* (Singapore: Oxford University Press, 1967), pp. 6–10; Song Ong Siang, *One Hundred Years' History of the Chinese in Singapore* (Singapore: University Malaya Press, 1967), pp. 110–11, 194–99, 222–23; 柯木林 Kua Bak Lim, ed., 新华历史人物列传 *Xinhua Lishi Renwu Liezhuan* [Who's Who in the Chinese Community of Singapore] (Singapore: EPB Publishers Pte. Ltd., 1995), pp. 50, 85, 90–91; *The Straits Times Overland Journal*, 26 February and 12 March 1870 and 11 January 1877; *The Singapore & Straits Directory 1901*, p. 170; Arnold Wright and H.A. Cartwright, *Twentieth Century Impressions of British Malaya: Its History, People, Commerce, Industries and Resources* (London: Lloyd's Greater Britain Publishing Company Ltd., 1908), pp. 497, 636, 640.

the main passenger and freight carriers in this stretch of the "liquid highway".

The Straits Steamship Company became more effective and competitive as a business venture when it began working in cooperation with the Straits Trading Company that had been established by Herman Muhlinghaus, a German, and James Sword, a Scot, in Singapore in 1887 to develop the business of tin trading and smelting in the Malay Peninsula (Drabble 2000, p. 43; Tregonning 1963, pp. 86–88). With financial backing from the Chartered Bank of India, Australia and China, the Straits Trading Company was able to pay for tin ore with cash on delivery (Tregonning 1963, p. 89; Wong 1965, p. 99). This cash deal offered impressed not only European miners but also Chinese ones, who were financially bound at the time to individual smelters or to merchants in Singapore or Penang. With cash in hand, the Chinese miners could provide themselves with provisions at competitive prices and not have to put up with the excessive charges they had previously been forced to accept from their financiers. Furthermore, they could also pay their labourers or coolies without having to borrow at an exorbitant rate. In sum, the new arrangement meant Chinese miners could escape the unequal relations that bound them to their creditors. By offering cash and having colonial government support, the Company succeeded in securing effective monopolies of tin export from Selangor and Sungei Ujong (Negeri Sembilan) and a right to export tin from Perak (Tregonning 1963, pp. 89–91; Chiang 1978, p. 109). In Selangor, Loke Yew, a tin magnate, was amongst the first to send his ore to the Company; Eu Kong and Eu Tong Sen, the father and son who were the leading tin miners in Perak, also sold their ores to the Company (Tregonning 1963, p. 102; Blythe 1969, p. 191). The Company commissioned the Straits Steamship Company to transport all the tin ore from those three Malay states to the smelting station in Singapore.

In 1906, the Straits Trading Company moved to Phuket, breaking another tin trading business monopoly of the Big Five. At this time, the Chinese mine owners of Phuket were in financial difficulty when Chip Hock & Co., an important Phuket-based trading and financial concern operated by the Big Five, went bankrupt. Chip Hock had started operation in Phuket around the 1880s, trading with the southwestern Siamese states as well as providing loans to merchants and miners.[11] By 1905, the Company had loaned out a sum of $200,000 but, when many debtors refused to repay their loans, the Company was declared bankrupt.¹² Thereafter the Big Five became reluctant to make loans. Seizing this opportunity, the Straits Trading Company opened a branch in Phuket, advancing capital to mine owners and collecting payment in tin. Through this method, the Straits Trading Company succeeded in capturing more than half of the Phuket tin output by 1908 (Prasertkul 1989, p. 256).

Together with the transport of tin and ore from the major and minor ports on the west coast, the Straits Steamship Company also expanded its general trading business. For example, the Company's 242-ton *Lady Weld*, a paddle steamer acquired in 1891, always sailed to Port Weld, a northern port of Perak, to pick up tin and land coolies and food supplies for the Chinese miners in Perak (Tregonning 1967, p. 26; Laxon and Tyers 1976, p. 5). By conducting this trade, the company now performed the same economic function as had the Big Five. Undoubtedly, the combination of coastal shipping and trading by the Straits Steamship Company posed an unprecedented threat to the Big Five. By the mid-1910s, the Ocean Steam Ship Company (or Blue Funnel Line) became the largest shareholder of the Straits Steamship Company and Alfred Holt, the director-cum-founder, made large capital funds available to the Straits Steamship Company to enable it to increase the size of its fleet.¹³ With the backing of this British heavyweight and international shipping company, the Straits Steamship Company was able to increase its fleet of vessels to twenty-four and expand its shipping services to southwestern Siam, southern Burma, and the East Coast of Sumatra (Laxon and Tyers 1976, p. 1; Tregonning 1967, p. 43), where the Big Five's shipping and trading activities were closely connected.

Hand-in-hand with its expanding shipping lines, the Straits Steamship Company also established a widespread network of agents. By 1920s, there was at least one agent at each of the fifty-four major and minor ports serviced by the Company in Southeast Asia (see Table 6.2). In some cases they were the local branches of big Western merchant houses — Harrisons & Crosfield Ltd. at Asahan and Belawan (East Sumatra), W.F. Stevenson & Co. Ltd. at Cebu, Jolo and Zamboanga (the Philippines), Mansfield & Co. Ltd. at Penang — and in other cases, they were Chinese concerns, shippers and traders of importance, such as Leong Hin at Krabi (southwestern Siam), Hokkien Guild at Kuantan (East Coast of the Malay Peninsula), and Ban Cheong Bee & Co. at Mergui (southern Burma). Occasionally, Malay firms would also be appointed as agents, such as Che Abdullah at Kuala Bahru (Perak). This diversity combined with the extensiveness of its

TABLE 6.2
The Shipping Agents of the Straits Steamship Company in Southeast Asia in the 1920s

Malaya	Southern Burma	Sumatra	Siam	Philippines	Borneo	Cochinchina
Guan Huat & Co. (Alor Star)	Ban Chong Bee & Co. (Mergui)	Teck Kee (Pangkalan Brandan)	Ban Hin Lee (Tanjong Star)	W.F. Stevenson & Co. Ltd. (Cebu, Jolo & Zamboanga)	Yat Fong Bros. (Kudat)	Companie de Commerce etde, Navigation Extreme Orient (Saigon)
Harrisons & Crosfield Ltd. and Soon Cheang (Bagan Datoh)	Lee Sen Chan & Co. (Moulmein)	Harrisons & Crosfield Ltd. (Belawan)	The Borneo Co. Ltd. (Bangkok)		Vanscolina & Co. (Labuan)	
Liew Lian Choon (Batu Pahat)			Leong Hin (Krabi)			
Lee Wah & Co. (Kelantan)	London Rangoon Trading Co. Ltd. (Rangoon)	Chew Beow Leng (Langkat)	Sin Gim Seng and Swee Hoe (Kopah)		Adamson Gilfillan & Co. Ltd. (Potianak)	
A.C.Harper & Co. Ltd. (Klang, Port Dickson, Port Swettenham, Seremban)	Chong Lee & Co. (Tavoy)	Harrisons & Crosfield Ltd. and Soon Cheang (Asahan)	Hong Cheang (Pungah)		Harrisons & Crosfield Ltd. (Sandakan and Jesselton)	
Che Abdullah (Kuala Bahru)			Lee Kim & Co. (Renong)			
A.C.Harper & Co. Ltd. (Kuala Lumpur)		Chin Bee (Batoe Bahra)	Swee Seng Moh (Setul)			
Sin Aik Joo (Kuala Selangor)		Harrisons & Crosfield Ltd. (Medan)	Swee Hin (Tongkah)			
The Hokkien Guild (Kuantan)			Ban Seng Hin and Swee Kee Co. (Trang)			
The Orient Stores & Agency and Kheng Thong (Lumut)						
Harrison & Crosfield Ltd. and Chop Soon Hup (Paneh River)						

TABLE 6.2 (Cont'd)

Malaya	Southern Burma	Sumatra	Siam	Philippines	Borneo	Cochinchina
Hock Chong Aun (Pangkor)						
Mansfield & Co. Ltd. (Penang)						
Soon Kee (Sabak Bernam)						
Hup Hin (Pulau Langkawi)						
The Orient Stores & Agency and Keat Sin Leong (Sitiawan)						
G.W. Wilson & Co. Ltd. (Sungei Patani)						
Boustead & Co. Ltd., Alylesburg & Nutter Ltd., and Yue Who & Co. (Teluk Anson)						
Heng Lee Chan (Terengganu)						
Boustead & Co. Ltd. and Ban Guan Bee (Utan Melintang)						
Hup Bee & Co. (Sungei Opis)						
Chop Eng Hock Hin (Muar)						
Straits Steamship Company (Melaka)						

Source: Directory of Malaya 1927.

port network gave the Company very good grass-roots contact with the local shippers and traders and helped enormously in its trade. It was at this point that the irreversible effect of the Company's penetration was most keenly felt by the Big Five.

ROYAL DUTCH PACKET COMPANY OR KONINKLIJKE PAKETVAART MAATSCHAPPIJ (KPM)

Along with the British Straits Steamship Company, the Dutch KPM, a regional and coastal shipping company established in Amsterdam in September 1888 (Pronk 1998, p. 34), was also actively extending its shipping services into the hub of the Big Five's shipping and trading activities. The establishment of the KPM was intended both to provide feeder and distribution services for the Dutch ocean-going lines of the Stoomvaart Maatschappij Nederland and the Rotterdamsche Lloyd, and to transport persons, bullion and goods for the Dutch colonial government (Campo 2002, pp. 67, 77). Strictly speaking, the KPM was a quasi-governmental enterprise granted a mandate for the coastal transport monopoly in the archipelago and a government subsidy for shipping services. Equipped with this "exclusive right" and supported by state funds, the KPM commenced the shipping service with twenty-nine vessels on 1 January 1891 (Campo 2002, p. 66; Lindeboom 1988, p. 20). Four of its thirteen shipping lines overlapped with the Big Five (see Table 6.3). The immediate effect of these four lines was to put the KPM in direct competition with the Big Five.

TABLE 6.3
The KPM's Four Shipping Lines to Sumatra

1. from Batavia via the south coast, west coast and north coast of Sumatra to Edie and back
2. from Padang to Olehleh and back
3. from Batavia via Bangka, Palembang, Riouw and the East Coast of Sumatra to Edie and back
4. from Batavia via Riouw and the East Coast of Sumatra to Edie and back

Source: Joseph Norbert Frans Marie Campo, *Engines Power: Steamshipping and State Formation in Colonial Indonesia* (Hilversum: Verloren, 2002), p. 67.

Competition from KPM's coastal shipping lines along Sumatra had a more serious effect than simply the taking away of certain trade from the Big Five; it could, and did, permanently divert the direction of trade away from Penang's port. For example, KPM, with its Batavia-East Coast Sumatra shipping line, was able to carve out a substantial share of the shipment of tobacco. By 1909, KPM had gained virtually half (49 per cent) of the control of tobacco transported from Deli to Java, which had previously gone through Penang (Campo 2002, p. 247). The competition was further intensified when the KPM opened its inter-regional shipping line, the Java-Bengal Line, in 1906 which connected the Java ports via Singapore and Sabang with the British Indian ports of Rangoon and Calcutta (Allen and Donnithorne 1957, p. 212). Export produce from Java was mainly sugar and treacle; reverse cargoes consisted of gunnies, and rice for Java and Deli (Campo 2002, p. 275). The transport of sugar and rice by KPM vessels in this cross-regional sea route inevitably competed with the Big Five's shipping and trading businesses since the two commodities also made up the main cargos of the Big Five's vessels that had always plied between Penang, Rangoon, and Deli.

However, the KPM realized that its large fleet of ships and sprawling web of shipping lines were not sufficient to consolidate its control over shipping and trade in the region where the Penang-oriented network was long established. In order to achieve predominance, the KPM decided to adopt other strategies, such as buy-out agreements, construction of deep-sea transshipment ports, and liberal credit extension to Chinese merchants in Aceh, all to divert trade and shipping and to eliminate competition.

The strategy of buying out smaller companies can be clearly illustrated by the rapprochement between KPM and the Ban Joo Hin Steamship Company of Penang. Ban Joo Hin (Wan Yu Xing 万裕兴) was established in 1886, by Thio Thiau Siat or Chang Pi-Shih 张弼士, a Dapu 大埔 Hakka entrepreneur and a close associate of the Big Five, who had built up his wealth by supplying provisions to the Dutch army and navy during the 1860s and 1870s.[14] Thiau Siat was an all-round businessman, whose interests extended to planting (coconut palms, coffee, tea) and revenue farming (opium, spirits and pawn-broking) in Sumatra and Penang as well as wine-making and railway construction in China.[15] Using Penang as a base, Ban Joo Hin operated three ships

— *Hok Canton*, *Pegu*, and *Raja Kongsee Atjeh* — which monopolized the trade of the west coast of Aceh (Reid 1969, p. 260). When KPM took over the provisioning contracts in 1895, Ban Joo Hin lost the lucrative military provisions trade with the Dutch. Despite this, Ban Joo Hin continued to operate its vessels to compete with KPM on the East and West Coasts of Sumatra. With its experience and connections, Ban Joo Hin proved to be an extremely annoying and tough competitor. In some cases, Ban Joo Hin defied the Dutch authorities by smuggling forbidden goods, such as firearms, across the Straits. For instance, in 1896 Ban Joo Hin joined with Kian Bi & Co., a firearm-trading company run by some members of the Big Five, to use the 423-ton coaster, *Hock Canton*, to ship a large quantity of arms and ammunition to Idi on the East Coast of Aceh.[16]

The dynamic trade of firearms between Aceh and Penang took place since the period 1847–56. Firearms imported by Penang from the United Kingdom and Singapore were mostly exported to Aceh. The Acehnese produced their own cannons and guns, but the more advanced European firearms were preferred. Penang, as a British trading place, became Aceh's major source for European firearms. When the Aceh war broke out in 1873, the strong demand for firearms continued unabatedly. Despite the ban on the export of firearms to Aceh during the war, Penang remained as the chief firearms supplier of Aceh. Firearms imported from Europe and Singapore to Penang were smuggled across the Straits to Aceh. This illegal flow of firearms fetched higher prices and profits. For example, small barrels of powder, which cost around two dollars a keg in Aceh before 1873, rose to ten dollars a keg in 1876, and their price jumped to nearly twenty dollars a keg by the early 1880s (Tagliacozzo 2005, pp. 292–93).

With such high profit margins, it is not surprising that smuggling of firearms became rampant. At the outset of the Aceh war, *The Penang Argus and Mercantile Advertiser*, a local weekly newspaper, reported in its 10 March 1873 issue: "Smuggling in unpowder is carried on, in Beach Street and in the harbor in Chinese vessels and junks, to a great extent. During the week several cases were brought forward before the authorities, and the delinquents dealt with summarily."[17] The firarms flow between Aceh and Penang was very important for the sultanate. They were not just a commodity sold for profit, but much needed weapons for Acehnese to resist Dutch encroachment and expansion.

To rid itself of this fierce competitor, KPM decided to negotiate with Ban Joo Hin by offering a cargo pool or a buyout around 1900. Given these two options, Ban Joo Hin chose the latter. Ban Joo Hin agreed to withdraw its ships from Aceh in return for a monthly payment of 1,000 guiders for ten years. On top of this, KPM also agreed to pay 30,000 guilders extra to Ban Joo Hin if those vessels stayed out of the Netherlands Indies, in the event that their ownership changed hands (Campo 2002, p. 328). Of course, the competing ships could be immediately removed by this measure, but there was no guarantee that the proprietor of the rival company would not become a partner with another company to re-engage in trade with Aceh by using different vessels. In 1907, this is what happened when Thio Thiau Siat joined the Eastern Shipping Company, which had seven ships plying between Penang and Sumatra.

What became a more effective and destructive strategy in weakening the Big Five's shipping and trading network in Sumatra, especially Aceh, was the liberal credit practised by KPM. Starting in 1896 KPM began to extend credit to a mass of small Chinese merchants in Aceh. Every KPM ship going to the coast of Aceh, carried a purse of 10,000 guilders from which advances were given (Campo 2002, p. 329). The interest rate on the advances charged by KPM was between 0.5 per cent and 1 per cent, which was the lowest in Sumatra.[18] In this way KPM became, quite informally, the largest banker in the colony for short-terms loans. It is no surprise that many local Chinese and indigenous merchants in Aceh turned to KPM for these low-interest loans. Within a few years' time millions of guilders were thus advanced in credit. To receive such generous loans, Chinese merchants had to put up their cargoes as security; and when KPM secured those cargoes it basically succeeded in gaining control of the transport of exports and imports in Aceh. The small Chinese merchants of Aceh were in fact a significant link in the flow of local produce and foreign foods in and out of Aceh. Jeroen Touwen notes that the Chinese in the Outer Islands, such as Sumatra, Borneo (Kalimantan), Sulawesi, Maluku, Bali and Lombok served as links in the chain between the big business end of imports and exports and the indigenous people; they penetrated deep into the villages to distribute imported products, such as rice and other foodstuffs, consumer goods and machines, as well as to gather cash crops both for sale in the coastal towns and for export (Touwen 2001, pp. 205, 207). In this regard, they formed the fibers of the shipping and trading network of the Big Five. By incorporating the small yet crucial Chinese merchants into its shipping and trade network through its liberal credit system, KPM was able to wrest an increasing share of the shipping and trading business from the Big Five.

THE RESPONSE OF THE BIG FIVE TO THE WESTERN SHIPPING AND TRADING CHALLENGE: THE EASTERN SHIPPING COMPANY

The Big Five and their associates did not remain passive in the face of the onslaught of Western interests on shipping and trading in the region. In 1907, they amalgamated five leading shipping and trading companies, namely Koe Guan Co., Beng Brothers, Hock Chong & Co., Kong Hock & Co., and Leng Cheak & Co., to form a joint-stock company, the Eastern Shipping Company (Campo 2002, p. 319). With an initial capital of $1,400,000 and a fleet of sixteen vessels, the Eastern Shipping Company was poised to meet the competition generated by the Straits Steamship Co. and the Dutch KPM (Cushman 1991, p. 67). The Company's fleet grew rapidly through the further purchase and construction of vessels after 1908. By 1912, its fleet had more than doubled to forty vessels.[19]

The essence of the Company lay in the Board of Directors, which was a group of sixteen prominent businessmen (see Table 6.4). There were three members of the Khaw family, the proprietors of Koe Guan Co., whose business interests involved mainly shipping, trading, tin mining, and revenue farming. Under Koe Guan Co., they operated ships sailing between Penang, Singapore, southwestern Siam, and southern Burma and dealing in tin, coolies and rice. The four members of the Lim family were also closely connected to the shipping and trading business. For instance Lim Eow Hong, who took over his father's Leng Cheak & Co. in 1901, managed an extensive and varied business which consisted of shipping and trading between Penang, Aceh, and Rangoon as well as milling factories for sugar, rice and tapioca. Another major shipper, Lee Teng See, the eldest son of the prominent trader, Lee Phee Ean, and a nephew of the shipping tycoon, Lee Phee Eow, together with cousins and brothers-in-law established Hock Chong & Co. to run at least six vessels between Penang and Province Wellesley.

TABLE 6.4
The Family and Business Backgrounds of the Directors of Eastern Shipping Company

Name of Directors	Family Relationship	Business Background

Khaw Sim Bee (许心美)	— Youngest son of Khaw Soo Cheang
	— Four wives:
	  1. Lim Seng Wan.
	  2. Lim Seng Kim.
	  3. Nuan Na Nakhon
	  4. Klao
		— Koe Guan Company
		— Trading & Shipping
		— Owned sixteen steamers by 1904 and became the largest shipping company in Penang.
		— Steamers sailed between Penang, southern Burma, southwestern Siam, west coast Malaya, East Coast Sumatra and China.
		— Revenue Farming
		— Tin mining

Khaw Joo Tok (许如琢)	— Third son of Khaw Sim Khim — Wife: Lim Chooi Hoon — A son Khaw Sim Kong	

Khaw Joo Ghee (许如义)	— Five wives:
	  1. Lim Pihatpoe
	  2. Lim Shai Hong
	  3. Prem Na Nakhon
	  4. Leu Yoo
	  5. Fuang	

Ong Hun Chong (王汉宗)	— Second son of Ong Guan Cheng — Wife: Lim Pek Mow (林碧貌), Second daughter of Lim Seok Chin (林淑振), a Kapitan of East Coast Sumatra. — His three brothers took their wives from the Cheah, the Khoo and the Tan families.	— Proprietor of Ban Tin Lam dealt in tin, pepper and salt. — A partner in revenue farming in Penang and Tongkah. — Owned coconut plantation

Foo Choo Choon (胡子春)	— Second son of Foo Yu Chio — Wife: a daughter of Chung family (niece of Chung Keng Kwee) — Had a cousin married into the Cheah family	— Proprietor of Chop Eng Hong in Lahat of Perak operated tin mining activities. — Owned tin mines in Selangor and southern Siam
Lim Soo Chee (林土志)	— Eldest son of Lim Kek Chuan — Wife: a granddaughter of Khaw Sim Chua	— Worked in Behn Meyer and Company. Later involved in revenue farming and tin mining.
Cheah Choo Yew (谢自友)	1. Lim Chye Geam 2. Lim Saw Yew	— Shipping business between Penang and Langkat — Involved in revenue farming in Deli, Penang, Kedah, Perak, Bangkok and Singapore
Cheah Tat Jin (谢达仁)	— Second son of Cheah Chen Eok (谢增煜) — Wife: Lim Kwee Guan (林桂元) (daughter of Lim Leng Cheak) — Brother-in-law of Lim Eow Hong	— Tat Brothers Company (financiers and merchants) — Involved in Penang Spirit and Opium Farm and Selangor Gambling Farm in 1910
Choong Cheng Kean (庄清建)	— Only son of Choong Chuo — Four wives: 1. Yeoh Khuan Neoh 2. Lim Gek Kee 3. Lim Gaik Teen Neoh 4. Ong Ee Gaik Neoh	— Involved in most revenue farms of Kedah — Rice milling and rubber planting
Lee Teng See (李鼎峙)	— Fourth son of Lee Pee Ean (李丕渊) First wife: a daughter of Khaw Sim Kong (died one month after) — Second wife: a daughter of Lim family	— A partner of Hock Chong & Co. and Hock Moh & Co. — These two shipping and trading companies operated eleven steamers sailing between Penang, west coast of Malaya and southern Burma.

TABLE 6.4 (Cont'd)

Name of Directors	Family Relationship	Business Background
Goh Teik Chee (吴德志)	— Youngest son of Goh Siang Kee (吴湘其) — Wife: Wong Tat Yong	— An importer of modern machineries from England and Europe. — An agent for Kwong Feng An Rubber Estate.
Lim Seng Hooi (林成辉)	— The fifth son of Lim Hua Chiam (林花钳) who had trading connection with Aceh. — Wife: a daughter of Khoo family	— Managing Director of Criterion Press
Quah Beng Kee (柯孟淇)	— Eighth son of Quah Joo Moey (柯汝梅) — Wife: a daughter of Chew Choo Inn, Kapitan China of Deli — Brother-in-law of Lee Phee Choon	— Worked in Behn Meyer and Company and later established Beng Brothers, a shipping and commission agency which operated ten steamers. — Established Guan Lee Hin Steamship Company in 1895 which provided ferry steamship service between Penang, Kedah, Province Wellesley and Perak. — Owned a 3,000-acre rubber estate in Penang

Lim Cheng Teik (林清德)	— Eldest son of Phuah Hin Leong @ Lim Choo Guan (潘兴隆/林浚川)
	— Wife: Khoo Guat Lee
	— His second brother Lim Cheng Law (林清露) married the only daughter Khoo Bean Leang; his niece, Lim Saw Kim, was wed to Ong Oh Leng, a son of Ong Beow Suan, a well-known businessman of Tongkah.
	— Proprietor of Khie Heng Bee Rice and Oil Mill (开恒美米油较)
	— Established Cheng Teik & Co., a shipping and trading firm, which operated a steamer Seang Leong, together with Lim Soo Hean & Co. of Rangoon, to carry cargo and passengers from Rangoon to Penang, Singapore and China.
Lim Eow Hong (林耀麽)	— Eldest son of Lim Leng Cheak (林宁绰)
	— Took over family business Leang Cheak & Co. which dealt in planting, shipping, revenue farming and rice-milling business
Hermann Jessen	— Export manager for Behn Meyer & Co.

Sources: Compiled from Lee Kam Hing and Chow Mun Seong, *Biographical Dictionary of the Chinese in Malaysia* (Kuala Lumpur: Pelanduk Publications, 1997), pp. 14, 18, 32, 42–43, 48–49, 58, 60–61, 106–8, 135, 139–40; Jennifer W. Cushman, *Family and State: The Formation of a Sino-Thai Tin mining Dynasty* (New York: Oxford University Press, 1991), pp. 20–24; 世界谢氏宗亲第五届恳亲大会纪念特刊 *Shijie Xieshe Zongqin Diwujie Kenqing Dabui Jinian Tekan* [Special Issue on the 5th World Cheah Clansmen Conference] (Penang; Beima XiesheZongci He Xieshe Fuhougong Gongsi 北马谢氏宗祠和槟城谢氏福侯公司 [North Malaya Cheah Si Chong Soo & Penang Cheah Si Hock Hew Kong Kongsi], 1989), pp. 85–86; Arnold Wright and H.A. Cartwright, *Twentieth Impressions of British Malaya – Its History, People, Commerce, Industries and Resources* (London: Lloyds Greater Britain Publishing Company Ltd., 1908), pp. 781, 803; *Pinang Gazette and Straits Chronicle*, 1 February 1900, p. 2; 张少宽 Teoh Shiaw Kuan, 槟榔屿福建公冢暨家碑铭集 *Binlangyu Fujian Gongzhong Ji Jiazhong Beimingji* [Epigraphic Inscriptions of Penang Hokkien Cemeteries] (Singapore: Singapore Society of Asian Studies, 1997), p. 63; *Straits Echo*, 28 June 1912, p. 485.

It is important to note that not all the Directors of the Company were drawn from shipping and trading circles. Foo Choo Choon, a Yoon Ting Hakka, was in fact a tin mining magnate. He owned Chop Eng Hong, a tin mining company which operated some of the largest tin mining fields in Perak.[20] In addition, his mining interests also spread to southern Siam and Selangor. In all he had 10,000 coolies in his employ (Lee and Chow 1997, p. 43). It is clear that Foo's economic mainstay was tin production. Hermann Jessen, the only non-Chinese director, was a German export manager of the Behn Meyer & Co. in Penang. This German trading and shipping company had opened a Penang branch in 1890, and was also the agent of the Norddeutchsher Lloyd steamship line, the Hamburg-Amerika line, the German Australian Steamship Company, the Indra, Atlantic Transport, Wilson Hill, East Asiatic Company, and Russian East Asiatic Company as well as a large number of important insurance companies (Wright and Cartwright 1908, p. 801).

Taking all this into consideration, it is clear that the Eastern Shipping Company was much more than an enterprise to pool capital and build up a single fleet of ships. The relatively large number of board members made it possible to maintain many contacts with other companies through interlocking directorates, thereby creating an integrated network of shipping, trading, processing, consumption, and production under the Eastern Shipping Company. The inclusion of Hermann Jessen, the Khaw, the Foo, and the Lim families well illustrated the integrated network. Rice was transported by the ships of the Khaw family from Rangoon to Penang and processed by the rice mill of the Lim family. Then the processed rice was sent to feed the mining coolies of the Foo family. Tin mined by the coolies was brought to the smelting factory at Penang, which was operated by some of the Eastern Shipping Company's directors. Finally, the refined tin was exported by the ships of the Company to the Chinese and Indian markets or by Behn Meyer & Co. to Europe and United States. Such an integrated network enabled the Eastern Shipping Company to enhance its competitiveness to face the Straits Steamship Company and the Dutch KPM.

INSURANCE BUSINESS: THE BIG FIVE VERSUS THE WESTERNERS

On 10 July 1885, the Penang Khean Guan Insurance Company Limited was duly registered at Penang to provide marine and fire insurance under the Indian Companies' Act 1866.[21] The establishment of this insurance company was not an accident. Its emergence was a direct consequence of the growing number of Western insurance companies that were operating under Western-managed agency firms in Penang. In the 1850s, there were only a handful of such insurance companies, such as the Calcutta Mercantile Marine Insurance Society and Sun Insurance Office under C.M. Shircore & Co, and the Eastern Marine Insurance Company under Franser & Co.; by 1895, their number had increased to at least fifteen.[22] This growth of Western insurance companies in Penang was inextricably linked with the extension of Western involvement in the coastal or local shipping of the Penang-centric region.

In the last two decades of the nineteenth century, Western penetration into Penang's commercial shipping orbit was gathering strength. This unprecedented expansion of Western shipping interests obviously spurred the growth of the marine insurance business in Penang. Marine insurance, to provide financial protection from loss or damage of seagoing ships and cargoes, had been an essential part of Western shipping and trade. Most, if not all, of the Western shipping companies had their ships insured against marine risks at that time. For example, the Ocean Steamship Company insured each vessel at £2,000 in 1870 and by 1875, its insurance premiums reached £36,225 (Hyde 1957, p. 145); the Straits Steamship fleet was insured through the old family firm of marine insurance broker, Willis Faber & Dumas (Tregonning 1967, p. 37). This Western shipping fleet coupled with insurance posed a serious challenge to the Penang Hokkien merchants, especially the Big Five who controlled most of the shipping firms of Penang and dominated the coastal or local shipping services in this Penang-centric region.

However, up to the mid-1860s most, if not all, of these Hokkien shipping companies operated without any insurance. This was not unusual since insured shipping was not a feature of traditional Chinese business methods. Indeed, the Hokkien merchants initially regarded having their ships insured as an extra cost. But the large-scale challenge of the Western shipping services backed by marine and fire insurance, as well as the growing number of multinational Western insurance firms in Penang, had raised the Penang Hokkien merchants' awareness of their own disadvantageous positions and the westerners' competitive edge in shipping and trading.

In 1878, the first Chinese insurance company entered Penang. It was probably the On Tai Insurance Company Limited 安泰保险公司

based in Hong Kong.²³ In 1877, a group of Hong Kong tradesmen had pulled together a sum of $400,000 to found this company to deal with marine insurance with a Western style of management.²⁴ Foo Tye Sin, the wealthy Hakka merchant and proprietor of Penang, was appointed as the local agent for the company in Penang in 1878.²⁵ Foo was an established merchant, who owned extensive business in tin mining, planting, revenue farming, and commerce, and a leading Chinese community leader who had been Justice of the Peace in 1872, Municipal Commissioner in 1883, and principal director of the Guangdong and Tingchou Association in 1885 (Lee and Chow 1997, p. 44). In becoming the agent of On Tai Insurance Company, Foo was probably the first Chinese merchant in Penang to gain experience and knowledge in marine insurance business. In 1885, equipped with this experience and knowledge, Foo and his crucial partner, Cheah Chen Eok of the Cheah family, founded the first Penang-based Chinese insurance company, the Penang Khean Guan Insurance Company Limited, based in Penang.²⁶

Out of the sixteen partners named in the Company's advertisement in the *Pinang Gazette and Straits Chronicle* of 9 February 1886, eight were prominent members of the Big Five families (see Table 6.5).

The rest were also the members of the established and well-to-do mercantile elite of Penang. The only non-Chinese partner was Logan & Ross, who was the company's legal advisor. This legal firm was jointly established by James Daniel Logan and Frederick John Caunter Ross in the 1850s. By 1886 both men were established and experienced advocates and attorneys of the supreme court of the Straits Settlements.²⁷ Logan, for example, became a wealthy proprietor who owned 18,000-acre estates in Province Wellesley and Penang.²⁸ The Khean Guan Insurance Company was thus organized by some of the main figures in the Penang mercantile elite, who were intricately and closely connected with each other by a series of marriages and business partnerships.

The Khean Guan was founded with a nominal capital of $1,200,000 in 24,000 shares of $50 each. Of these, $332,800 was paid up and 16,640 shares of $20 each were issued.²⁹ By the year 1891, the paid-up capital amounted to $339,400 and the number of shares issued reached 16,970.³⁰ Most of these shares were in the hands of the promoters and their family members as well as close business associates. The ownership of shares was always transferred within the family circle. For example, Khoo Eu Yong, whose father, Khoo Sim Bee, was one of the directors of Khean Guan (1885–91) had his shares of the insurance company transferred to a clan

TABLE 6.5
The Board of Directors of the Penang Khean Guan Insurance Company, 1886

槟榔屿乾元保安公司
The Penang Khean Guan Insurance Company Limited Board of Directors
(9th February 1886)

Tan Ley Kum (Chairman)	陈俪琴	Chop Lai Shang
Lee Phee Yeow	李丕耀	Chong Moh & Co.
Cheah Eu Ghee	谢有义	Chie Hin & Co.
Khoo Thean Teik	邱天德	Chin Bee & Co.
Khoo Sim Bee	邱心美	Ee Soon & Co.
Cheah Tek Soon	谢德顺	Sin Eng Moh & Co.
Ong Beng Tek	王明德	Ban Chin Hong & Co.
Foo Tye Sin	胡泰兴	Tye Sin Tat & Co.
Yeoh Cheng Tek	杨清德	Hong Thye & Co.
Khaw Sim Bee	许心美	Koe Guan & Co.
Cheah Leng Hoon	谢凌云	Eng Ban Hong & Co.
Gan Kim Swee	颜金水	Aing Joo & Co.
Tan Kim Keng	陈锦庆	Kim Cheang & Co.
Cheah Cheng Eok (Secretary)	谢增煜	Chen Eok & Co.
Ong Boon Tek (Treasurer)	王文德	Boon Tek & Co.
Logan & Ross		Solicitors

Note: Tan Ley Kum was also known as Chun Ley Kum or Chan Lai Kham. He was a Cantonese originated from Nanhai (南海) district in Guangdong province of China. He was a revenue farmer and tin mining financier. He owned a tin smelting house, Chop Lai Shang, and a trading shop, Lai Shang Tsan, in Larut.

Source: Pinang Gazette and Straits Chronicle, 9 February 1886, p. 2; *The Singapore & Straits Directory*, for the years 1890, 1894, 1895.

kinsman, Khoo Heng Cheak in 1896.[31] By so doing, the Big Five and their close associates could firmly secure a controlling interest in the Company. The establishment of Khean Guan by the Big Five and their associates served two main purposes. It enabled the Big Five to compete with the Western enterprises for the growing insurance market in Penang, and at the same time to provide insurance for their own ships and godowns.

Despite being a latecomer, this Penang-based and Hokkien-owned insurance company emerged as a major and dynamic competitor in the Western-dominated insurance world of Penang. In order to undercut its Western rivals, the Penang Khean Guan joined with the Hong Kong-based On Tai Insurance Company and the Shanghai-based China Merchants' Insurance Company, through their insurance agents in Penang, to reach an agreement to offer lower premium rates and to adopt a bonus system which gave yearly bonuses to agents as a means to motivate their representatives to give more business.[32] These two strategies greatly concerned the Western insurance companies, which hardly ever reduced their premium rates and never gave bonuses to their agents. In 1886, some Western insurance companies, especially the London-based ones, reluctantly reduced their premium rates and adopted the bonus system.[33] The Marine Insurance Company Limited of London, for example, took out an advertisement in the *Pinang Gazette and Straits Chronicle* to announce a discount of 10 per cent for its premium rates.[34]

Having the Khean Guan Insurance Company in operation, the Big Five and their associates could have their ships and godowns insured against marine and fire risks and gain profit from it themselves, instead of paying others. In a way, the Khean Guan Insurance Company served to provide internal insurance for the trading and shipping companies of the Big Five. With this internal insurance, the leaders of the Big Five families saved thousands of dollars on their external insurance premiums. Indeed it is likely that the premiums from the Big Five families and their associates contributed a substantial portion of the Penang Khean Guan's earnings. The Company's financial statements of 1886 to 1895 registered a progressive growth of net premiums, which were $100,426.91 in 1886 and rose to $157,252.99 in 1895 (see Table 6.6).

A handsome yearly bonus was delivered to shareholders of the Company, the lowest amount was $14,534.98 and the highest amount reached $59,402.78 in the period of 1891–95. With the increasing profits, the capital allocated for a reserve insurance fund was no less than $10,000 and by 1895, the accumulated reserve fund of the Company was $250,000.

However, in 1896 and 1897 the Company suffered a sharp drop in profits. The net premiums earned in those two years fell to $75,708.55 and $63,272.23 respectively, both less than half of the amount in 1895. This decline was most probably due to two factors: the increase of disbursements

TABLE 6.6
The Financial Accounts of the Penang Khean Guan Insurance Co., 1886, 1891–1900, and 1905–6

	Net Premiums	Disbursements for Loss and Claims	Add in Reserve Fund	Bonus for supporters	Reserve Fund
	$	$	$	$	$
1886	100,426.91	36,793.64	20,000	25,523.47	10,000
1891	138,653.49	53,865.92	20,000	24,967.19	120,000
1892	147,143.64	64,620.48	20,000	23,514.89	140,000
1893	148,397.49	21,276.90	20,000	59,402.78	160,000
1894	159,444.22	53,929.58	60,000	36,779.96	220,000
1895	157,252.99	61,915.16	30,000	14,534.99	250,000
1896	75,708.55	33,681.10	N/A	N/A	N/A
1897	63,272.23	61,982.19	Nil	Nil	N/A
1898	87,772.95	81,516.36	N/A	N/A	N/A
1899	94,085.88	86,328.64	N/A	N/A	N/A
1900	102,421.70	93,332.18	10,000	N/A	N/A
1905–6	62,662.56	15,525.58	2,000	44,122	200,000

Note: N/A = Not Available
Source: Pinang Gazette and Straits Chronicle, 29 November 1887, p. 3; 28 November 1891, p. 6; 16 December 1892, p. 3; 6 December 1893, p. 3; 28 November 1894, p. 2; 13 December 1895, p. 3; 29 November 1896, p. 2; 23 November 1897, p. 2; 24 November 1899, p. 2; 17 December 1900, p. 2; *Straits Echo*, 23 November 1906.

for claims and a damaging proposal to wind up the Company. In September 1896, a claim for Rs.75,000 and expenses equivalent to $47,548.83 from Mauritius, caused by the total loss of 7,594 bags of sugar, put the company in a rather difficult position.[35] Following this claim, the company secretary, Cheah Chen Eok resigned in 1896. Then, on 13 July 1897, an extraordinary and general meeting was held to consider whether to wind up the company, brought on by several prominent shareholders.[36] It failed to get two-thirds of the shareholders to agree,[37] but the move to end the company had already shaken confidence in the Penang Khean Guan as a stable insurer.

Despite these two setbacks, however, the Penang Khean Guan, under the leadership of a new secretary, Cheah Tek Thye, the brother-in-law of Khaw Sim Bee, regrouped and recovered (see Table 6.7).

TABLE 6.7
The Board of Directors of the Penang Khean Guan Insurance Company, 1897

槟榔屿乾元保安公司 The Penang Khean Guan Insurance Company Limited Board of Directors (26th November 1897)		
Cheah Eu Ghee	谢有义	
Chuah Yu Kay	蔡有格	
Lim Teang Hooi	林长辉	
Khoo Heng Cheak	邱衡赤	
Khaw Joo Took	许如义	
Cheah Tek Soon	谢德顺	
Cheah Tek Lee	谢德利	
Cheah Leng Hoon	谢凌云	
Cheah Oon Heap	谢允协	
Lim Sun Ho	林山河	
Tan Kim Keng	陈锦庆	
Ong Boon Tek	王文德	
Teh Keng Quee	郑景贵	
Khoo Chew Eng	邱秋荣	
Lim Gim Seang	林锦祥	
Cheah Toon Haw	谢敦厚	
Lim Gim Thuan	林锦传	
Cheah Tek Thye	谢德泰	Secretary
Goh Khuan Leang	吴寛量	Treasurer
Lim Chee Boo	林紫雾	Auditor
Logan & Ross		Solicitors

Source: *Pinang Gazette and Straits Chronicle*, 23 July 1897, p. 2 and 6 August 1897, p. 2.

From 1898, the net premiums earned by the Company picked up again increasing from $87,772.94 to $102,421.70 by October 1900 (see Table 6.6). Apart from providing marine and fire insurance, the Company also played a role as a financial institution, which made loans on promissory notes and investments in mortgages of real property in Penang. By 1887, the amounts invested in mortgages and the loans made on promissory notes were $203,160.80 and $128,680 respectively.[38] In addition, the Company also spread its business to other countries, such as China, Siam, Hong Kong, Burma, Nederland Indies, the Philippines, and Siberia (see Table 6.8). Koh Hong Tek 辜鴻德, better known in South China as Kaw Hong Take, who served as a Justice of the Peace of Hong Kong in 1886, 1891 and 1904, was the person who supervised the business at the open ports of those countries.[39]

Taking all this into consideration, it is clear that the Penang Khean Guan Insurance Company was not identical to the Western insurance companies, but rather a combination of financial and insurance enterprises. Besides the opium revenue farm syndicate, Khean Guan was another avenue that the Big Five used to generate and accumulate a large pool of capital. It represented not only an attempt to meet a growing economic demand, but also to compete with the Western insurers who were already well-established in the region.

IMPLICATIONS OF THE WESTERN COMPETITION FOR THE BIG FIVE

The encroachment of these Western interests on the shipping, trading and insurance business had not only made the Big Five conscious of another powerful and threatening economic force, but also of their own economic weaknesses and vulnerability. The two major and imperative inadequacies confronting the Big Five and their closest associates were the relative lack of capital and the well-integrated methods of modern business operations. Both were important, as the economic development of the local region became increasingly based on capital-intensive technological systems. In order to overcome these two inadequacies, the Big Five had moved to marshall all their most important and well-connected business associates to form the Eastern Shipping Company and the Khean Guan Insurance Company. However, the establishment of these two companies was a prelude to a more ambitious organizational endeavour — the Khaw Group. It was a conglomerate intended to integrate vertically six companies (Khean Guan

TABLE 6.8
The Overseas Agents of the Penang Khean Guan Insurance Company

China	Singapore	Netherlands East Indies	Burma	Philippines
Hong Kee (Amoy)	Gim Moh	Teow Joo Ho (Batavia)	Ho Hin (Moulmein)	Chin Hup (Manila)
Chin Cheang (Amoy)	Gim Lam Hin	Sea ng Hup (Samarang)	Ee Seng (Rangoon)	Kwong Seang Ho (IlO-IlO)
Chuan Cheang Cheng (Canton)	Joo Seing Chan	Moh Guan (Sourabaya)	Soon Thye (Rangoon)	
Tong Sin (Canton)		Sin Joo Hin (Edie)		
Jin Seing (Swatow)		Joo Cheang (Oleh-leh)		
Chin Hin (Shanghai)		Tong Guan (Padang)		
Tong Sing Ho Kee (Shanghai)				
Hong Cheang (Ningpo)				
Lee Kee (Chin-Kiang)				
Chuan Cheang Cheng (Hangkow)				
Guan Seing (Chefoo)				
Jin Joo (Newchang)				
Tong Huat Seang (Tien-Tsin)				
Tan Teck Hong (Wu Hu)				
Ho Kee (Pak-Hoi)				

Source: *The Singapore & Straits Directory 1904.*

Western Mercantile Elite and Their Challenge to the Penang Chinese

Siam	Cochinchina	Malaya	Hong Kong	Taiwan	Siberia
Tek Guan Huat Kee (Bangkok)	Ban Soon Ann (Saigon)	Loke Chow Kit (Klang)	Joo Tek Seing	Pang Kee	Eng Heng Ann (Wladiwostock)
Hock Thye (Bangkok)				Hong Kee Chan (Tamsui)	
				Ho Hin Kongsee (Takow)	

Insurance Co., Opium Farm Syndicate, Eastern Shipping Co., Eastern Trading Co., Eastern Smelting Co., and Tongkah Harbour Tin Dredging Co.) and centralize them under the inter-directorship of the Big Five and their associates (Cushman 1991, p. 63).

Although the conglomerate was led by the Khaw family, the Big Five still played influential managerial and financial roles. Leading members of the Big Five could be found among all the various companies' Boards of Directors, and were also the main partners or shareholders of those companies. What is important about this conglomerate was the inclusion of a group of outside businessmen who were not only non-Hokkien speaking Chinese (Hakka and Cantonese), but also Indian Chettiar,[40] German, and Australian. This diversity was the key to vast capital and relevant expertise. For example, Edward T. Miles and Edward Leslie Miles, the two Australians, who had considerable maritime experience and engineering skills, served as directors of the Eastern Shipping Co. and Tongkah Harbour Tin Dredging Co. (Cushman 1991, p. 64). As well as contributing their experience and skill, together with the Khaw family these two Australians contributed a large proportion of the $250,000 capital assets of the Tongkah Harbour Tin Dredging Co.[41] In the case of the Eastern Shipping Co., apart from the Chinese, German and Australian directors and partners, certain Chettiars were also major shareholders. A.M.K. Raman Chettiar, for instance, had investments amounting to $900,000 in the Eastern Shipping Company.[42]

With such various companies to be managed by a group of the most powerful and well-to-do economic figures under an umbrella organization, the Big Five were able to create and vertically integrate production, transportation, trade, and finance businesses. The conglomerate also tried to achieve a horizontal integration of the widespread personal business networks. With Foo Choo Chun, Ng Boo Bee and Chung Thye Phin from Perak, Loke Chow Kit and Loke Chow Thye from Kuala Lumpur, Khaw Sim Bee and Khaw Joo Tok from southern Siam, Choong Cheng Kean from Kedah, Thio Thiauw Siat from Sumatra, and Tan Kheam Hock from Singapore, acting as the directors and partners, the conglomerate became a confluence of networks linking to the surrounding states of Penang. Equipped with this umbrella of interlocking companies, the Big Five and their associates seemed well placed to defend their business interests as well as put up a counter attack against their competitors. More importantly, the launch of such a collective corporation was a clear indication of the ability and flexibility of the Big Five and their associates in creating not only greater intra-dialect and inter-dialect but also inter-ethnic cooperation and networks to deal with the unprecedented Western challenge.

CONCLUSION

In the last decade of the nineteenth century, the Big Five encountered serious business competition for the first time, with the entry of a group of aggressive Western enterprises in the Penang-centred region. The Western enterprises drew upon larger sources of capital and new technology as well as modern management methods to penetrate the shipping, tin trading and smelting enclaves of the Big Five. The Dutch KPM, the British Straits Steamship Company, and the Straits Trading Company were the prime cases in point. With their shipping companies supported by insurance and financial institutions, the Western business interests were able to make inroads into the shipping, tin smelting and tin trading domain of the Big Five. Such an aggressive western challenge elicited competitive response from the Big Five. The Big Five attempted to meet the challenge by forming the Eastern Shipping Company and Penang Khean Guan Insurance Company, which created a united shipping network coupled with insurance and large capital. The initial success of these two companies prompted the Big Five and their associates to try something more ambitious — the Khaw Group. By establishing the Khaw Group, the Big Five intended not only to consolidate themselves within the Hokkien dialect group, but also connect the Hokkiens with other dialect communities and link themselves with the other ethnic groups. As such, the Big Five could source technology, management skills and larger amounts of capital to rival the western enterprises. By embarking on the Khaw Group, the Big Five and their associates appeared to have reinvented themselves by emulating Western business practices as a way to guard their business empire. But at the turn of the century, a set of Western-oriented political and economic systems and networks began to take root in Penang and the surrounding states, the twin loci of the Big Five's economic power. This new economic and political order provided a more favourable business environment for Western enterprises and more seriously eroded the Big Five's economic ascendancy.

Notes

1. Carl A. Trocki, *Opium and Empire: Chinese Society in Colonial Singapore, 1800–1910* (Ithaca, N.Y: Cornell University Press, 1990), p. 183. See also Robert E. Elson, "International Commerce, the State and Society: Economic and Social Change", in *The Cambridge History of Southeast Asia*, vol. II, edited by Nicholas Tarling (Cambridge: Cambridge University Press, 1992), p. 137.
2. Nicholas Tarling, "The Establishment of the Colonial Regimes", in *The Cambridge History of Southeast Asia*, vol. II, edited by Nicholas Tarling (Cambridge: Cambridge University Press, 1992), pp. 50–51. See also Ronald Hyam, *Britain's Imperial Century, 1815–1914: A Study of Empire and Expansion* (New York: Palgrave Macmillan, 2002), pp. 197–202.
3. Carl A. Trocki, "Political Structures in the Nineteenth and Early Twentieth Centuries", in *The Cambridge History of Southeast Asia*, vol. II, edited by Nicholas Tarling (Cambridge: Cambridge University Press, 1992), pp. 83–104. See also Elson, "International Commerce, the State and Society", pp. 149–54.
4. *Pinang Gazette and Straits Chronicle*, 9 December 1890, p. 5.
5. *The Penang Argus and Mercantile Advertiser*, 17 October 1872, p. 3.
6. *PAMA*, 21 November 1868, p. 3.
7. *PAMA*, 22 October 1868, p. 4. See also Chuleeporn Pongsupath, "The Mercantile Community of Penang and the Changing Pattern of Trade, 1890–1940", PhD thesis, University of London, 1990, pp. 244, 247; and Nadia H. Wright, *Respected Citizens: The History of Armenians in Singapore and Malaysia* (Middle Park, Vic.: Amassia Pub., 2003), p. 96.
8. *The Colonial Directory of the Straits Settlements including Sarawak, Labuan, Bangkok and Saigon for 1875*, p. F10.
9. *Melaka* 404 tons, *Billiton* 335 tons, and *Hye Leong* 406 tons. W.A. Laxon and R.K. Tyers, *The Straits Steamship Fleet 1890–1975* (Singapore: Straits Steamship Co., 1976), p. 1. See also K.G. Tregonning, *Home Port Singapore: A History of Straits Steamship Company Limited, 1890–1965* (Singapore: Oxford University Press, 1967), pp. 17–18.
10. *PGSC*, 27 April 1886, p. 5.
11. *Penang Chamber of Commerce and Agriculture Report for the year 1905* (Penang: Pinang Gazette Press Ltd., 1906), pp. 61, 72.
12. Ibid., pp. 72–79.
13. Francis E. Hyde, "British Shipping Companies and East and Southeast Asia, 1860–1939", in *The Economic Development of Southeast Asia*, edited by C.D. Cowan (U.S.A.: Frederick A. Praeger, 1964), pp. 38–39. Alfred Holt, the director-cum-founder of Ocean Steamship Company, had close connection with two banks, the Liverpool Union Bank and the Bank of Liverpool. His father, George Holt, was a shareholder and Chairman of the latter bank in 1847–49. Three relatives of Alfred, William Durning Holt, Robert Durning

Holt, and Sir Richard Durning Holt, took turns to serve as the Chairman during 1884–1938.
14. Michael R. Godley, "Thio Thiau Siat's Network", in *The Rise and Fall of Revenue Farming*, edited by John Butcher and Howard Dick (New York: St. Martuin's Press, 1993), p. 263.
15. Godley, "Thio Thiau Siat's Network", pp. 263–66. See also Lee Kam Hing and Chow Mun Seong, *Biographical Dictionary of the Chinese in Malaysia* (Petaling Jaya: Pelanduk Publications, 1997), pp. 10–11.
16. *PGSC*, 14 November 1896, p. 2.
17. *PAMA*, 10 March 1873, p. 3.
18. Joseph Norbert Frans Marie Campo, *Engines Power: Steamshipping and State Formation in Colonial Indonesia* (Hilversum: Verloren, 2002), p. 329. The interest rate charged by the Penang merchants was between 10 and 30 per cent.
19. Jennifer Cushman, *Family and State: The Formation of a Sino-Thai Tin-Mining Dynasty 1797–1932* (Singapore: Oxford University Press, 1991), p. 86. The company also had six water-boats, a workshop, and a plant. See also *Straits Echo*, 29 November 1907, p. 1157.
20. *The Singapore and Straits Directory 1904*, p. 281.
21. *PGSC*, 9 February 1886, p. 2.
22. *PGSC*, 12 July 1856, p. 5, 13 September and 26 December 1895, p. 4.
23. *PGSC*, 7 January 1879, p. 5.
24. 冯邦彦 [Feng Bang Yan], 香港金融业百年 *Xianggang Jingrongye Bainian* [A Century of Hong Kong Financial Development] (Hong Kong: Sanlian Shudian Youxiangongsi 三联书店有限公司, 2002), p. 35. See also Carl Smith, "A Sense of History: Part 1", *Journal of the Hong Kong Branch of the Royal Asiatic Society*, vol. 26 (1986): 225.
25. *PGSC*, 7 January 1879, p. 5.
26. Cheah Chen Eok, a son-in-law of Foo, was also a prominent and wealthy businessman with experience in finance and shipping. Born in Penang in 1852, Cheah was educated at the Penang Free School before, at the age of 16, joining Boon Tek & Co., a shipping and trading firm. He left shortly after to join the Penang branch of Chartered Mercantile Bank of India, London and China where he served for eight years. Lee and Chow, *Biographical Dictionary of the Chinese in Malaysia*, p. 13.
27. *The Penang Almanack and Directory for 1876*, pp. 18, 62, 66. James Daniel Logan, after practising law in Singapore for about ten years, came to Penang in 1853 where he often served as a legal advisor to the Chinese community in their conflicts with the colonial government. See Jean Debernardi, *Rite of Belonging: Memory, Modernity, and Identity in a Malaysian Chinese Community* (California: Stanford University Press, 2004), p. 49.
28. *The Penang Almanack and Directory for 1876*, pp. 40–41.
29. *PGSC*, 29 November 1887, p. 3.

30. *PGSC*, 28 November 1891, p. 6, 16 December 1890, p. 3, and 11 December 1893, p. 3.
31. *PGSC*, 20 November 1896, p. 2.
32. *PGSC*, 26 November 1886, p. 5.
33. Ibid.
34. *PGSC*, 18 March 1887, p. 3.
35. *PGSC*, 23 November 1897, p. 2.
36. *PGSC*, 17 November 1896, p. 3.
37. *PGSC*, 14 July 1897, p. 2.
38. *PGSC*, 29 November 1887, p. 3.
39. *PGSC*, 25 March 1895, p. 2. See also Wong Choon San, *A Gallery of Chinese Kapitans* (Singapore: Ministry of Culture, 1963), pp. 20–21 and Carl T. Smith, *Chinese Christians: Elites, Middlemen, and the Church in Hong Kong* (Hong Kong: Hong Kong University Press, 2005), pp. 162, 164. Koh Hong Tek was the grandson of Koh Leong Tee, who was the third son of Kapitan Koh Lay Huan. He was the uncle of Koh Cheng Sian, a son of Koh Seang Tat, who secured the Hong Kong opium farm in 1899.
40. A merchant-banking caste of ethnic Tamil originated from Tamil Nadu of South India.
41. Rajeswary Brown, "Chettiar Capital and Southeast Asian Credit Networks in the Interwar period", in *Local Suppliers of Credit in the Third World, 1750–1960*, edited by Gareth Austin and Kaoru Sugiharn (New York: St. Martin's Press, 1993), p. 271.
42. Ibid., p. 270.

7

NEW REGIONAL ORDER AND THE DECLINE OF THE BIG FIVE

The Western inroads into the Big Five's shipping and trading enclaves, as discussed in the previous chapter, were not the full extent of the Western business challenge. From the 1910s onwards, Western enterprises extended their business interests towards the primary production sector, especially in tin mining and plantation agriculture. It was at this point that the full force of Western commercial powers first descended on this Penang-centred region. By organizing as public joint-stock companies, Western mercantile interests were able to gather the larger amounts of capital necessary to adopt new technologies and to attract the skilled management that would enable them to establish their supremacy in the tin and rubber industries. On top of this, the modernization and expansion of Western-style political and administrative apparatus, which increased state power, had adverse effects on revenue farms and landownership. In the face of these changes, the Big Five lost their ability to compete and began to disintegrate. This was not a natural or inevitable process, but a result of their unsuccessful attempt to cope with the problems and challenges that emerged in a dynamically changing economic and political order.

This chapter broadly outlines the economic and political changes that would ultimately disadvantage the Big Five and considers why the Big Five failed to survive as the dominant economic force in the new order. We will consider two main arenas of change in turn, beginning with tin.

THE TIN INDUSTRY

Western enterprises began to gain ground in this traditionally Chinese-dominated industry from the late nineteenth century. Their first inroads were in the smelting sector. From the late 1880s, Western companies began to break the practical monopoly of smelting held by the Chinese (Brown 1994, p. 77; Yip 1969, p. 105). The Straits Trading Company was most successful in this respect and by 1902, it was smelting 55 per cent of the tin exported from the Straits (Cushman 1991, p. 76). Challenged by this growing Western control over tin smelting, in August 1907 the Big Five and their associates established a local limited company — Eastern Smelting Company — with modern smelting facilities as part of the Khaw Group (Wong 1965, p. 229; Cushman 1991, pp. 76, 78). This enterprise was floated in England with a capital of $1.5 million.[1] With a group of prominent tin-mine operators and smelters owners as directors, the Company initially proved an effective vehicle for competing with the Western smelting enterprise. Despite the tin depression of 1908–9, the Company was able to dramatically increase its production over the three years it was in operation. In 1908, it smelted 11,400 tons of ore and unrefined tin, or 18 per cent of the tin shipped from the Straits; in 1909, the quantity increased to 16,000 tons or 29 per cent of total shipments (Brown 1994, p. 87; Wong 1965, p. 229). This progressive growth of the smelting business suggested that the Chinese company was on a firm commercial footing and could compete with the British-owned Straits Trading Company.

However, in early 1911 this promising enterprise had to be sold to British interests for £133,000.[2] The problem was a lack of capital for expansion. At this time, the Big Five and their associates had incurred heavy debts in their opium farming operations, which created a shortage of funds for other enterprises in the Khaw Group (as is discussed in later part of this chapter). The sale of the Eastern Smelting Company formed a watershed for Western commercial dominance in the Penang-centred area: the most important Chinese tin smelting enterprise in the Straits was now in Western hands, bringing in an era of nearly-complete Western domination of the tin smelting business in the region. From 1911 to 1940, the two British-controlled companies smelted 85 per cent of the output of Malayan tin, accounting for one-third of world production (Courtenay 1972, p. 92).

On the production side, however, the Chinese still occupied the prominent position. At the turn of the century, Chinese mines contributed

90 per cent of the total tin output of Malaya, Siam and Burma (Brown 1994, p. 89). It was not until 1912 that Western enterprises posed a serious threat to the Chinese mining monopoly, with their growing use of expensive dredging techniques (Brown 1997, p. 195; Brown 1994, p. 79; Yip 1969, p. 132). Meanwhile, the Chinese were not unaware of these technological innovations in tin mining. In 1906, the Big Five and their associates started to adopt dredging in their mining operations in southern Siam. Together with the Khaw family, the Big Five embarked on a listed dredging enterprise, the Tongkah Harbour Tin Dredging Company, in collaboration with some Australian entrepreneurs. By adopting this modern technology, the Big Five hoped to defend their interests in tin mining, if not necessarily to maintain their previously predominant share. But they were completely squeezed out of the business by the Westerners in the early 1930s. The story was as follows.

The Tongkah Harbour Tin Dredging Company was a Chinese–Australian joint venture initiated by two key promoters, Khaw Sim Bee of southern Siam and Edward Thomas Miles of Australia. The former was economically successful and politically influential in southern Siam while the latter was an experienced and established entrepreneur in Tasmania. Khaw operated his Penang-based family shipping firm Koe Guan & Co., which had a fleet of sixteen steamers by 1904. It was the largest shipping firm in early twentieth-century Penang.[3] Khaw was first appointed Governor of Kraburi in 1885, and then of Trang in 1890, before being appointed Superintendent Commissioner of Monthorn Phuket in 1900, a position empowering him to administer all the southwestern Siamese states (Lee and Chow 1997, pp. 60–61). Miles, a Hobart-born Tasmanian who first worked as a ship's boy, started his own shipping company and became involved in the property business in the 1880s and 1890s. In 1903, he became a shipping broker for the Union Steamship Co. of New Zealand and a trade representative for Henry Jones & Co.[4] Both men were undoubtedly enterprising and sophisticated figures, but more importantly, they played the major role in bringing together their close associates, the Big Five and the directors of Henry Jones & Co. (Henry Jones and Achalen Wooliscroft Palfreyman), under an umbrella organization for common business pursuits. Strictly speaking, the Tongkah Harbour Tin Dredging Company was a strategy of the Big Five to tap Australian capital, technology and management.

Under the stewardship of Khaw and Miles, within three years the company had five offshore tin dredges working its Phuket tin leases. By 1910, it was the only company using dredges in Siam and it accounted for 25 per cent of Siam's tin output (Cushman 1991, p. 75). Between 1908 and 1911, the Company paid out over £30,000 in dividends and, in 1911 alone, its profits were £60,000 (Brown 1994, p. 87). The spectacular success of this pioneering company was a great spur to the growth of more dredging companies in southern Siam. Between 1911 and 1914, Miles and Palfreyman formed three more companies in association with the Khaw family — Deebook Dredging, Katoo Deebook, and Bangnon Dredging Tin Company.[5] All three companies were equipped with four dredges from Melbourne to carry out tin mining in Ranong (Miles 1967, p. 13; Hillman 2005, p. 167). This Khaw–Australian syndicate went from strength to strength and in the 1920s, it established seven more dredging companies to explore more tin mines in Phuket, Ranong, Takuapa, Songkhla, and the Federated Malay States (Cushman 1991, p. 104).

Given the close connection between the Khaws and the Big Five, it is not wrong to say that the Big Five were also involved in those dredging companies, along with the Tongkah Harbour. However, the Big Five had no role in the running of those companies: their day-to-day business, like organizational management and engineering, was in the hands of the Australian partners. Under this arrangement, E.T. Miles and his two sons took charge of at least four dredging companies (Miles 1967, p. 13; Hillman 2005, p. 167), while Khaw Joo Tok, the leading figure of the Khaw family after the death of his uncle, Khaw Sim Bee, showed no interest in management of the dredging companies. His role was to obtain tin concessions for his Australian partners in exchange for a nominal directorship along with a parcel of free shares.[6] In this regard, the Khaw–Australian syndicate was formed more on the basis of patron–client relationships rather than a genuine business partnership. This syndicate never established a professional regional administration and remained only a loosely-knit interest group.

In 1928, a dispute over the title to mining properties in Takuapa erupted that shook the Khaw–Australian syndicate to its foundations. Frustrated with Lim Hock Seng's delay in securing the mining leases for the Satupulo Tin Company, and believing the leases were held up in Bangkok, Miles and his associates complained to Prince Purachatra, Minister for Commerce and Communications and chairman of Siam's Board of Commercial Development. A sympathetic Purachatra requested the Minister for Lands and Agriculture, Chalerm Na Nakhon, investigate the Australian complaints in person. To the outrage and dismay of Miles and his associates, Khaw Joo Tok was revealed as the mastermind behind the hold-up in the Satupulo's acquisition of the mining leases in Takuapa. Khaw argued that he was the real owner of the land and Lim was just his agent.[7] Therefore, Joo Tok insisted that Satupulo had to pay an extra $49,000 on top of the original purchase consideration of $300,000, which was to be paid half in cash and half in shares (Cushman 1991, p. 107). Miles and his associates rejected the demand, perceiving this to be duplicity on Joo Tok's part. It became evident that Joo Tok's prime interest lay less in establishing a successful dredging company than in the immediate returns to be gained from brokering the mining lease. However, the "scandal" surrounding the mining lease provoked Chalerm Na Nakhon to introduce a central committee presided over by the Minister for Agriculture to scrutinize all mining permits and lease applications.[8] In other words, Khaw Joo Tok's role as influential lease-broker was effectively checked, while the results of the investigation of the dispute caused an immediate breakdown of relations between Khaw Joo Tok and his Australian associates.

If Joo Tok remained a director of the Australian companies, relations between the Australian investors and their Penang associates had degenerated into mutual suspicion and contempt. As a consequence of the conflict, the Australian capitalists were encouraged to circumvent the Khaw connection and successfully establish direct contact with the Siamese central government. Thanks to this direct connection, relations between the Australians and Siamese improved significantly. Symbolic of this new relationship, the Siamese Chamber of Mines was created in August 1928 and its inaugural president was Thomas Miles, a son of Edward Thomas Miles.[9] With a predominately Australian membership, the Chamber became an Australian-controlled association from which, not surprisingly, the Khaw family and their Penang associates were excluded.

The collapse of the Khaw–Australian syndicate was a blow to the Big Five's ambitions to use new technology (dredging) and management procedures (joint-stock company) to protect and enhance their tin mining business. At the same time, the Big Five also faced the aggressive expansion of British mining enterprises. By 1929, there were thirty-six British mining companies operating in Siam. The Siamese Tin Syndicate Ltd. and the Anglo-Oriental Mining Corporation were the most prominent. Siamese Tin was established in 1906 by Henry G. Scott, former director of the Mining and Geology Department of Siam. With the help of his brother, T.G. Scott, a London stockbroker, Henry Scott floated the company in London. By the late 1920s, Siamese Tin operated at least six dredges which became the most productive in Siam.[10] Anglo-Oriental Mining

Corporation, which was founded by John Howeson, launched its first mining venture, Talerng Tin Dredging, in 1927. John Haweson was a merchant and financier with no mining experience but with extensive international connections. He was closely linked not only with Patino Mines and Enterprises, the world's largest company in Bolivia, but also Yuba Manufacturing of California, which built the world's best and most expensive dredges (Myers 1937, p. 106; Hillman 1988, pp. 239–40; Hillman 2005, p. 175).

By the early 1930s, Anglo-Oriental had acquired a number of dredging companies, including Tongkah Harbour Tin Dredging which they took over in 1934 (Brown 1994, p. 88; Hillman 2005, pp. 180–81). The acquisition of those dredging companies was made possible when the Great Depression set in and caused hundreds of tin mines to cease operation in the region.[11] Within just a few years, Anglo-Oriental was producing 20 per cent of Siamese tin output (Brown 1994, p. 89). Anglo-Oriental also became a leading force in Malaya's tin mining sector. By the 1930s, it controlled twenty mining companies there which were probably responsible for half of Malayan tin output (Yip 1969, p. 21). Anglo-Oriental also played a major role in Burma, where it financed the Calcutta-based Indo-General Tin Corporation and the Rangoon-based Tavoy Tin Dredging. These companies dominated tin mining along the Tenasserim coast of southern Burma (Hillman 2005, p. 171).

The expansion of these Western mining enterprises brought about significant changes in the balance between the Western and Chinese sectors of the industry, securing an increased share of the total output for the Westerners and proportionately reducing that of the Chinese (see Table 7.1).

The growing ascendancy of Western interests in the tin industry was not only due to their larger capital reserves and advanced technology. Rather, their horizontal and vertical integration of different business activities, interweaving finance, mining and smelting with trading by international Western interests, was the crucial factor. This business integration enabled the creation of a superior international trade network compared to the regionally-based one that the Big Five had been able to achieve, using very similar methods on a smaller scale. Anglo-Oriental was the best example of this integrated network. As a major tin miner, Anglo-Oriental moved to consolidate its control over smelting by forming a large international smelting combine — Consolidated Tin Smelters (CTS) (Brown 1994, p. 90; Thoburn 1994, pp. 75–76; Puthucheary 1979, p. 87). The CTS created a tremendous horizontal combination of

TABLE 7.1
Share of Malayan and Siamese Tin Output held by Western and Chinese, 1906–40
(in percentage)

Year	Malaya		Siam	
	Western	Chinese	Western	Chinese
1906	10–15	80–90	7	93
1910	22	78	25	75
1914	25	75	37	63
1918	32	68	47	53
1920	36	64	47	53
1926	64	36	35	65
1929	61	39	32	68
1936	68	32	68	32
1940	62	38	70	30

Source: Rajeswary Ampalavanor Brown, *Capital and Entrepreneurship in South-East Asia* (New York: St. Martin Press, 1994), p. 7.

four companies, which were the Cornish Tin Company, the Penpoll Tin Smelting Company, Williams Harvey and Company, U.K. and the Eastern Smelting Company in Penang (Brown 1994, p. 90; Yip 1969, p. 182). As a result, the CTS became the world's largest tin smelting organization: in the 1930s, it smelted at least half of the Southeast Asia's tin and more than one-third of the world's tin (Thoburn 1994, p. 75; Brown 1994, p. 90).

Besides, Anglo-Oriental was financially connected to some international enterprises like the New Consolidated Goldfield, Aramayo Mines of Bolivia, Guggenheim Brothers of Bolivia and the banking firm of Cull and Company (Yip 1969, pp. 182–83). The New Consolidated Goldfield, primarily a holding company, was a major shareholder in a number of mining companies throughout the world. The boards of directors of the Goldfields and of Anglo-Oriental had three directors in common. The Guggenheim Brothers, an American firm of mining engineers which had considerable investments in tin mining business in Bolivia and Malaya, also had a substantial holding in Anglo-Oriental. With such a sound internationally-linked financial network, Anglo-Oriental was able to mobilize huge capital for its tin business venture. Indeed, Anglo-Oriental poured £7,270,000 into the tin industry in Malaya, Burma, Nigeria and Cornwall in the 1920s.

Through the agency firms, Anglo-Oriental was able to access an international network of shipping and trading firms for the transport and sale of its tin produce. Henry Waugh & Co., for instance, was an agency firm based in Singapore that worked closely with Anglo-Oriental in tin-related businesses (Puthucheary 1979, pp. 57, 89–90). By providing management, shipping and trading services to Anglo-Oriental, Henry Waugh became a subsidiary of Jardine, Matheson of Hong Kong, the company that ran the fastest and best-handled ships (Blake 1999, p. 230). Thus tin ores produced by Anglo-Oriental in Burma, Siam and Malaya could be sent to Eastern Smelting Co. in Penang and the smelted tin shipped out by Henry Waugh & Co.'s ships to Europe and the United States. Each link in this business chain bypassed the Big Five's enterprises. With the presence of this highly integrated network of Western tin enterprises, the role of the Big Five as tin miners, smelters, traders or shippers became indefensible. Tin mining in the Penang-centred region was permanently transformed from a predominantly Big Five-controlled operation to a mostly Western-controlled industry.

A similar story ultimately unfolded in regard to rubber, with a promising start finally giving way to decline, as the next section shows.

THE RUBBER INDUSTRY

In the nineteenth century, the agricultural landscape of the Penang-centred region was primarily characterized by the cultivation of commercial crops, such as pepper, sugar, coconut, and tobacco. The local rubber tree (*guttah percha*) was still a wild plant growing in the forests of Sumatra, Borneo, Java, and Riau-Lingga, with only small amounts of latex collected by the natives for export (Drabble 2000, p. 51). The turn of the century witnessed the introduction of the South American rubber tree (*Hevea brasiliensis*) by British speculators. This came at the time of an increased demand for rubber from the automobile manufacturing industry in the United States. This rubber was converted into a commercial crop which quickly dominated the plantations of Southeast Asia. Thanks to the formation of two of the world's largest tyre manufacturing companies to meet the rising demand of the automobile industry, Goodyear in 1898 and Firestone in 1899, rubber became a product in rising demand (Tate 1996, p. 207). This is reflected in its high initial price on the London market, where it rose from 2 shillings 3 pence per pound in 1900 to 12 shillings 9 pence per pound in 1910 (Lim 1967, p. 73; Drabble 2000, p. 53; Brown 1997, p. 145).

Realizing early the potential profitability of rubber, the Big Five had started planting rubber on a commercial scale in the late 1890s and in the early 1900s. Cheah Tek Thye and his partners owned the Eng–Moh–Hui–Thye–Kee 榮茂輝泰记 Estate in Kedah, which was planted with 30,000 rubber trees on 1,000 acres (Wright and Cartwright 1908, p. 489); Tan Kay Beng in partnership with Chew Choo Heang invested in Kean Ann Estate in Province Wellesley, where they planted 60,000 rubber trees on 1,400 acres (Wright and Cartwright 1908, p. 384); Lim Boon Haw and Lim Seng Hooi together built up a rubber estate of 5,538 acres in Kedah.[12] The Big Five's rubber-planting interest also extended to the East Coast of Sumatra and Southern Siam. Khoo Hun Yeang, a prominent figure of the Penang Opium Syndicate, was a shareholder of Tjong A Fie's rubber-planting business in Medan. Tjong was the Chinese Captain of Medan who managed to acquire large tracts of rubber plantation in 1908 when the Westerners had just begun to promote and organize large-scale cultivation of rubber in Sumatra.[13] In southwestern Siam, the Big Five worked closely with their associate, Khaw Sim Bee, to develop rubber planting. In 1901, Khaw shipped large quantities of rubber seeds to Trang from Perak via Penang and urged local Chinese and Siamese to establish rubber plantations (Montesano 1998, pp. 296–302; Silcock 1970, p. 41). Trang eventually emerged as the first important rubber-producing state on the west coast of the Siamese peninsula. By the early 1920s, about two thirds of rubber exports from the southwestern Siamese states were shipped to Penang (Stifel 1973, p. 124).

While it is clear that the Big Five were among the first to engage in the commercial cultivation of rubber and to develop this new cash crop as an economic base, and continued to make their mark in the mercantile circles of Penang, the rubber interests did not afford the Big Five the same degree of economic control and influence as they enjoyed in the nineteenth century. Despite being experienced and established agriculturalists, the Big Five failed to assume a dominating role in the rubber industry. Instead they were overshadowed by Western planters, thanks largely to the rise of Western agency houses.

The presence of Western agency houses in the early twentieth-century Penang-centred economic arena was not a new phenomenon. The agency houses, such as Guthrie & Co., Boustead & Co., Harrisons & Crosfield, and Katz Brothers, had been operating in the region since the early nineteenth century. Most of the agency houses were naturally associated with export–import trade (Drabble and Drake 1981, pp. 304–5; Puthucheary 1979, pp. 23–24). Operating in Singapore or Penang, they acted as the selling and purchasing agents for foreign manufactures based in Europe and the United States, thus providing the major link between local producers and western markets on the one hand, and between Western manufacturers and local consumers on the other hand. They also served as shipping, insurance, and managing agents.

At the turn of the century, these agency houses became increasingly indispensable in the development of the rubber plantations. The commercial cultivation of rubber was no less demanding than other agricultural endeavours; but, to be successful, and unlike rice, sugar, coconuts or gambier, rubber growing needed a real degree of global economic knowledge and contacts. Locally commercial rubber cultivation required the acquisition of land, imports of labour and consumer necessities for workers, imports of capital goods for the estates, and the provision of transportation services to the ports. Beyond all that, however, it also required access to shipping capacity to Europe and the United States, familiarity with Western markets, and a means of raising large capital sums for financing all these activities (Tate 1996, p. 238). With their marketing and financial knowledge, strong connections in Europe, shipping and insurance experience and networks, the agency houses were exceptionally well placed to provide for all these needs. Above all, the ability of the agency houses to float rubber companies on the London Stock Exchange to obtain finance was a crucial advantage. Their intimate involvement in publicly floating rubber companies enabled the agency houses to invest some of their large capital resources in shares in the companies they helped to float (Tate 1996, p. 253).The initial difficulties involved in setting up colonial plantations, especially of new products like rubber, almost inevitably gave them opportunities to gain a controlling interest in many such public companies (Puthucheary 1979, pp. 37–40). As a result of floating rubber plantation companies, over time agency houses came to achieve an almost unassailable position in the rubber planting business. In 1914–15, the Western agency houses controlled about 455 rubber companies that owned 372,810 hectares of plantations in British and Dutch territories in Southeast Asia (Voon 1976, p. 156).

Unlike the agency houses, the Big Five preferred family-based and private partnerships to develop their rubber estates, since establishing public companies went against the traditions of family ownership. As a result, the Big Five had to source their capital from the clan organizations (*kongsis*), Western and Chinese banks, and Chettiar creditors. However, as only a few banks were willing to provide loans for such a slow-maturing and capital intensive crop,[14] they were forced to rely on the clan organizations and Chettiars as primary credit providers. Lim Boon Haw, the president of Lim Kongsi in 1910s–20s, for instance, was able to raise a $400,000 loan from the Lim Kongsi and Penang Chettiars to invest in rubber planting (Wu 2003, p. 155). But these credit facilities had crippling limitations. Loans advanced to the Big Five involved stringent terms and conditions, such as short repayment periods, high interest rates (12 to 36 per cent per annum) and security of rubber land.[15] Constrained by such terms and conditions, the Big Five had difficulty in acquiring large amounts of capital quickly for the expansion of their rubber businesses. Western rubber companies floated by the agency houses, however, did not face this problem. Ayer Kuning (FMS) Rubber Co. Ltd. affords a good illustration. The company was floated by Thomas Barlow & Co. and had an authorized capital of £140,000, of which £128,000 was paid up (Tate 1996, p. 252). In 1910, the Ayer Kuning Co., as a listed company, could easily raise £100,000 by issuing shares to the public to procure more lands and expand its operations. Thanks to the willingness of distant investors to pour money into what was, in fact, a very long-term and risky investment, British agency houses became the leading rubber planting interest group in Southeast Asia. By 1921, they owned 684,551 hectares of rubber estates that could produce about 111,714 metric tons of rubber. This production accounted for approximately 50 per cent of the total rubber export of Southeast Asia (Voon 1976, p. 176).

Although important, capital shortage was not the only obstacle that handicapped the development of the Big Five's rubber business. A closely-woven labour network controlled by the agency houses also created a formidable hurdle for them. The success of British plantation rubber production could not have happened without Indian labourers from South India. In order to secure an increase and steady labour supply, the agency houses and the colonial government worked together to establish the Indian Immigration Committee and the Tamil Immigration Fund in 1907 (Parmer 1960, pp. 38–40; Voon 1976, p. 134). The Committee, which comprised five European planters and three officials (superintendent of Indian Immigration, the general manager of the government-owned railway, and the government surgeon of Perak) aimed to advise the Governors on Indian immigration; while the Fund was intended to subsidize the cost of transporting a labourer from India to his place of employment in Malaya (Voon 1976, p. 134; Parmer 1960, pp. 38–40). This subsidization subsequently made the cost of recruiting an Indian (£3.5 or $17) cheaper than a Chinese labourer (£4.5 or $22) (Voon 1976, p. 135).

This promotion of Indian immigrants was thus deliberately conducted at the expense of Chinese immigrants, and of those who had brought them to Malaya. In 1912, the colonial government went further and enacted a law to prohibit the practice of indentured Chinese labour system in Malaya; then in 1928 the Immigration Restriction Ordinance was passed to regulate Chinese immigration in the Straits Settlements (Parmer 1960, p. 92; Beeman 1985, p. 114). Essentially, these measures enabled the British agency houses to have exclusive control of the recruitment and importation of a large pool of cheap Indian labour. From 1907 to 1938, the Indian composition of the total estate labour force averaged 73.7 per cent (Beeman 1985, p. 142), while the Chinese component was only about 19.2 per cent (Beeman 1985, p. 142). Within two decades, Indians had become the dominant labour force in all the rubber estates of Malaya. In the East Coast of Sumatra and Aceh, Javanese labourers played the same role as Indians in Malaya (Thee 1977, p. 38; Stoler 1995, p. 2; Voon 1976, p. 102). By 1906, the Javanese were the fastest growing estate labour force on the East Coast of Sumatra and quickly outstripped the Chinese; in 1913, their numbers reached 118,517 or double that of Chinese labourers (see Table 7.2).

TABLE 7.2
Number of Chinese, Javanese and Indian Workers in East Sumatra, 1883–1930

Year	Chinese	Javanese	Indians
1883	21,136	1,711	1,528
1893	41,700	18,000	2,000
1898	50,846	22,256	3,360
1906	53,105	33,802	3,260
1913	53,617	118,517	4,172
1920	27,715	209,459	2,010
1930	26,037	234,554	1,021

Source: Thee Kian-Wie, *Plantation Agriculture and Export Growth: An Economic History of East Sumatra, 1863–1942* (Jakarta: LIPI, 1977), p. 39.

The tremendous influx of Javanese labourers was initiated by the General Association of Rubber Planters of the East Coast of Sumatra or A.V.R.O.S. (Algemeene Vereeniging Van Rubber Planters tier Osstkust Van Sumatra) to meet the growing demand for labourers in the booming rubber plantations. This association was made up of the major Western rubber companies, which controlled most of the estates in the East Coast of Sumatra. In 1912, it set up the Java Immigration Bureau to standardize recruiting, reduce costs, and to abolish competition among estates seeking Javanese labourers. Together with DPV (the Deli Tobacco Planters' Association), the A.V.R.O.S. also set a uniform wage standard that avoided competitive wage wars between the companies (Blandin 1924, p. 210; Stoler 1995, p. 42).

Under the aegis of the A.V.R.O.S., Western planters were able to secure a constant and assured supply of cheap Javanese labour. By standardizing and streamlining these processes to their own advantage, Western planters were able to recruit a Javanese labourer for 79 to 127.50 guiders (£6.5–£10.5) compared to a Chinese labourer at 132 to 151 guiders (£11–£12.5) (Blandin 1924, pp. 213–14). Consequently, the Western planters no longer needed to rely on Chinese labour and Javanese labourers supplanted Chinese labours as the major workforce in the East Coast of Sumatra. The ethnic shift in both labour forces clearly indicated the success of Western agency houses in creating and controlling an alternative labour supply that displaced the Big Five's formerly dominant Chinese supply system. It is ironic that the Big Five and their associates now faced with the high cost of recruiting Chinese labourers, turned to the Western agency houses for cheap Indians or Javaneses.[16]

In addition to technology, management and labour control, the Western planting interest groups together with the colonial governments also developed a well-integrated network of land and sea communications to support the commercial planting of rubber. For example, the west coast of the Malay Peninsula, where most of the rubber estates were located, was provided with a well-spread rail links connecting rubber estates directly with the ports (see Map 7.1).

Except for Penang, all the ports (Port Weld, Teluk Anson, Kuala Selangor, Port Swettenham, Port Dickson and Melaka) along the western coastline were well served with railways to facilitate the carriage of goods in and out of the inland production areas. Commodities like rubber could be carried from the interior straight to the ports while imported foodstuffs and labourers could be sent from the ports directly to the interior in a short time. Undeniably, the railways provided a big expansion in freight

MAP 7.1
Railway Network and the Distribution of Rubber in Malaya, 1924

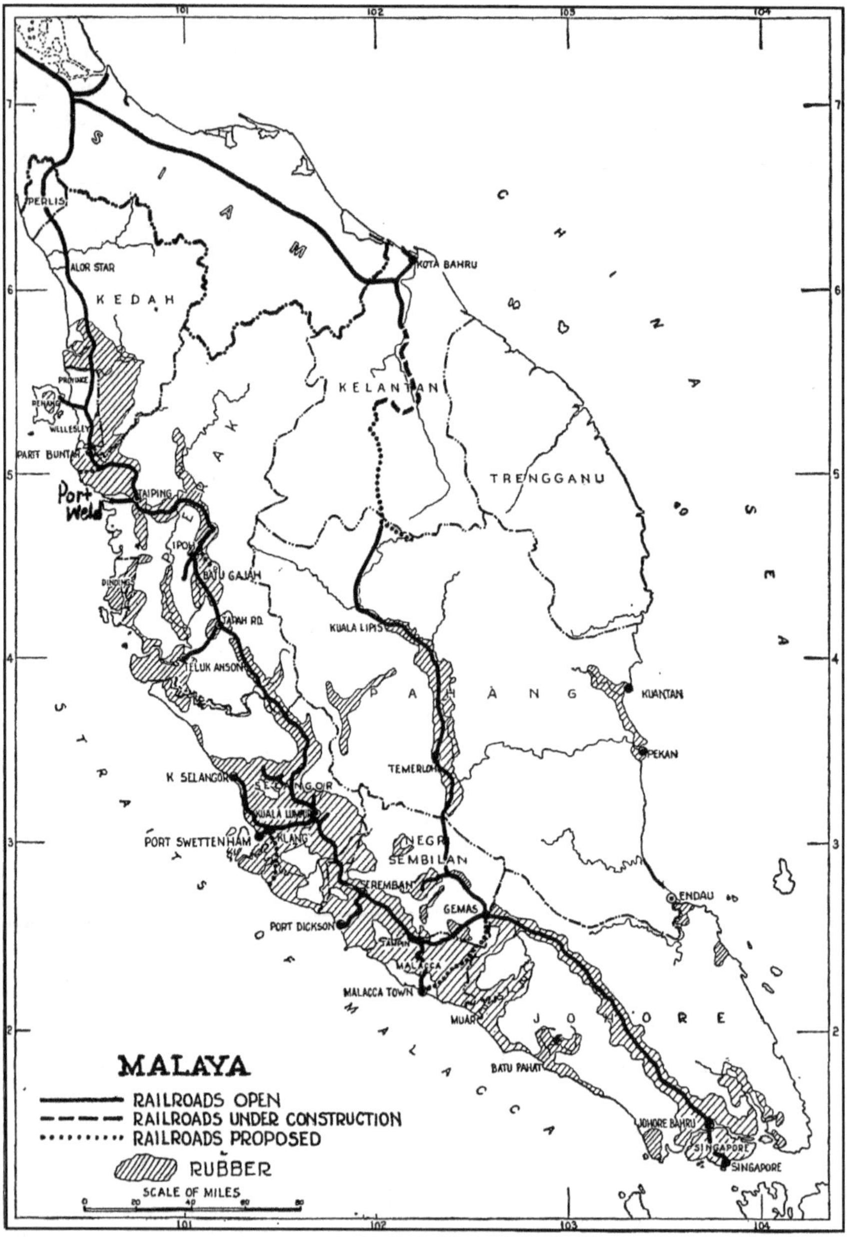

Source: J.J. Blandin, *Crude Rubber Survey* (Washington: The Bureau of Foreign and Domestic Commerce, 1924), p. 210.

capacity and considerable savings in costs and time compared to other modes of transport (see Table 7.3).

Similar networks of railways also linked production areas with ports on the East Coast of Sumatra. By 1924, there was a total of 950 km of railroad tracks and tramlines connecting all the estates to two major ports, Kota Raja in Aceh and Belawan in Deli.[17] The establishment of this railway system paralleling the coast and traversing the estates regularized transportation between productive hinterland and coastal ports and allowed for better coordination between land and sea transport modes. Most importantly, the linkage of the railway network with the ports enabled the Western planters to cease their reliance on the riverine transport which was dearer and subject to indefinite delays on account of the tides and weather (Kaur 1985, p. 151). Although the use of rivers in conjunction with traditional land transport (elephant, oxcart, human porters) had been the primary means of transportation for many decades, the railways competed effectively with them and became the most important and efficient means of land transport in the early twentieth century. The railways not only brought about an unprecedented change in port-hinterland communication, but also a very different business landscape.

TABLE 7.3
Freight Capacity and Cost of Rail/Land/Water in Malaya

Type of Carrier	Freight Capacity	Freight Cost
Bullock (oxen cart)	Average 15 cwt (762 kg) (up to a max of 1½ tons or 1,524 kg)	$0.90 per coyan (2,419 kg)
Elephants	Average 800 lbs (370 kg)	—
Boat	—	$25.00 per coyan
Porters (coolies)	Averages 100 lbs (46 kg) (up to max of 150 lbs)	$0.05 per kati (0.6 kg) (up to 15 miles a day)
		$0.06–$0.07 per kati (above 15 miles a day)
Train	12 tons (12,192 kg)	$3.36 per ton (1,016 kg)

Note: — No information available.
Source: Amarjit Kaur, *Bridge and Barrier: Transport and Communications in Colonial Malaya 1870–1957* (Singapore: Oxford University Press, 1985), pp. 151–52.

As railways spread, Western mercantile interests obtained more lands, especially along the railway lines, to develop and expand large-scale planting business in the hinterlands since the railways guaranteed a fast and convenient movement of rubber, labour and consumer goods between ports and plantations. In the face of the expanding railway network, the Big Five's controlled river system suffered a severe commercial decline, as did the rubber interests of the Big Five. Not only did they experience real difficulties in establishing more inland rubber plantations but also in transporting their commodities, since their plantations were located away from the railways. With the greater speed to market and greater carrying capacity of the railways, Western mercantile interests succeeded in revolutionizing commercial rubber planting in the region. The cultivation, tapping, preparations and transport of rubber were all carried out in a different way from earlier agricultural cash-crop production, due to the industry's role in the global capitalist economy. Despite being the pioneer, the Big Five's investments in the rubber industry were not only out-matched but overwhelmed by the Western interests operating in a transnational business arena.

THE END OF BIG FIVE REVENUE FARMS AND THE RISE OF GOVERNMENT MONOPOLIES

As is well known, profound changes were also taking place in the political order within the Penang-centred region in the late nineteenth and early twentieth centuries.[18] Seeking to consolidate their sovereignty in the high colonial age, British, Dutch and Siamese authorities increasingly pushed towards Western-style state administrative structures, with their characteristic central control of the fiscal system via restrictive laws regulated by a centralized bureaucracy. There were two important economic consequences of this change that particularly impacted on the future commercial viability of the Big Five and their closest associates. They were the abolition of opium revenue farming in favour of a state monopoly on processing and distributing the drug; and the application of a Crown Land policy to the Federated Malay States by which the state asserted ultimate control over all its territories. We consider them in turn, beginning with the opium revenue farm.

The turn of the century marked a watershed in the business landscape of the region as far as opium farming was concerned. The Dutch, British and Siamese governments took turns in abolishing the opium farming system and establishing direct control over the processing, trade, and sale of opium in their respective territories.[19] In Siam, the opium farms were brought to an end in 1907; by 1910, all revenue farms in the Straits Settlements and the Federated Malay States were largely abolished; in the Netherlands Indies, the process of abolition started in the 1880s and was virtually completed in 1925. Undeniably, the main factor that induced the takeover of the opium business by the state was the low return from Chinese revenue farming caused by the severe economic depression of 1904–9. During the depression, the prices of most commodities in the region dropped drastically (Trocki 1990, pp. 187–89; Chiang 1978, pp. 115–18). Major commodities, such as tin, pepper, sugar, gambier, and tobacco, were especially hit. The falling market values of these commodities led to the closure of many businesses, such as trading and shipping companies, and tin mines. From 1906 to 1910, fifty-six Chinese companies in Penang went bankrupt, with at least half of the companies related to the Big Five. In 1907, 60 per cent of mines in the Federated Malay States were running at a loss while the area planted with sugar dropped sharply from 11,233 acres in 1905 to 4,594 acres in 1909.[20]

Large numbers of Chinese coolies were laid off and Chinese migration was inhibited, both factors that tremendously reduced both the import of opium into the Strait Settlements and the level of *chandu* (cooked opium) consumption. The quantity of imported opium had already been dropping progressively before the depression, from 16,699 chests in 1903 to 12,658 chests in 1906,[21] while the consumption of *chandu* decreased by 43,732 kg in Singapore and 28,596 kg in Penang during the period 1904–6.[22] Such an unexpected drop put the Big Five in great difficulty. They could not run their monopolies profitably and consequently it weakened their ability to pay their exorbitant rents. Furthermore, the removal of the brotherhood *hui* (Kian Teik Tong) and the truck system — the basis of the opium farm operation of the Big Five — had an even more devastating effect.

These two institutions, the *hui* and the truck system, had been integral parts of the opium revenue farming system since at least the mid-nineteenth century. They played a crucial role in keeping the opium farms profitable. With its widespread multi-branch network, as we saw in Chapter 4, the *hui* of the Big Five served as an effective means to safeguard the monopoly rights of the opium farms. Through the *hui*, the Big Five were able to recruit squads of *chintengs*, or revenue farm police, to check smuggling and promote the sale of opium (Yen 1986, p. 122; Trocki 1990, p. 126; Blythe 1969, p. 250). In addition, the *hui* was a significant mechanism in the coolie trade network of the Big Five, since it controlled their movement as well as supervising them. Coolies, of course, were the largest Chinese immigrant group in the region. The truck system was the name of the arrangement by which the mines advanced provisions (rice, opium, liquor, tobacco, oil) to coolies at mark-ups of as much as 200 to 300 per cent (Drabble 2000, p. 55; Wong 1965, p. 75). In the nineteenth century, this prevailing practice in the tin mines and plantations aimed to ensure coolies remained in their workplace by keeping them in perpetual debt to mine or plantation owners, on whom they relied for consumables, especially opium. The *hui* and the truck system together created a large, effectively captive, labour force who became regular customers of opium farms.

By the turn of the century, these two institutions were eliminated by state legislation. The Societies Suppression Ordinance of 1889, which came into force on 1 January 1890, required the *hui* to wind up their affairs and dispose of their property and funds within six months (Blythe 1969, p. 236). In early March, the Big Five dissolved their *hui* in accord with the ordinance (Blythe 1969, pp. 239–40). The introduction of a series of liberal labour laws, beginning with the Labour Code of 1895 that made the Chinese coolie a free and independent man, ended in 1911 by terminating the truck system. First the Labourers' Wages Priority Enactment of 1899 gave coolies' wages legal priority over the claims of other unsecured creditors upon the sale of mines and estates (Chai 1964, p. 123). Then the Truck Enactment of 1909 prohibited the supply of opium and liquor to labourers as a form of remuneration (Parmer 1960, p. 116). In addition to these enactments, the Federal Council, which was responsible for labour policy and legislation, passed the Estate Labourers (Protection of Health) Enactment of 1910, the Chinese Immigrants Enactment of 1910, and the Labour Enactment of 1911.[23] If all this legislation intended to put an end to abusive practices and improve the welfare of Chinese coolies, in practice the measure also seriously undermined the Big Five's control over the Chinese coolies who were the lifeblood of the opium revenue farms.

Without the *hui* and truck system to control the coolies, the Big Five lost a secure market for their opium. When the economic depression set in, the Big Five's already weakened opium farming businesses suffered further loss. The inability of the Big Five to settle their farm rent provided an opportunity for the government to take back the state's monopoly right which had been leased out since the late eighteenth century. There was a fiscal incentive to do so by the early twentieth century, which was an era of intensified political centralization. Bureaucratic expansion and

TABLE 7.4
Straits Settlements Government's Expenditure, 1900–5

Year	Expenditure
1900	$6,030,740
1901	$7,315,001
1902	$7,601,354
1903	$8,185,952
1904	$10,848,988
1905	$10,976,525

Source: Compiled from Robert L. Jarman, ed., *Annual Reports of Straits Settlements 1901–07* (Slough, U.K.: Archive Editions, 1998), pp. 66, 166, 250, 356, 642.

infrastructural development were speeding up, as was clearly reflected in a 40 per cent increase in government expenditure during the period 1900–5. Public works, personnel costs and the military took up at least 60 per cent of the expanding budget (see Table 7.4).

In the Netherlands East Indies, the Dutch also relied on the revenue from the tax farms to support their power expansion and colonial development. In 1905, 40 per cent of the colonial budget was spent on warfare and administration.[24] In order to finance this immense expenditure, the colonial government could not afford the opium revenue farms to run at a loss, since they had been the major contributor to state revenue.[25]

Direct government control over opium spelt the end of the Big Five's opium business. British, Dutch and Siamese governments all enshrined the new state monopolies in legislation, with expensive new administrative apparatuses to operate them. In Malaya, the change occurred following the Chandu Revenue Ordinance 1909, which abolished the lease of the state monopoly right to revenue farmers and replaced it with a direct government monopoly. Henceforth, the Straits Settlements Government enjoyed the exclusive right to deal in the drug, whether to import or export opium and *chandu*, or to manufacture and sell wholesale *chandu*.[26] A Government Monopolies Department, staffed by revenue officers and equipped with some motor launches, was also established to stop smuggling and otherwise enforce the laws governing the opium monopoly.[27]

Two years later, in 1911, the Dutch successfully introduced the Opium Régie (or state monopoly) to replace the revenue farm in eastern Sumatra.[28] This gave the Dutch direct control of the manufacturing, wholesaling and retailing of opium in this part of Sumatra. To guard its monopoly, the colonial government mobilized the army, the navy, the police force and the law to enforce surveillance and interdict smuggling. More and more steamers and small craft became involved in coastal and upriver patrols along the East Coast of Sumatra in the early 1900s (Tagliacozzo 2005, p. 61); while legal codes concerning excise, deportation and extradition were also enacted to buttress border enforcement (Tagliacozzo 2005, p. 68).

In Siam, the growing disagreements between farmers (the Penang Big Five and the local partners), coupled with their inability to meet contractual payments, helped bring about the collapse of the revenue farming system there.[29] In January 1907, the Siamese government decided to abolish the opium farms and take over the administration of the opium monopoly throughout the country. With all this in view, it is clear that the appearance of government-run monopolies not only marked the end of the Big Five's opium business empire, but the rise of the state's active and direct role in managing the opium business.

CENTRALIZED LAND POLICY

The commercially-disastrous change in the fiscal treatment of opium was not the only result of the new political circumstances emerging in the region. There was another — the imposition of British norms in land ownership which would have a far-reaching impact on tin mining and planting activities. In the early twentieth century, the territory of Malaya was legally transformed by a radical land policy that vested ultimate control of land in the state: "to fix and stabilise the whole land situation by vesting supreme control of all land in the territory in the Governor on behalf of His Majesty, and thus to establish effective control by the state over the whole land of the territory and over all changes in it whether of tenure, title, alienation or transfer" (Lim 1976, p. 143). In other words, the ultimate control over land was vested in the state. A set of restrictive rules was subsequently introduced to administer the land distribution and usage in the colony.[30] This was particularly the case in regard to the land allocated for tin mining and rubber planting. To enable European companies to obtain large areas of mining land at practically no cost, the Perak Government, for example, decided in 1906 to resume all the idle or inadequately-exploited land owned by Chinese and Malays for redistribution to others (Yip 1969, p. 152). In the alienation of land for rubber cultivation, land with the best location, with frontage onto a main road or railway, was almost invariably allocated to a European planter (Brown 1997, pp. 148–49). The restriction was further intensified when the Malay Reservations Enactment was passed in the Federal Council on 25 November 1913 (Lim 1977, p. 112). The legislation not only gave the British Resident powers to declare any land within a Malay Reservation but also ruled that land within a Malay Reservation was not to be sold, leased or otherwise disposed of to a non-Malay.

In Siam, a similar tightening of central control occurred, when King Vajiravudh moved to further consolidate the power of the central government over the provincial administration. As a result, the economic privileges of the Khaw–Big Five combination, especially their easy access to mining concessions in the southwestern Siamese states, was severely affected. By removing the Mines Department from the Ministry of the Interior in 1909, King Vajiravudh curbed the power of Prince Damrong, the Minister of the Interior and a patron of the Khaw family (Brown 1988, p. 107; Bunnag 1977, p. 226). Prince Damrong thus lost the authority to issue mining concessions and the Department's new minister, Chaophraya Wongsanupraphat, showed preference for the Western mining interests who could bring in larger capital and more advanced mining technology (Brown 1988, p. 108).

When viewed from a political economy angle, it is clear that the new political order in the region was not simply a matter of the introduction of Western-style administrations and systems of law that intended to achieve political centralization and rationalization. It was also aimed at removing the long-standing regional socioeconomic configuration that had enabled the Big Five to establish their economic domination of the Penang-based area. The new political order thus laid a foundation for Western penetration while setting up a real stumbling block for the Big Five in business and political pursuits. One of its important victims was the Khaw Group.

THE COLLAPSE OF THE KHAW GROUP AND THE DEMISE OF THE BIG FIVE BUSINESS EMPIRE

The Khaw Group was certainly an impressive business endeavour launched by the Big Five and the Khaw families to meet the pressing Western challenge in the early twentieth century. With a conglomeration of mining companies, smelters, shipping lines, financial and insurance companies, the Khaw Group was intended to become self-sustaining and competitive. The Opium Syndicate controlling a chain of opium farms, which were abundant producers of profits, ideally should have served as the cash cow for other enterprises in the group.[31] However, the opium revenue farms turned out to be the bane of the group. The unexpected change of direction in the economic and political order delivered a fatal blow to opium revenue farming, as we have just seen. The Big Five and their associates suffered a great loss and became heavily in debt to the governments. On the Selangor opium revenue farm alone, for instance, the revenue farmers like Ng Boo Bee, Khaw Joo Tok, and Lim Teang Hooi, incurred a debt of $688,677 from 1908–11.[32] Without financial support from the farms, the growth and expansion of other enterprises in the Khaw Group could not be sustained. The sale of the Eastern Smelting Company in 1911 was a case in point. In the same year, another enterprise, the Penang Khean Guan Insurance Company was liquidated. The Eastern Shipping Company, which remained as a viable operation until after World War I, was eventually sold to the Straits Steamship Company in 1922.[33] The last component of the Khaw Group, the Tongkah Harbour Tin Dredging Co., was taken over by the British in 1934.

However, the failure of the opium revenue farms as capital generator was not the only factor that caused the collapse of the Khaw Group. The unfavourable political-economic background within which the different enterprises of the group operated was also a contributory factor. For example, the Eastern Shipping Company encountered fierce competition from Western shipping interests at the same time that Penang's role as a regional entrepot was declining. The development of the mainland's minor ports into deep-water ports by colonial governments to establish direct shipping links with the West had a great impact on Penang. Port Swettenham of Selangor, for instance, which was converted from a coastal port into an ocean port in 1915, became the premier port on the west coast of Malay Peninsula with direct shipping to Burma, India and Europe.[34] The construction of the deep-sea harbour at Belawan on the East Coast of Sumatra set in motion direct calls by ocean-going vessels and direct shipping links with the surrounding states (Java and Burma) and the West (Holland and England) (Airries 1989, pp. 123–25). The emergence of these ports facilitated the mainland's direct trade with the surrounding states and the West, and hence reduced the importance of Penang as an entrepot centre. With this changing pattern of shipping and trading operation, the Eastern Shipping Company, which had its base in Penang, lost control of coastal shipping lines and entrepot exchange trade.

Undeniably, the Khaw Group was at serious risk from the series of undesirable economic and political changes initiated by the colonial authorities and Western mercantile elite just when it was established in 1907. These changes affected almost all the enterprises of the Khaw Group and hence undermined the business competitiveness of the group. At the same time the Big Five and their associates became entangled in a series of internal legal conflicts which eventually eroded the values and trust among them. The external changes coupled with family feuds progressively brought down the Khaw Group and effectively destroyed the Big Five's business empire.

FAMILY FEUDS

In the early twentieth century, the Big Five found themselves confronted not only by tremendous changes in the economic and political order, but also with conflicts of interest within families and with other families. Of course, conflicts of interest within or between families did not crop up only at this time. This was already a problem faced by the Big Five in the nineteenth century. For example, in 1886, Koh Seang Thye and Khoo Thean Teik filed a lawsuit against Chung Keng Kwee for a breach of agreement.[35] Koh and Khoo demanded compensation, but the court ruled in Chung's favour. Despite the legal wrangle, Koh, Khoo and Chung remained close partners in tin mining and trading as well as the revenue farming business.[36] In 1897, some directors of the Penang Khean Guan Insurance Co., who were supporters of Cheah Chen Eok, the former secretary, who resigned in 1896, urged the winding up of the Company.[37] The new secretary, Cheah Tek Thye, stepped in and resolved the differences among the directors.

It is clear from these examples that earlier conflicts did not develop to the extent of undermining family relationships and damaging business partnerships. Those arising in the early twentieth century, on the other hand, plunged the Big Five and their associates into protracted and bitter legal disputes involving huge monied interests that were highly damaging. In the absence of personal papers or other direct evidence from the participants, it is impossible to analyse the inner reasons for these disputes. It is surely nevertheless significant that all the most important ones broke out in the insecure decades after the abolition of the Big Five's dominance in coolie trading, shipping, tin mining, and revenue farming. Unlike past disputes, the twentieth-century conflicts seem to be symptoms of the Big Five's decline, carried out in an era of reduced opportunities and limited possibilities, and far more bitter because there was much more to lose. In this respect, they can also be seen as a consequence of the way that Western penetration had revolutionized to political economy of the Penang-centred region.[38]

On 6 January 1919, the Eastern Shipping Company, which was being sued by the Peninsular and Oriental Steam Navigation Company (P&O Company) for damaging its wharf at Belawan in Sumatra, brought in Quah Beng Kee, the managing director, under third-party procedure for the defence and to appear at the trial.[39] In the proceedings, the P&O Company made a compensation claim of $79,860 from the Eastern Shipping Company, which in turn pressed a claim for an indemnity from Beng Kee.[40] According to the Eastern Shipping Company's charges, Beng Kee had abused his power by giving instructions without company authority to a ship which he himself had chartered for his own benefit to berth at the wharf.[41] Therefore, Beng Kee should be held liable for the damage not the company. But the court ruled that the Eastern Shipping Company had to pay the compensation and had no right of indemnity against Beng Kee since he had acted within the scope of his power as managing director.

This lawsuit definitely dented Quah Beng Kee's relationship with the Big Five and the Khaw family, who were the core directors and partners of the Eastern Shipping Company. Apart from this, Quah Beng Kee was also involved in another wrangle with the Big Five and the Khaw family over company policy. As World War I was drawing to a close, the British government requisitioned the Eastern Shipping Company's nine steamers.[42] Disagreeing with the rates and compensation offered, the directors of the Company, except for Beng Kee, refused to sign the agreement and turn over their vessels. Dissatisfied with the majority decision, Beng Kee and Yeoh Seng Chang, the treasurer, resigned from the company. Under relentless pressure from the Colonial Secretary, the Big Five and the Khaw family eventually handed over the management of their vessels to Beng Kee, who was appointed by the British as the caretaker (Cushman 1991, pp. 110–11). With this power, Beng Kee became even more uncompromising when he dealt with the directors of the Eastern Shipping Company. In one case, he rejected the company requests for payment of coal and stores on the steamers at the time they were delivered to the British. Beng Kee did not rejoin the company when the steamers were returned in 1919. This incident clearly revealed a growing dissension within the partnership that ended by causing the exit of one of the most experienced and prominent shippers in the region.

The pursuit of lucrative revenue farming contracts could pull together the Big Five and their associates but it could also tear them apart. The first legal dispute over the opium revenue farming in October 1909 was the first to crop up. Cheah Choo Yew, the chief manager of the Siam opium revenue farm, and other partners were indicted by Yeoh Ooi Gark, who was also a partner of the opium farm, for fraud. In February 1905, a syndicate was formed by Cheah, Yeoh and other Penang towkays to take control of the Siam opium farm, running from 1 April 1905 to 31 May 1908.[43] But, in August 1905, the Penang interests group, who was confronted with some financial difficulties, decided to relinquish the farm with a full compensation of 752,800 baht ($451,680) from the Siamese government.[44] With the termination of this opium farming contract, Yeoh, who had a share of $100,000 in the syndicate of which $61,000 was paid up, was only given back an amount of $38,798.[45] Realizing his partners' unaccountability and their conspiracy to defraud, Yeoh hence resorted to court action.

On 16 January 1911, Khoo Hun Yeang took legal action for embezzlement against his partners, Khaw Joo Choe and thirteen others, who controlled the Singapore and affiliated farms from 1907 to 1909.[46] As a guarantor of the opium farm syndicate, Khoo Hun Yeang discovered that nearly $61,000 in the books of the Chartered Bank had been withdrawn by Khaw Joo Choe and others without making any account of it.[47] The proceedings dragged on for years and were only dropped when Khoo Hun Yeang died in a car accident during a visit to Medan in 1917 (Buiskool 2003, p. 4; Chang 1981, pp. 148–49). In 1914, the opium farmers were entangled in another legal dispute. Khaw Joo Tok, who was a partner in the Selangor Opium, Gaming and Spirit Farms, 1908–9 under the name of Ban Bee, filed a law suit against the manager, Ng Boo Bee, for breach of duty as a partner. By probing into the account books of the partnership kept by Boo Bee, Joo Tok found that the manager used the assets of the partnership for trading on his own account without the knowledge or consent of his partners, and without accounting to them for the profits.[48] Worst of all, Boo Bee had in some matters acted in fraud of his partners. In one case, Boo Bee did not obtain the consent of other partners to execute a deed, on behalf of the syndicate, to act as surety for Ewe Keok Neo's mortgage debt.[49] Ewe Keok Neo, a wife of Ng Boo Bee, became heavily in debt after an unsuccessful speculation in landed property. In order to bail out his wife, Ng Boo Bee planned to debit the debt ($242,357) against the syndicate's account.[50]

Apart from these legal conflicts with other families, the family members within each of the Big Five were also embroiled in launching legal battle against each other. In March 1913, Yeoh Paik Tatt of the Yeoh family filed a law suit against the president and the committee of trustees of the Seh Yeoh Kongsi for abusing their power to mismanage the *kongsi*'s funds and properties. Since 1901, Yeoh Paik Tatt conducted inquiries and investigations on the *kongsi*'s account books and found substantial amount of money remitted to China, which was improperly disposed of the funds of the *kongsi*.[51] There was a sum of $60,000 remitted between the years 1885–93 and another sum of $33,224 remitted between the years 1904–12.[52] The books did not detail for what purposes these remittances were made. Besides, some of the *kongsi*'s funds were also used to lend to the members without interest or security. The litigation lasted for three years and the Supreme Court eventually ruled in favour of Yeoh Paik Tatt. This court decision resulted in the appointment of John Mitchell, a close business associate of Yeoh Paik Tatt, as the receiver to take over the books and accounts of the *kongsi*.[53] In July 1917, a new scheme for the management and administration of the *kongsi* was approved by the Supreme Court and Yeoh Paik Tatt and his supporters formed a new committee of trustees to replace those discredited in the scandal.

The Lim family was another house in chaos. Lim Boon Haw and Lim Seng Hooi, who were president and vice-president of the Seh Lim Kongsi respectively, became entangled in a legal dispute. In 1931, Lim Seng Hooi took legal action against Lim Boon Haw to recover a loan (Wu 2003, p. 154). In June 1932, the case was settled and Lim Boon Haw promised to pay two charges of $16,000 for part of his land in Kedah to Lim Seng Hooi. But in 1934, Lim Boon Haw suddenly passed away and left his debt unsettled. Lim Seng Hooi immediately took legal action against Lim Boon Haw's sons to secure a repayment of his loan. At the same time, Lim Seng Hooi also faced two legal actions taken by a public officer of the Lim Kongsi. One claim was for $135,000 and another was for $17,102. The case was later settled by an agreement approved by the court. Lim Eow Thoon, a trustee of the Lim Kongsi, was sued for the recovery of a debt by his brothers-in-law, Cheah Tatto and Cheah Tat Jin[54] in 1931. In the judgement, Eow Thoon was ordered to pay the two brothers $135,720 plus interest.[55] As a result, Eow Thoon had to put his family estate up for sale, which was bought by the Cheah brothers.

Taking all this into consideration, it is clear that the conflicts of interest ending in lawsuits created great tension and division within the leading elements of the Big Five and their associates. The court cases soured relations between family members and their business partners, which degenerated into mutual distrust and contempt. Spoiled personal relationship not only led to the departure of business partners, but also to the disintegration of a powerful economic alliance. Although some members of the Big Five remained active in business from the 1930s to the early post-war period, their economic activities become more locally-oriented compared to those of the colonial or *singkeh* Chinese business elites, their former economic significance in regional and international spheres increasingly forgotten.

CONCLUSION

Western business expansion was first gradual in the late nineteenth century, then rapid and comprehensive by the turn of the twentieth century. This was particularly evident in tin mining and rubber planting. The Big Five could, and did, continue to compete with the Western economic interests by adopting new technologies and management skills. Teaming up with some Australians, the Big Five intended to employ dredging technology and the management of listed corporate companies to enhance their tin mining business. But personal profiteering and impropriety spoiled the relationship and damaged the partnership between the Big Five and the Australians. Besides, the capital-rich and well-organized British mining interests proved to be too powerful for the Big Five to compete. When the rubber boom started, the Big Five were fast to channel their capital into rubber planting. But the business was largely carried out in the form of family-based and small private partnerships rather than through the formalized organizational structures of public companies and the agency house system. As a result, the Big Five could only rely on limited sources of capital from clan associations, banks, and Chettiars to develop their business. By contrast, the Western agency houses, which possessed political and financial connections, were able to tap large capital resources in the West through the floatation of rubber companies to become by far the most important owners of rubber estates. On top of this, a well-organized supply network of Indian and Javanese labour and a transportation system was developed by the agency houses to establish ultimate Western control of the industry.

Contemporaneously, the Big Five found themselves increasingly at a disadvantage as state power shaped the context in which they could operate. The turn of the century saw a dramatic change in a region where the Chinese networks used to extend in a more or less unbounded fashion, was carved into discrete political and administrative units. In Malaya, British power penetrated from the Straits Settlements into the Peninsula and brought all the Malay states under colonial control. In the Indies, the Dutch expanded their Java-based political machine to draw the outer islands together to form a "Netherlands East Indies". In Siam, the Bangkok-based government adopted a Western-modelled "self-strengthening" strategy to consolidate its control over the peripheral territories. All these political actions inexorably and inevitably demarcated and tightened the boundaries of the respective regimes. Restrictive laws and regulations were introduced progressively by the state to consolidate centralization power and dismantle the quasi-political and socioeconomic institutions that the Big Five had relied upon. This eventually and ultimately deprived the Big Five of the economic privileges (monopoly of opium farms and mining concessions) they had enjoyed for many decades. In others words, strong colonial and indigenous states emerged to take control of affairs. In this new context, the Big Five found that not only their role as middleman or conduit was unnecessary, but also their economic activities were relentlessly restricted.

The dredging machines and the Indian/Javanese coolies took the place of the Chinese coolies; the joint-stock companies and government machinery supplanted the old *kongsi* houses; the railways and roads replaced the river transportation. All the forces that used to uphold the system created by the Big Five together lost significance and even meaning in the face of the new economic and political order. Alongside this order, the Big Five were confronted with growing conflicts of interest among themselves and with their associates. Bringing the conflicts to court, the Big Five and their associates fell foul of each other. Troubled by internal conflicts, the Big Five confronted with the new and unfavourable political and economic conditions at the same time, proved unable to adapt to the new demands and eventually saw their economic alliance disintegrating and they faded into oblivion. The century-long economic dominance of the Big Five in the Penang region came to an end under the impact of modern Western business methods and colonial political supremacy.

Notes

1. Jennifer Cushman, *Family and State: The Formation of a Sino-Thai Tin-Mining Dynasty 1797–1932* (Singapore: Oxford University Press, 1991), pp. 76–78. See also *Penang Centenary Number*, 1833–1933, Penang, 1933, p. 20.
2. The British interests consisted of Sir Ernest Woodford, Sir Cecil Lindsay Budd and David Currie. The selling price of Eastern Smelting Company was almost four times that of the setting up cost (£35,000) of the enterprise. Cushman, *Family and State*, p. 98. See also John T. Thoburn, *Commodities in the International Economy* (Edinburgh: Edinburgh University Press Ltd., 1994), p. 59.
3. *The Singapore & Straits Directory 1904*, p. 12.
4. *Australian Dictionary of Biography*, vol. 10 (Melbourne: Melbourne University Press, 1986), pp. 500–1.
5. Paul Battersby, "Diggers and Diplomats: Australian Mining Entrepreneurs and the Evolution of the Australia–Thailand Bilateral Relationship, 1903–1941", in *Thai–Australian Relations in the Twentieth Century*, edited by M. Hayes and S. Smith (Bangkok: Kasetsart University, 2000), p. 5 (online book).
6. Battersby, "Diggers and Diplomats", p. 7; see also Cushman, *Family and State*, pp. 104–5. On 8 January 1922, E.L. Miles wrote a letter to the editor of the *Straits Observer*, a local newspaper in Penang, and complained that the holders for prospecting licences in Phuket rather sold their licences for profit than worked the lands for tin. *Straits Echo*, 17 January 1922, p. 64.
7. Battersby, "Diggers and Diplomats", p. 7; see also Cushman, *Family and State*, p. 105.
8. Battersby, "Diggers and Diplomats", p. 8.
9. Battersby, "Diggers and Diplomats", p. 8. See also Paul Battersby, "An Uneasy Peace: Britain, the United States and Australia's Pursuit of War Reparations from Thailand, 1945–1952", *Australian Journal of International Affairs*, vol. 54, no. 1 (2000): 16.
10. Suehiro Akira, *Capital Accumulation in Thailand 1855–1985* (Tokyo: Centre for East Asian Cultural Studies, 1989), p. 66. See also Battersby, "Diggers and Diplomats", p. 4.
11. In 1929–33, eighty-two tin mines which were worked by dredges ceased operation in Malaya. Yip Yat Hoong, *The Development of the Tin Mining Industry of Malaya* (Kuala Lumpur: University of Malaya Press. 1969), p. 209.
12. Wu Xiao An, *Chinese Business in the Making of a Malay State, 1882–1941: Kedah and Penang* (London; New York: RoutledgeCurzon, 2003), p. 154. See also Jas Baillie, "Rubber", in *Directory of Malaya 1927*, edited by Broughton Richmond (Singapore: Directory of Malaya, 1927).

13. Dirk A. Buiskool, "The Chinese Commercial Elite of Medan, 1890–1942", a paper presented in Shared Histories Conference in Penang 30 July 2003–3 August 2003, p. 5. See also Dirk A. Buiskool, "Medan: A Plantation City on the East Coast of Sumatra 1870–1942", in *Kota Lama, Kota Baru di Indonesia Sebelum and Setelah Kemerdekaan* [Old City, New City: The History of the Indonesian City Before and After Independence], edited by Freek Colombijn, Martin Barwegen, Purnawan Basundoro and Johny Alfian Khusyairi (Yogyakarta: Ombak & NIOD, 2005), p. 287. Tjong A Fei bought his first plantation in 1908, and by 1919 he owned almost twenty estates.
14. D.J.M. Tate, *The RGA History of the Plantation Industry in the Malay Peninsula* (New York: Oxford University Press, 1996), pp. 236–37. Gambier needs 12 to 14 months to mature; pepper needs 2 to 3 years and coffee needs 3 to 4 years. Rubber needs at least 5 or 6 years before the trees become tappable. According to John Drabble, it costs on average around £21 per acre to plant a rubber estate in the early 1900s.
15. John H. Drabble, *An Economic History of Malaysia, 1800–1990: The Transition to Modern Economic Growth* (Canberra, New York: St. Martin's Press in association with the Australian National University, 2000), p. 138. In 1919, the Chettiars held over approximately 28,000 hectares of land in Federated Malay States (FMS). By 1922, they had foreclosed on an estimated 8,000 hectares of Chinese-owned rubber holdings.
16. Arnold Wright and H.A. Cartwright, eds., *Twentieth Century Impressions of British Malaya: Its History, People, Commerce, Industries, and Resources* (London: Lloyd's Greater Britain Publishing Company Ltd., 1908), p. 377. Chung Ah Yong, the eldest son of Chung Keng Kwee who was the Big Five's close associate, employed only Tamil and Javanese coolies (about 200) to work in his 500-acre Hearwood Rubber Estate in Perak. Cheah Chim Yean, a rubber planter and merchant, also recruited mainly Indian coolies to work in his estates in Kedah.
17. *Handbook of the Netherlands East Indies, 1924*, p. 288. See also J.J. Blandin, *Crude Rubber Survey* (Washington: The Bureau of Foreign and Domestic Commerce, 1924), p. 205.
18. Carl A. Trocki, "Political Structures in the Nineteenth and Early Twentieth Centuries", in *The Cambridge History of Southeast Asia*, vol. II, edited by Nicholas Tarling (Cambridge: Cambridge University Press, 1992), pp. 75–126; Robert E. Elson, "International Commerce, the State and Society: Economic and Social Change", in *The Cambridge History of Southeast Asia*, vol. II, edited by Nicholas Tarling (Cambridge: Cambridge University Press, 1992), pp. 127–58; Eric Tagliacozzo, *Secret Trades, Porous Borders: Smuggling and States along a Southeast Asian Frontier, 1865-1915* (New Haven: Yale University Press, 2005), pp. 9–15.

19. John Butcher, "Revenue Farming and the Changing State in Southeast Asia", in *The Rise and Fall of Revenue Farming: Business Elite and the Emergence of the Modern States in Southeast Asia*, edited by John Butcher and Howard Dick (New York: St,.Martin Press, 1993), pp. 35–36.
20. *Penang Chamber of Commerce Report for the year 1910*, p. 77.
21. Robert L. Jarman, ed., *Annual Reports of Straits Settlements 1855–1941* (Slough, Berkshire: Archive Editions, 1998), pp. 391, 506, 650. One chest contained around 135 pounds of the substance.
22. "Correspondence regarding the Report of the Commission appointed to enquire into matters relating to the use of Opium in the Straits Settlements and the Federated Malay States", *Straits Settlements Legislative Council Proceedings 1909*, p. C44. The original unit for chandu in the document is tahil (one tahil is equivalent to about 38 grams).
23. "Shorthand Report–Minutes of 1 and 3 November 1910", *Proceedings of the Federal Council of the Federated Malay States for the year 1910*, pp. 92–95 and 120–25. See also J. Norman Parmer, *Colonial Labor Policy and Administration: A History of Labor in the Rubber Plantation Industry in Malaya, c. 1910–1941* (New York: J.J. Augustin Incorporated Publisher, 1960), p. 117.
24. J. Thomas Lindbald, "The Late Colonial State and Economic Expansion, 1900–1930s", in *The Emergence of a National Economy: An Economic History of Indonesia, 1800–2000*, by Howard Dick et al. (N.S.W. and Honolulu: Asian Studies Association of Australia in association with Allen & Unwin and University of Hawaii Press, 2002), p. 118.
25. In 1875–1905, the opium duty alone accounted for 45 to 55 per cent of the total Straits Settlements revenue. Cheng U Wen, "Opium in the Straits Settlements, 1867–1910", *Journal of Southeast Asian History*, vol. 1, no. 1 (March 1961): 52.
26. *Straits Settlements Government Gazette*, 15 October 1909, p. 3135. See also Laurentia Magchilina van Lottum-van Leeuwen, *From Source to Scourge* (Rotterdam: University Erasmus, 1992), p. 84. The Ordinance aimed to give the Government the exclusive right to import and export opium and to prepare and sell *chandu* (cooked opium).
27. *Annual Departmental Reports of the Straits Settlements for the year 1910*, pp. 88, 95. See also Derek Mackay, *Eastern Customs: The Customs Service in British Malaya and the Opium Trade* (London: The Radcliffe Press, 2005), pp. 31–32.
28. F.W. Diehl, "Revenue Farming and Colonial Finances in the Netherlands East Indies, 1816–1925", in *The Rise and Fall of Revenue Farming*, edited by John Butcher and Howard Dick (New York: St. Martin's Press, 1993), p. 218. Opium Régie was a government department which was first established in Java.

29. Ian Brown, "The End of the Opium Farm in Siam, 1905–7", in *The Rise and Fall of Revenue Farming*, edited by John Butcher and Howard Dick (New York: St. Martin's Press, 1993), pp. 233–41.
30. *Straits Settlements Government Gazette*, 31 December 1885, pp. 1960–64; 14 May 1886, pp. 695–702.
31. Carl Trocki, "Boundaries and Transgressions: Chinese Enterprise in Eighteenth- and Nineteenth-Century Southeast Asia", in *Ungrounded Empires: The Cultural Politics of Modern Chinese Transnationalism*, edited by Ong Aihwa and Donald M. Nonini (New York: Routledge, 1997), p. 79. Also see Cushman, *Family and States*, p. 80.
32. Selangor Secretariat File 2164/1911.
33. *Straits Echo*, 10 October 1922, p. 1257. The Company was sold at the price of $1,351,000. Lee Chin Tuan, who negotiated the sale, was given a commission of 7.5 per cent on the sum of $1,351,000. Lim Chin Guan was paid $12,000 for his services as liquidator of the Company.
34. Most of the ships which visited this port were owned by the British India Steam Navigation (B.I.S.N) and P & O Navigation Company. The main exports were tin and rubber and the imports were rice, Indian immigrants, and western manufactures. Mon Bin Jamaluddin, *A History of Port Swettenham* (Singapore: Malaya Publishing House Limited, 1963), p. 7. See also Marion W. Ward, "Port Swettenham and Its Hinterland", *Journal of Tropical Geography*, vol. 19 (December 1964): 72–73.
35. *Cases Heard and Determined in Her Majesty's Supreme Court of the Straits Settlements*, vol. 4, 1885–90, p. 137.
36. Koh Siang Thye and Khoo Thean Tek were partners with Chung Keng Kwee in winning the control of Penang's opium farm for 1889–91.
37. *PGSC*, 17 November 1896, p. 3.
38. I would like to thank Nola Cooke for this particular insight.
39. *The Privy Council Cases: Malaysia, Singapore and Brunei, 1875–1954* (Kuala Lumpur: Professional Law Books, 1990), p. 205.
40. Ibid., p. 206. Also see *Straits Echo*, 9 May 1922, p. 547 and 22 August 1922, p. 1036.
41. *The Privy Council Cases*, p. 203. Also see *Straits Echo*, 9 May 1922, p. 553 and 22 August 1922, p. 1036. Quah Beng Kee was also an agent at Penang of the Yamashita Kishen Kaisha Limited. A ship, s.s. *Kumakata Maru*, belonged to the Yamashita Kishen Kaisha Limited, was chartered to Quah Beng Kee on 22 May 1908 to carry rice between Rangoon or Moulmein and Penang or Deli. In July 1918, Beng Kee entered into an arrangement with the Hollandia Rice Milling Company of Rangoon, whereby the ship was loaded at Rangoon with rice consigned to Van Nie & Co. of Medan. The ship arrived at Belawan port on 10 July 1918 and a large quantity of bags of rice was discharged and piled upon the wharf. On the night of 11 July 1918, part of the wharf sank.

42. CO273/469, Requisitioning of local shipping, 7 August 1918, pp. 465–67. See also Cushman, *Family and State*, p. 110.
43. *Straits Echo*, 24 February 1905, p. 147. Also see Ian Brown, "The End of the Opium Farm in Siam, 1905–7", in *The Rise and Fall of Revenue Farming: Business Elites and the Emergence of the Modern State in Southeast Asia*, edited by John Butcher and Howard Dick (New York: St. Martin Press, 1993), pp. 234–36.
44. Brown, "The End of the Opium Farm in Siam", p. 239.
45. *Straits Echo*, 22 October 1909, p. 1176.
46. *Malayan Cases*, vol. I (Singapore: Malayan Law Journal Pte. Ltd., 1939), p. 16.
47. Ibid.
48. *Straits Echo*, 19 November 1914, p. 1586.
49. *Straits Settlements Law Reports*, vol. 15 (Singapore: Pub. for the Committee of the Singapore Bar, 1922), p. 186.
50. *Straits Settlements Law Reports*, p. 184.
51. *Straits Echo*, 5 March 1913, p. 209; 11 April 1913, p. 357.
52. *Straits Echo*, 11 April 1913, pp. 357–58.
53. *Straits Echo*, 5 September 1917, p. 1327.
54. In 1906, Cheah Tat Jin married Lim Eow Thoon's sister, Lim Kui Guan (林桂元).
55. Civil Case of High Court II Alor Star No. 227/49, 1931. Also see Wu, *Chinese Business in the Making of a Malay State*, p. 153.

8

CONCLUSION

The Big Five Hokkien business families of the nineteenth century controlled the most crucial economic elements of the age and the region, namely labour, capital, organizations, and business networks. The family alliances and power relationships that they formed in and around Penang crucially and profoundly shaped the development of the region. Hence, they serve well as a point of access to recover the vibrant socioeconomic and political life at local and regional levels, to contextualize the subtle interaction between the business elite, the grass roots, and the colonial and indigenous political powers, and to reconstruct the local state and wider regional history. My work serves not only as a complement to the scarce literature on the Hokkien business families and their business networks, but also another trajectory to use the Hokkien business families as a tool of analysis for the study of Southeast Asian economic history in the nineteenth century. This is in contrast to some previous studies which tended to take a Euro-centric approach. It has led us to believe that Western interests played the leading role, while this study on the Big Five tries to deconstruct the conventional narratives and restore the long-neglected local agency and show a more nuanced picture of the Southeast Asian communities, societies and histories in the nineteenth century, where the Hokkien business elite families played such a central role.

My work has also shown that the economic importance of the local Chinese merchants and their crucial business networks in transforming Penang into not just a trading port, but also a financial and business centre from which numerous enterprises were launched and controlled. This development helped to consolidate the business leadership of the Hokkien elite families during the colonial period of rapid economic expansion. A detailed analysis of the Big Five's business operations, family relationships, inter-*hui* conflicts, economic cooperation and competition has led us to see a wide-ranging web of hybrid and fluid regional business networks that contributed to the Big Five's economic ascendancy and fashioned the contours and patterns of Penang and its surrounding states (southern Burma, southwestern Siam, western Malay states, and the north and eastern coasts of Sumatra) as a single economic unit in the nineteenth century.

Despite the rise of Singapore, Penang, being a maritime base of the Big Five, remained as a regional entrepot. The Big Five operated the biggest fleet of vessels criss-crossing the seas around Penang and carrying Straits produce, Indian and China goods, and European merchandise between Penang and the surrounding states, sometimes as far as to China and India. The trade goods the Big Five shipped and traded were in demand and good profits could be made in both regional and international markets. This orbit of shipping and trade rendered Penang quite independent from Singapore in some ways while in others creating interlocking interests. The Big Five were also involved in agricultural and mineral production. They owned vast acres of estates to cultivate coconut and sugar in Penang, Province Wellesley and Kedah. For pepper and rice, the Big Five had direct links to the source of supply in southern Burma and the East coast of Sumatra. In tin production, the Big Five owned and financed most of the mines stretching from the southwestern Siamese coast to the West Malay states. Coolies who worked in the plantations and mines were supplied by the Big Five. This immigrant labour force was the mainstay of production, and also provided a huge new profitable market for consumption.

To exercise control over their workforce and secure great profits, the Big Five and their associates pooled their capital and acquired a ring of opium revenue farms to provide the highly-demanded opium. Opium revenue farming business was in fact the most important. The farm was not only a centre to import raw opium but also to manufacture and distribute the *chandu* (cooked opium) to thousands of mining and plantation coolies who were addicted to the drug. With the opium farms, the Big Five could maintain their control of commodity production (agriculture and tin) and hence strengthen their hold on trade. Recognizing this crucial nexus between opium revenue farm, trade, labour organization and commodity production, the Big Five moved to control not only the opium farms in Penang and its surrounding states, but also the farms in Melaka, Selangor, Johor, Borneo, Bangkok, Singapore and Hong Kong.

By controlling this highly diversified range of businesses (shipping, entrepot trade, commodity production, coolie trade, and revenue farms), the Big Five not only linked Penang and its surrounding states together but also created a web of interconnected economic sectors — production, transportation, trade, and consumption. The integrated whole of these various economic sectors clearly revealed that the structure and function of capital, labour force, commodities, and market driven by the Hokkien entrepreneurial flair formed a regional market economy and capitalism in the Penang-centric region.

To succeed in these diverse and extensive enterprises, the Big Five developed and commanded a web of regional business networks which encompassed family relationships, sworn brotherhood *hui*, and business partnerships. The family network of the Big Five went beyond the prominent Hokkien to Hakka, Indo-Malay, and Siamese families, and beyond Penang. Having this pool of kin, the Big Five relied upon and utilized family members as trustworthy business partners or assistants. By doing so the Big Five were able to take advantage not only of the wealth of their business partners, but also of some crucial socioeconomic and political connections. This can be clearly seen in the commercial companies and opium farm syndicate organized by the Big Five. The sworn brotherhood *hui*, Kian Teik Tong, provided an important vehicle for the Big Five as not only did they have their own *hui*, but they also established a *hui* network through the alliance with other *hui* through which they mobilized thousands of coolies to compete with rivals in attaining their economic goals.

In the pursuit of their dominance in opium revenue farming and tin mining, the two most lucrative businesses, the Big Five faced intense challenges from the Cantonese-dominant sworn brotherhood *hui*, the Ghee Hin, the Singapore Hokkien mercantile elite, the Siamese local chiefs, and the British officers. In order to secure or defend their economic interests, the Big Five grouped together under their *hui*, and formed alliances with other *hui* like the Ho Seng, which comprised Hokkien, Malay, Indian and Jawi-Peranakan members, the Hakka-dominant Hai San, and the Indo-Malay Red Flag. With this alliance of *hui*, the Big Five could effectively and conveniently mobilize troops of coolies to support their commercial competition. Such support always involved violence and bloodshed as occurred in the cases of the 1867 Penang riot, the Krabi riot of 1878, the 1879 coolie riot of Taiping, the Deli plantation coolies' revolt of 1884, the Phuket coolie riot of 1876, and the Larut Wars of 1861, 1862 and 1872. However, in some cases, the

Big Five also collaborated with their rivals. Adopting these two strategies, the Big Five were able to outmanoeuvre and defeat their business rivals and achieve dominance in opium revenue farming and tin mining businesses. The Big Five's business networks were more than simply the leverage for wealth accumulation, they were instrumental in the rise and transformation of the Big Five as a regional power, profoundly influencing the economic organization and integration of Penang and its surrounding states throughout the nineteenth century.

By the late nineteenth century, a group of large-scale and financially powerful Western trading and shipping interests, such as the British Straits Steamship Company and Straits Trading Company as well as the Royal Dutch Packet Company (KPM), sought to expand their business interest in the Penang-centred region. These British and Dutch enterprises operated a large shipping fleet coupled with insurance, sailing and trading extensively between Penang and its surrounding states. This posed a serious threat to the Big Five's shipping and trading domain in the region. In order to enhance their competitiveness, the Big Five established the first Chinese insurance company, the Penang Khean Guan Insurance Company in 1885 and amalgamated their leading shipping companies to form the Eastern Shipping Company in 1907. These two enterprises were later combined with the other four companies (Eastern Trading Co., Tongkah Harbour Tin Dredging Co., Eastern Smelting Co., and Opium Farm Syndicate) to form a conglomerate — the Khaw Group. The Khaw Group was not only an ambitious venture launched to meet the Western encroaching competition, but also a ground breaking attempt taken by the Big Five to reorganize and revitalize their business strategies and operations. With this archetypal conglomerate, the Big Five intended to establish a financially, technologically, and managerially integrated and sustainable super corporation. However, the group disintegrated in the face of a wave of Western-oriented economic and political changes in the Penang region.

A new economic and political order emerged in the early twentieth century and created an unfavourable environment for the Big Five. On top of shipping and trading, Western enterprises also extended their interest into the commodity production sectors — tin mining and plantation agriculture. Equipped with large capital reserves, advanced technology and a horizontally and vertically integrated international network of finance, trading, shipping, mining and smelting, the British Anglo-Oriental succeeded to wrestle the control of the tin industry from the Big Five. In the rubber production sector, the Big Five were among the first to pour money in commercial rubber planting. But their investments were quickly overshadowed by the Western agency houses which commanded access to the large supply of capital in London, the supply of Indian and Javanese labours, and a closely knit network of land and sea transportation.

The early twentieth century saw not only the rise of large-scale and capital-intensive Western interests, which gained ground in the shipping, trading and commodity production, but also the consolidation of state political power through centralization. The British, Dutch and the Siamese authorities introduced a series of restrictive laws and created an expanding bureaucratic machinery to strengthen their grip on all affairs. This political assertion by ruling powers had a devastating effect on the Big Five's business interests, especially the opium revenue farms and land ownership. The introduction of the Societies Suppression Ordinance of 1889, and a series of labour-related enactments between 1895 and 1911, eliminated the Big Five's *hui* and truck system which were the essential mechanism for operating the opium revenue farms profitably. The economic depression during 1904–7 further weakened their viability. As a result, the opium revenue farm business collapsed and the Big Five and their associates became heavily in debt to the governments and went bankrupt. The opium revenue farming system was ultimately abolished and converted into government monopolies. By centralizing the land policy, the colonial and the Siamese governments succeeded in restricting the Big Five's easy acquisition of lands in their territories for economic exploitation. Coincidentally, in this troubled time, the Big Five became embroiled in conflicts of interest among themselves and with their business associates. The conflicts of interest relating to control of business and the huge monied interests which ended in court eventually broke up the economic cohesion of the Big Five and made them go their own ways.

The Western-inspired revolution in commercial, financial, technological, and administrative practices emerged as the engines of change in the early twentieth-century Penang region and altered the rules of the game. With their access to abundant capital, superior corporate organization and advanced technology, coupled with favourable administrative arrangements, Western interests were able to out-compete the Big Five and gained ascendancy in the economic mainstream. More importantly, Western interests commanding the new economic and political elements succeeded in establishing a new global business network that replaced the Big Five's regional one as the economic framework and commercial mechanisms of the capitalist economy in the Penang region.

The decline of the Big Five, however, did not mark the end of Chinese economic power in the region. Instead, it signified the rise of another group of notable economic players — the *singkeh* Chinese. Unlike the *Baba* or *Peranakan* (the local-born and acculturated Chinese in Malaya and Indonesia), the *singkeh* Chinese came to the region in late nineteenth century or early twentieth century. The size of this group of newly arrived Chinese immigrants reached several hundred thousand. Some fared well in their business pursuits and became prominent capitalists and merchants. Among them, Yeap Chor Ee 葉祖意, a Hokkien, and Lim Lean Teng 林連登, a Teochew, serve as the best examples of the successful *singkeh* business elite. They showed little or no connection with the old established Big Five families. Their meteoric rise as the leading merchants in Penang was no coincidence. Some new business networks were developed by this group of *singkeh* businessmen to achieve their economic pre-eminence in the new economic and socio-political order in which the Big Five had failed. The business operation of the *singkeh* Chinese still displayed the multifaceted characteristics of the old days, but rubber and banking had become the cornerstones of their businesses. Transnational cooperation, cross-dialect alliances, and inter-family marriages were still judiciously and strategically formed and capitalized by the *singkeh* Chinese to achieve their economic ends. The rise of these Penang *singkeh* Chinese businessmen represented a fascinating new chapter but it will have to await further research.

This work enables us to see not only the rise and fall of a leading and powerful economic force in the Penang region, but also to have a better understanding of the Chinese in nineteenth-century Southeast Asia. It is clear that those we call the "Chinese" were made up of several dialect groups of different classes rather than one. They were the Hokkiens, Hakkas, Teochews, and Cantonese establishing as coolies, merchants, traders, agriculturalists, miners, and capitalists that constituted the dominant force in the local economy. But not all were influential players. Only a handful of mercantile elite families were able to display considerable economic power. It was these families commanding a web of business networks that took the leading roles in the economic and socio-political arenas. The business networks of the mercantile elite families were not one-dialect or one-ethnic group oriented and one-state bounded, but multi-ethnic, multi-dialect and cross-state mechanism linking horizontally to other families, *kongsis*, *hui* and various business enterprises and vertically to the grassroots. With this versatile and extensive web of business networks, the Chinese business families were successful in adapting the capacities that enabled them to succeed in family-clan business and to meet the very different requirements needed to make a change to international limited liability corporation. This is clearly reflected in the case of the Big Five. From controlling the junk shipping and trade, labour-intensive planting and mining to adopting steamship and dredging technologies and insurance institution, the Big Five had exhibited the remarkable dynamism and innovation in capital formation and regeneration as well as entrepreneurship. This contrasts sharply with what Yoshihara Kunio has described the Chinese entrepreneurs in Southeast Asia as rent-seekers or "ersatz capitalists", who only relied on concessions, licences, and monopoly rights to succeed in business. More importantly, my investigation of the Big Five acknowledges that the key concepts at issue in the framing and writing of Southeast Asian Chinese narrative are a sense of networks, polyvalence, fluidity, and permeability.

It is time to have more in-depth studies on Chinese business families in Southeast Asia as their significance and influence are still not well identified and understood. Chinese business families and their networks have been the fundamental and dynamic force that plays a leading role in the economic life, social formation, and political processes of different parts of Southeast Asia over the centuries. Even today, the Chinese big businesses in Southeast Asia are all essentially family-owned. Although the present business networks of the Chinese business families have changed and adapted to new demands and circumstances, some attributes (strategic marriages and kinship) remain and persist. Robert Kuok Hock Nien 郭鹤年 of the Kuok family, for example, the richest businessman in Malaysia, who has built up a multifarious business empire (hotel, media, mining, shipping, planting, manufacturing) stretching from Southeast Asia to China, India and as far as to Europe and North America, has recruited his children and relatives as business assistants and formed marriage alliances with other Chinese and non-Chinese families in Malaysia and Hong Kong.

APPENDICES

APPENDIX 1
Comparison of Number of Native Vessels and Square Rigged Vessels between Penang and Singapore, 1843–96

Name of Places	1843–44	1844–45	1843–44	1844–45
	Number of Native Vessels Entered into Penang		Number of Native Vessels Entered into Singapore	
Acheen	330	209	—	—
Deli	160	194	—	—
Moulmein	41	45	—	—
Pungah	73	159	—	—
Kedah	170	284	—	—
Sumatra	—	—	510	573
West-side Peninsula	—	—	44	28
Siam	—	—	22	18
Total	*774*	*891*	*576*	*619*
	Number of Native Vessels Departed from Penang		Number of Native Vessels Departed from Singapore	
Acheen	312	216	—	—
Deli	181	224	—	—
Moulmein	45	55	—	—
Pungah	155	183	—	—
Kedah	301	423	—	—
Sumatra	—	—	506	468
West-side Peninsula	—	—	92	47
Siam	—	—	21	21
Total	*994*	*1,101*	*619*	*536*

Note: N/V = No Vessel

APPENDIX 1 (Cont'd)

	Number of Square Rigged Vessels Entered into Penang		Number of Square Rigged Vessels Entered into Singapore	
Acheen	29	24	—	—
Deli	6	9	—	—
Maulmain	22	14	1	17
Pungah	3	N/V	—	—
Kedah	N/V	1	—	—
Sumatra	—	—	28	25
Rangoon	—	—	5	N/V
Siam	—	—	13	13
Total	60	48	47	55

	Number of Square Rigged Vessels Departed from Penang		Number of Square Rigged Vessels Departed from Singapore	
Acheen	24	27	—	—
Deli	5	9	—	—
Moulmein	27	27	5	19
Pungah	5	N/V	—	—
Kedah	N/V	1	—	—
Sumatra	—	—	27	32
Rangoon	—	—	3	3
Siam	—	—	12	9
Total	61	64	47	63

Note: N/V = No Vessel

APPENDIX 1   (Cont'd)

Name of Places	1846–47	1847–48	1846–47	1847–48
	Number of Native Vessels Entered into Penang		Number of Native Vessels Entered into Singapore	
Sumatra	551	536	507	445
Moulmein	88	91	7	3
Pungah	162	161	—	—
West-side Peninsula	645	721	30	57
Siam	—	—	17	20
Total	1,446	1,509	561	525
	Number of Native Vessels Departed from Penang		Number of Native Vessels Departed from Singapore	
Sumatra	582	559	490	504
Maulmain	80	105	3	5
Pungah	232	142	—	—
West-side Peninsula	818	1071	75	132
Siam	—	—	21	32
Total	1,712	1,877	589	673
	Number of Square Rigged Vessels Entered into Penang		Number of Square Rigged Vessels Entered into Singapore	
Sumatra	26	32	30	22
Rangoon & Moulmein	22	22	4	7
Pungah	1	2	—	—
West-side Peninsula	6	7	—	—
Siam	—	—	16	21
Total	55	63	50	50
	Number of Square Rigged Vessels Departed from Penang		Number of Square Rigged Vessels Departed from Singapore	
Sumatra	33	34	23	24
Rangoon & Moulmein	23	30	10	8
Pungah	1	N/V	—	—
West-side Peninsula	4	7	—	—
Siam	—	—	14	19
Total	61	71	47	51

Note: N/V = No Vessel

APPENDIX 1 (Cont'd)

Name of Places	1848–49	1849–50	1848–49	1849–50
	Number of Native Vessels Entered into Penang		**Number of Native Vessels Entered into Singapore**	
Sumatra	607	576	616	538
Moulmein	76	76	2	1
Pungah	195	144	—	—
West Side Peninsula	574	508	22	36
Siam	—	—	29	42
Total	1,452	1,304	669	617
	Number of Native Vessels Departed from Penang		**Number of Native Vessels Departed from Singapore**	
Sumatra	624	634	711	577
Moulmein	69	73	3	2
Pungah	224	186	—	—
West Coast Peninsula	1035	884	54	39
Siam	—	—	50	38
Total	1,952	1,777	818	656
	Number of Square Rigged Vessels Entered into Penang		**Number of Square Rigged Vessels Entered into Singapore**	
Sumatra	30	36	21	20
Rangoon & Moulmein	25	24	11	5
Pungah	1	1	—	—
West Coast Peninsula	6	4	—	—
Siam	—	—	14	20
Total	62	65	46	45
	Number of Square Rigged Vessels Departed from Penang		**Number of Square Rigged Vessels Departed from Singapore**	
Sumatra	27	42	13	18
Rangoon & Moulmein	31	22	4	10
Pungah	N/V	1	—	—
West Coast Peninsula	6	5	—	—
Siam	—	—	14	20
Total	64	70	31	48

Note: N/V = No Vessel

APPENDIX 1 (Cont'd)

	1851–52	1852–53	1851–52	1852–53
Name of Places	Number of Native Vessels Entered into Penang		Number of Native Vessels Entered into Singapore	
Sumatra	625	584	488	466
Moulmein	43	38	8	1
Pungah	110	113	—	—
West Coast Peninsula	530	565	32	55
Siam	—	—	47	67
Total	*1,308*	*1,300*	*575*	*589*
	Number of Native Vessels Departed from Penang		Number of Native Vessels Departed from Singapore	
Sumatra	653	654	498	421
Moulmein	54	49	5	1
Pungah	196	130	—	—
West Coast Peninsula	1,014	1,037	26	81
Siam	—	—	47	93
Total	*1,917*	*1,870*	*576*	*596*
	Number of Square Rigged Vessels Entered into Penang		Number of Square Rigged Vessels Entered into Singapore	
Sumatra	44	48	20	20
Rangoon & Moulmein	14	15	8	2
Pungah	1	1	—	—
West Coast Peninsula	6	9	—	—
Siam	—	—	29	31
Total	*65*	*73*	*57*	*53*
	Number of Square Rigged Vessels Departed from Penang		Number of Square Rigged Vessels Departed from Singapore	
Sumatra	56	59	16	18
Rangoon & Moulmein	23	13	19	3
Pungah	1	2	—	—
West Coast Peninsula	6	8	—	—
Siam	—	—	31	27
Total	*86*	*82*	*66*	*48*

APPENDIX 1 (Cont'd)

Name of Places	1868		1868	
	Number of Native Vessels Entered & Cleared at Penang		Number of Native Vessels Entered & Cleared at Singapore	
	Entered	Cleared	Entered	Cleared
Sumatra	541	838	397	394
Moulmein	41	37	N/A	N/A
Siam	125	217	14	18
West Side Peninsula	289	678	58	62
Total	*996*	*1,770*	*469*	*474*
	1890		1890	
	Number of Native Craft Entered & Cleared at Penang		Number of Native Craft Entered & Cleared at Singapore	
	Entered	Cleared	Entered	Cleared
Sumatra	628	657	873	762
British Burma	17	15	Nil	Nil
Siam West Coast	2,454	2,300	61	74
Malay Peninsula	2,500	2,618	N/A	N/A
Kedah	N/A	N/A	N/V	N/V
Perak	N/A	N/A	7	9
Total	*5,599*	*5,590*	*941*	*845*

APPENDIX 1 (Cont'd)

	1892		1892	
	Number of Native Craft Entered & Cleared at Penang		Number of Native Craft Entered & Cleared at Singapore	
	Entered	Cleared	Entered	Cleared
Sumatra	388	436	1,756	1,825
British Burma	15	12	N/V	N/V
Siam West Coast	1,000	1,014	18	27
Kedah	1,342	1,310	N/V	N/V
Perak	1,514	1,517	17	4
Selangor	44	53	96	15
Total	*4,303*	*4,342*	*1,887*	*1,871*
	1896		1896	
	Number of Native Craft Entered & Cleared at Penang		Number of Native Craft Entered & Cleared at Singapore	
	Entered	Cleared	Entered	Cleared
Sumatra	410	433	1,926	2,004
British Burma	37	30	Nil	7
Siam West Coast	1,173	1,072	62	53
Kedah	1,308	1,344	1	N/V
Perak	1,697	1,687	11	8
Selangor	68	94	158	125
Total	*4,693*	*4,660*	*2,158*	*2,197*

Sources: Compiled from *Tabular Statement of the Commerce and Shipping of Prince of Wales Island, Singapore and Malacca* from 1843–53 and *Straits Settlements Blue Books* 1868, 1890, 1892 and 1896.

APPENDIX 2
The Intermarriages of the Big Five Families
(the Khoo, the Cheah, the Yeoh, the Lim, and the Tan) in Penang

Family	Member	Marriage Partner	Comments
KHOO 邱	Khoo Beng San 邱明山 (1787–1843)	1. Xu Yu Nian 许玉娘	Wife in China
		2. Zhou Han Nian 周汉娘	Wife in Penang
		3. Cheah Yin Neo 谢荫娘	Wife in Penang
	Khoo Sim Bee 邱心美 (?–1895)	Tan Li Neo 陈理娘	
	Khoo Thean Teik 邱天德 (1818–90)	1. Chew Fong Neo 周凤娘	
		2. Ooi Kiaw Neo 黄乔娘	
		3. Boey Kwee Lan 梅桂蘭 (春姐)	
	Khoo Thean Poh 邱天保 (1833 — ?)	Toh Mee Neo 杜媚娘	They had a daughter married to Syed Mohamed Alatas, an Acehnese of Arab descent.
	Khoo Thean Choe 邱天佐	Tan Kwee Neo 陈贵娘	
	Khoo Cheng Lim 邱清临 (1808–53)	1. Lim Seh 林氏	First wife in China
		2. Koh Keng Yean 辜轻烟	Daughter of Koh Kee Jin, one of the sons of Koh Lay Huan.
	Khoo Cheow Teong 邱昭忠 (1840–1916)	Lim Siam Neoh 林氏	Eldest daughter of Lim Cheoh 林石, who was a rice merchant in Melaka.

APPENDIX 2 (Cont'd)

Family	Member	Marriage Partner	Comments
	Khoo Sian Ewe 邱善佑 (1886–1964)	Lee Yoke (Gaik) Thye 李玉娣	Only daughter of Lee Bian Leong and granddaughter of Khoo Tiong Poh 邱忠波
	Khoo Sek Chuan 邱石泉 (?–1871)	1. Cheah Seh 谢氏	First wife in China
		2. Yap Kuang Bee 叶匡美	Second wife in Penang. She was the younger sister of Yap Hap Keat 叶合吉, a revenue farmer and tin financier.
	Khoo Guet Cheng 邱月清 (1862–1922)	1. Koh Chin Poh	
		2. Cheah Kooi Yoong *alias* Cheah Choo Neo 谢朱娘	Daughter of Cheah Hin Chien
	Khoo Hun Yeang 邱漢阳 (1860–1917)	Ong Gaik Thay 王玉钗	
	Khoo Siew Ghee	Gan Seh	Second son of Khoo Hun Yeang married the second daughter of Gan Ngoh Bee
	Khoo Thay Jin 邱体仁 (1884–?)	Lim Kim Hong	Eldest daughter of Lim Chian Ek
	Khoo Sian Tan 邱仙丹 (1869–1948)	Yeoh Seh 楊氏	
	Khoo Ban Seng 邱万成	Yeoh Cheam Neo	

APPENDIX 2 (Cont'd)

Family	Member	Marriage Partner	Comments
	Khoo Being Hock	Khaw Swee Ee	A son of Khoo Guet Cheng married a daughter of Khaw Sim Kong, the Governor of Ranong.
	Khoo Hong Tat	Khaw Phaik Chin	Second daughter of Khaw Joo Tok
	Khoo Keng Tong	Gan Cheow Eng 颜昭容	Daughter of Gan Ngoh Bee
	Khoo Heng Chuan	Khaw Swee Suat	Third daughter of Khaw Sim Bee
LIM 林	Lim Mah Chye 林吗栽 (1857–1927)	Cheah Geok Kee	Daughter of Cheah Geok
	Lim Chin Guan 林振元 (1881–1963)	Yeoh Saw Heang	Daughter of Yeoh Cheang Chye
	Lim Eu Toh 林有道 (1871–?)	1. Khoo Soon Neoh 邱顺娘	Second daughter of Khoo Thean Poh 邱天保
		2. Khoo Khuat Siew 邱氏	Daughter of a merchant in Rangoon
	Lim Cheow Kam	Yeoh Gim See	Eldest daughter of Yeoh Guan Seok
	Lim Ang Kee 林红柿 (1853–1901)	Cheah Geok Kin	One of their daughters, Lim Meh Beow, married the son of Phraya Wichitsongkhram, the Governor of Phuket.

APPENDIX 2 (Cont'd)

Family	Member	Marriage Partner	Comments
	Lim Hwa Chiam 林花钻 (1837–1912)	1. Wang (Ooi) Shu Shen 黄淑慎 2. Khoo Shu Qin 邱淑勤	
	Lim Seng Tek 林成德	Ong Chooi Bee	A daughter of Ong Kean Sean and sister-in-law of Lim Kek Chuan.
	Lim Saing	Cheah Geok Keat	Both are parents of Lim Kek Chuan.
	Lim Kek Chuan 林克全 (1858–1907)	1. Oh (Foo) Kee Neo	Third daughter of Foo Tye Sin
		2. Oh (Foo) Jim Neo	Fourth daughter of Foo Tye Sin
		3. Ong Cheow Bee	
	Lim Soo Chee 林士志 (1880–?)	Chuah Hooi Ngoh (1882–1964)	A granddaughter of Khaw Sim Chua married Soo Chee in 1901.
	Lim Cheng Cheang 林正昌	Cheah Shu Shen 谢淑慎	
	Lim Leng Cheak 林宁绰	1. Tan Say Seang 陈西祥 2. Leow Thye Hai	
	Lim Eow Thoon 林耀椿 (1886–1976)	Goh Saw Chooi	Second daughter of Goh Ewe Keong of Penang

APPENDIX 2 (Cont'd)

Family	Member	Marriage Partner	Comments
	Lim Seong Wah	Yeoh Cheng Ee	A son of Lim Eow Thoon married a daughter of Yeoh Seng Hoe.
	Lim Kong Wah 林光华	Oh Yeo Neo	
	Lim Cheng Keat 林清傑	Khoo Sew Jeong 邱绣绒	Eldest daughter of Khoo Sek Chuan
YEOH 杨	Yeoh Kok Boon 杨国文	1. Lu/Loh Seh 卢氏	A son married a daughter from the Lim family. A daughter married into the Khoo family.
		2. Yap Har Neo 叶霞娘	Three daughters married into the Khoo family and one married into the Lim family.
		3. Keng Seh 龚氏	
	Yeoh Cheng Teik 杨清德 (?–1894)	1. Khoo Siew Jin 邱绣巾	Eldest daughter married into the Lee family and second daughter married into the Khoo family.
		2. Tang Ce Shi 唐侧室	
		3. Khoo Siew Soon 邱绣顺	
	Yeoh Seng Lim 杨升霖	Khoo Seh 邱氏	Eldest daughter of Khoo Pek Haw 邱碧侯
	Yeoh Shuan Tow 杨双滔	Kang Bee Geok 江美玉	Eldest daughter married into the Khoo family and the second one married into the Lee family.

APPENDIX 2 (Cont'd)

Family	Member	Marriage Partner	Comments
	Yeoh Chin Long 杨真龙	Lim Seh 林氏	
	Yeoh Paik Keat 杨碧杰	Khoo Seh 邱氏	Fourth daughter of Khoo Thean Poh 邱天保
	Yeoh Paik Tatt 杨碧達 (1872–1925)	Cheah Seh 谢氏	
	Yeoh Cheang Seng 杨章成	Khoo Seh 邱氏	
	Yeoh Heng Keat 杨允吉	Lim Hock Neoh	
	Yeoh Cheng Kung	Cheah Seh 谢氏	The wife was an elder sister of Cheah Tek Soon.
	Yeoh Boon Tean	Foo Seh 胡氏	Second daughter of Foo Choo Choon
	Yeoh Wee Yang	Lim Suan Paik	Second son of Yeoh Boon Wan married the second daughter of Lim Chin Guan.
	Yeoh Guan Seok 杨元绩 (1883–1926)	Khoo Chooi Lian 邱规奋	Second daughter of Khoo Cheow Teong
CHEAH 谢	Cheah Chow Pan 谢昭盼	Khoo Rong Ying 邱蓉荧	
	Cheah Tek Thye 谢德泰 (1860–?)	Koh Seh 辜氏	A daughter of Koh Teng Choon, the eldest son of Koh Kok Chye.

APPENDIX 2 (Cont'd)

Family	Member	Marriage Partner	Comments
	Cheah Toon Jin 谢敦仁	Khoo Cheng Sooi	Daughter of Khoo Swee Bok and granddaughter of Yeo Ooi Gark
	Cheah Toon Loke 谢敦禄	Yeoh She 杨氏	
	Cheah Ewe Ghee 谢有义 (?–1892)	Ong Chi Neo 王织娘	
	Cheah Chen Eok 谢增煜 (1852–1922)	Foo It Nyong Neoh	A daughter of Foo Thye Sin 胡泰兴.
	Cheah Tat Jin 谢達仁 (1885–1967)	Lim Kwee Guan 林桂元	A daughter of Lim Leng Cheak 林宁綽.
	Cheah Tat Tee	Lim Kwee Kim	Daughter of Lim Ewe Sian
	Cheah Tat Thye	Foo Seh	Third daughter of Foo Choo Choon
	Cheah Wat Hye 谢日海	Low Leong Chow	The only daughter of Low Leong Huat and granddaughter of Low Boon Kim (Low Kim) of Kuala Lumpur.
	Cheah Wat Lum 谢日南	Lim Bin Ai	Eldest daughter of Lim Kar Chang
	Cheah Oon Yeap 谢允协	Lim Choon Geck	
	Cheah Choo Yew/Eu 谢自友	1. Lim Chye Geam 2. Lim Saw Yew 3. Lim Hoon Neo 林云娘	

APPENDIX 2 (Cont'd)

Family	Member	Marriage Partner	Comments
	Cheah Seng Khim 谢成金	Lim Swee Bee 林瑞美	
	Cheah Boon Hean 谢文贤	Foo Kang Nyong 胡氏	A cousin of Foo Choo Choon 胡子春.
	Cheah Cheang Lim 谢昌霖 (1875–1948)	Khoo Pek Hua 邱百花	
	Cheah Cheang Hooi 谢昌辉	Yeap Paik Kim	
	Cheah Ghim Leng 谢锦铃 (1902—?)	Seet Suat Hay Tan Lian Eng 陈氏	Later separated or divorced
TAN 陈	Tan Sim Hoe 陈心和 (?–1901)	1. Khoo Soo Guet 邱素月 2. Yeoh Cheng Guet 楊清月 3. Chan Gan Neoh 曾然娘 4. Yau Sut Neo 姚述娘	
	Tan Hup Swee 陈合水	Kam Kian Neo 甘捷娘	Second daughter of Kam Su Kau 甘四教
	Tan Swee Keat 陈瑞吉	1. Teh Guet Kee 郑玉枝 2. Neo Suet Neo 梁雪娘	

APPENDIX 2 (Cont'd)

Family	Member	Marriage Partner	Comments
	Tan Lean Kee 陈连枝	Cheah Voon Sean	Two daughters married to the grandsons of Chung Keng Kwee and granddaughters and a great-granddaughter also married into the Chung family.
	Tan Chor Kay	1. Son Meh Rai	A daughter from the wealthy Na Thip Thalang family in southern Siam.
		2. Ng Gaik Phoay	
	Tan Chor Sin	Ang Tan Soo	A granddaughter of Khaw Soo Cheang.
	Tan Kheam Hock 陈谦福	Foo Bing Neo 胡丙娘	Sixth daughter of Foo Thye Sin 胡泰兴

Sources: Lee Kam Hing and Chow Mun Seong, *Biographical Dictionary of the Chinese in Malaysia* (Malaysia: Pelanduk Publications (M) Sdn. Bhd., 1997); 张少宽 Teoh Shiaw Kuan, 槟榔屿福建公冢暨家冢碑铭集 *Binlangyu Fujian Gongzhong Ji Jiazhong Beimingji* [Epigraphic Inscriptions of Penang Hokkien Cemeteries] (Singapore: Singapore Society of Asian Studies, 1997); Wong Choon San, *A Gallery of Chinese Kapitans* (Singapore: Ministry of Culture, 1963); 颖川堂陈公司:神主簿 *Yinchuantang Chengongsi: Shenzubu* [Tan Kongsi's Record Book of Spirit Tablet], compiled in 1969; 南洋名人集传 *Nanyang Mingren Jizhuan* [South Sea Chinese Biography], no. 1 vol. 2; 新江邱曾氏族谱 *Xinjiang Qiuzeng She Zubu* [The Genealogy of the Sin Kang Khoo and Chan Clans]; *The Penang Argus and Merchantile Advertisers*; *Pinang Gazette and Straits Chronicle*; 世界谢氏宗亲第五届恳亲大会纪念特刊 *Shije Xieshe Zongqing Diwujie Kenqin Dahui Jinian Tekan* [Special Issue on the 5th World Cheah Clansmen Conference] (Penang: Beima Xieshe Zongci He Bincheng Xieshe Fuhougong Gongsi 北马谢氏宗祠和槟城谢氏福侯公公司 [North Malaya Cheah Si Chong Soo and Penang Cheah Si Hock Hew Kong Kongsi], 1989); 槟州華人大會堂慶祝成立一百週年新厦落成開幕纪念特刊 *Binzhou Huaren Dahuitang Qingzu Chengli Yibai Zhounian Xinxia Luocheng Kaimu Jinian Tekan* [Commemorative Publication of Centenary Celebrations and Inauguration of New Building, Penang Chinese Town Hall] (Penang: Binzhou Huaren

Dahuitang 檳州華人大會堂, 1983); Arnold Wright and H.A. Cartwright, eds., *Twentieth Century Impressions of British Malaya: Its History, People, Commerce, Industries, and Resources* (London: Lloyd's Greater Britain Publishing Company Ltd., 1908); G.A.C. Beattie, "A Forgotten Tan Family of Penang and Phuket", Paper presented at the Shared Histories Conference, Penang, 2003; 柯木林 Kua Bak Lim, 新华历史人物列传 *Xinhua Lishi Renwu Liezhuan* [Who's Who in the Chinese Community of Singapore] (Singapore: EPB Publishers Pte. Ltd., 1995); *Straits Echo* 1904, 1905, 1906, 1909, 1911, 1915, 1919, 1921, 1924.

APPENDIX 3
The Intermarriages of Other Prominent Hokkien and Hakka Families in Penang

Family	Member	Marriage Partners	Comments
THE HOKKIEN			
CHUNG 辜	Koh Kok Chye 辜国彩 (?–1849)	Cheah Thoe Neoh	
	Koh Leong Tee 辜龙池	Goh Kooi Neoh	
	Koh Teng Choon 辜登春 (?–1874)	Khoo Sim Neoh	
	Koh Seang Tat 辜尚达 (1833–1910)	Oon Geok Teah 温玉锭	Sister of Oon Gan Thay, Kapitan China of Deli
	Koh Cheng Sian 辜祯善 (1863–1928)	Cheah Keow Moh	Daughter of Cheah Siang of Penang One of their daughters (Koh Chooi Pheng) married Chung Thye Seong, eighth son of Chung Keng Kwee.
	Koh Leok Hup 辜六合	Ooi Phek Eong	The only son of Koh Cheng Sian married the granddaughter of Lee Phee Chuan.
	Koh Leap Teng 辜立亭 (1875–1956)	Cheah Liu Qing	Eldest daughter of Cheah Tek Thye
	Koh Sin Hock 辜承福 (1898–1986)	Cheah Yue Yin	

APPENDIX 3 (Cont'd)

Family	Member	Marriage Partners	Comments
KHAW 许	Khaw Sim Kong 许心光 (1840–1912)	1. Cheah Lean Kee 谢莲枝 2. Phan	Daughter of Cheah Chow Phan. Their daughters married into the Goh, the Lee, and the Tan families.
	Khaw Sim Khim 许心钦 (1845–1903)	Lim Kim Teen	
	Khaw Sim Tek 许心德 (1820–1920)	Cheah Lean Looi 谢莲蕊	Daughter of Cheah Chow Phan
	Khaw Sim Chuah 许心泉 (1846–75)	Yeoh Siew Chee 杨秀市	
	Khaw Sim Bee 许心美 (1856–1913)	1. Lim Seng Kim 2. Lim Seng Wan 3. Nuan Na Nakhon 4. Klao	A daughter of the Na Nakhon family.
	Khaw Joo Ghee 许如义 (?–1932)	1. Lim Shai Hong 2. Lim Phatpoe 3. Prem Na Nakhon 4. Leu Yoo 5. Fuang	A daughter of the Na Nakhon family.
	Khaw Joo Choe 许如初 (1868–1925)	Lee Cheng Chuan 李精专	Eldest daughter of Lee Pee Choon 李丕峻

APPENDIX 3 (Cont'd)

Family	Member	Marriage Partners	Comments
	Khaw Joo Tok 许如琢 (1897–1972)	Lim Chooi Hoon	Their daughters married into the Ong, the Khoo, the Cheah, and the Lim families.
	Khaw Joo Ley 许如利	Klub Bunnag	A daughter of the Bunnag family. One of their daughters married Mom Chao Vibul Sawatwong, a son of Prince Sommot.
	Khaw Joo Jeang 许如讓	Oh Chooi Har 胡翠霞	A daughter of Oh Paik Hock. They married in 1908.
	Khaw Bian Chee (1896–1971)	Lee Soo Poey	
	Khaw Bian Tatt (?–1959)	1. Cheah Saw See 2. Tan Kiat Neo	
	Khaw Bian Hoe (1897–1972)	Gan Keng Wah	Daughter of Gan Ngoh Bee 颜五美
	Khaw Bian Wan (1850–1920)	Chew Gaik Tuan	
	Khaw Bian Teong (?–1972)	Goh Kooi Looi	
	Khaw Bian Howe (?–1985)	Yeoh Saw Kooi	Granddaughter of Yeoh Wee Gark 杨维岳
	Khaw Bian Ang (1902–?)	Tan Suat Chit	
	Khaw Bian Soon (1903–?)	Tan Suat See	
	Khaw Bian Kee	Tan Lam Heang	

APPENDIX 3 (Cont'd)

Family	Member	Marriage Partners	Comments
Ong 王	Ong Guan Cheng 王元清 (1835–89)	Yeap Geok Eee 叶玉意	Sister of Yeap Hup Keat. Their daughters married into the Cheah, the Ong, and the Tan families.
	Ong Hun Teng 王汉鼎 (?–1903)	Cheah Joo Se 谢如丝	
	Ong Hun Chong 王汉宗 (1865–1922)	Lim Paik Mow 林碧貌	Second daughter of Lim Seok Chin 林淑振, a Kapitan of Sumatra.
	Ong Hun Siew 王汉寿 (1866–1920)	Khoo Kwai Kee 邱桂枝	
	Ong Hun Chi 王汉墀	Tan Seh 陈氏	
	Ong Huck Shi 王学诗	Lim Seh 林氏	
	Ong Huck Chuan 王学铨	Khaw Phaik Yong	Eldest daughter of Khaw Joo Tok
	Ong Huck Leng 王学宁	Cheah Gay Hoon	Fifth daughter of Cheah Kee Ee
	Ong Oh Leng	Lim Saw Khim	Sister of Lim Cheng Teik
	Ong Boon Swee	Lim Quee Giak	Youngest daughter of Lim Leng Cheak
GAN 颜	Gan Guan Teat 颜元哲	Tan Suk Cheng 陈淑贞	
	Gan Hong Kee 颜宏基 (?–1895)	Lee Seok Kim	Daughter of Lee Choe Guan

APPENDIX 3 (Cont'd)

Family	Member	Marriage Partners	Comments
	Gan Ngoh Bee 颜五美 (1850–1922)	1. Khoo Kuat Keong	Second daughter of Khoo Cheng of Penang
		2. Lim Aik Kheng	Their eldest daughter married Cheah Teong Ho and second daughter married Khoo Siew Bee, manager of the revenue farm in Sarawak.
	Gan Teong Tat 颜仲达	Kam Chooi Lean	Fourth daughter of Kam Beng Chan of Penang. Their daughter Gan Keng Kooi married to Khoo Soon Keong, second son of Khoo Jin Tuo of Rangoon.
	Gan Teong Teng	Khoo Joo Choo	
	Gan Teong Kum	Thio Chon Nhong	A daughter of Thio Tiauw Siat (Chang Pi Shih).
	Gan Teong Yang 颜仲炎	Cheah Paik Suat	
LEE 李	Lee Sim Geang 李心研	Goh Cheng Khoon 吴贞坤	
	Lee Phee Hian 李丕显	Goh Su You 吴素佑	
	Lee Phee Tat 李丕达	Goh Su Chin 吴素锦	
	Lee Phee Yeow 李丕耀	Cheah Chun Bi 谢純璧	
	Lee Phee Choon 李丕峻	Quah Say Keow 柯西娇	Eldest sister of Quah Beng Kee. One of their daughters married into the Khaw family.

APPENDIX 3 (Cont'd)

Family	Member	Marriage Partners	Comments
	Lee Toon Tock 李纯篤	Khoo Seh 邱氏	A daughter of Khoo Chew Eng 邱秋荣.
	Lee Hai Thye	Nee Khoo Gaik Hoe Neoh	
	Lee Cheng Ewe	Khoo Seh	Only daughter of Khoo Ewe Yong
	Lee Peng Tong	Ong Seh	Eldest daughter of Ong Hun Chung
	Lee Hong Kock 李鸿国	Gan Chooi Gnoh	A daughter of Gan Hong Kee.
	Lee Chin Ho 李振和	1. Cheah Chooi Kheng 谢水庆娘 (1869–1919) 2. Lim Poh Neoh 林施娘 (1889–1960) 3. Khaw Saw Lean 许绣莲 (1894–1969)	

THE HAKKA

Family	Member	Marriage Partners	Comments
FOO 胡	Foo Tye Sin 胡泰兴 (1825–?)	1. Kam Lian Neoh 甘连娘 2. Lim Cheok Bee 林石美	Daughter of Kam Tan Keng, a merchant in Penang.
	Foo Boon Sean 胡文宣	Lim Moey Moey 林妹妹	
	Foo Joo Hoe 胡裕和	Khoo Bee Lan 邱美蘭	

APPENDIX 3 (Cont'd)

Family	Member	Marriage Partners	Comments
	Foo Choo Choon 胡子春 (1860–1921)	1. Chung Siew Lian 郑绣莲	A daughter of Chung Keng Seng and niece of Chung Keng Kwee.
		2. Eu Seh 余循娘	
	Foo Mow Sang	Lim Seh	Eldest daughter of Lim Kheng Kee.
	Foo Mow Ching 胡茂精	Choo Sim Kenn	Eldest daughter of Choo Kia Peng 朱嘉炳
CHUNG 郑	Chung Keng Kwee 郑景贵 (1821–1901)	1. Lim Ah Chen	
		2. Foo Teng Nyong	
		3. Lee See Mui	
		4. Tan Gaik Im Neoh 陈玉蔭娘	
		5. Tan Ah Loi	
	Chung Thye Phin 郑大平 (1879–1935)	1. Khoo Joo Bee 邱如美	Died in 1924 at the age of 45
		2. Lee Sau Yeng 李秀英	
		3. Tan Sim Hiang	
		4. Chan Kwai Chee	
		5. Oh Jit Kwai	
		6. Wong Yoon Hoe	
		7. Ho Foon Kaee	

APPENDIX 3 (Cont'd)

Family	Member	Marriage Partners	Comments
	Chung Thye Seong 郑大祥	Koh Chooi Pheng	Eldest daughter of Koh Cheng Sian and granddaughter of Koh Seang Tat
	Chung Ah Ming	Tan Wan Saik	Fourth daughter of Tan Lean Kee
	Chung Kok Ming	Lim Seh	The eldest son of Chung Thye Yong married a daughter of Lim Teow Siang.
	Chung Yoke Sang	Tan Sok Yeow	A daughter of Tan Chor Kay and granddaughter of Tan Lean Kee.

Note: Names are spelled according to Hokkien pronunciation or otherwise in *pinyin*.

Sources: Wong Choon San, *A Gallery of Chinese Kapitans* (Singapore: Ministry of Culture, 1963); J.W. Cushman, *Family and State: The Formation of Sino-Thai Tin-Mining Dynasty 1797–1932* (Singapore: Oxford University Press, 1991); 张少宽 Teoh Shiaw Kuan, 槟榔屿福建公冢暨家冢碑铭集 *Binlangyu Fujian Gongzhong Ji Jiazhong Beimingji* [Epigraphic Inscriptions of Penang Hokkien Cemeteries] (Singapore: Singapore Society of Asian Studies, 1997); Lee Kam Hing and Chow Min Seong, *Biographical Dictionary of the Chinese in Malaysia* (Petaling Jaya: Pelanduk Publications (M) Sdn. Bhd., 1997); 陈耀威 Tan Yeow Wooi, 慎之家塾: 室内可移动文物普查 *Shenzhi Jiashu: Shinei Ke Yidong Wenwu Pucha* [Inventory of Movable Artifacts for Private School of Chung Keng Kwee] (Penang: Tan Yeow Wooi Culture and Heritage Research Studio, 2004); *Pinang Gazette and Straits Chronicle*; 南洋名人集传 *Nanyang Mingren Jizhuan* [South Sea Chinese Biography], no. 1 vol. 2; *Singapore and Straits Directory 1904*, p. 218; *Straits Echo*, 1904, 1905, 1908, 1910, 1911, 1919, 1920, 1922, 1924; *Malay Daily Chronicle*, 1913; *Times of Malaya and Commercial Advertiser*, 1904; Jeffrey Seow, "Chung Thye Phin", in *Biographical Dictionary of Mercantile Personalities of Penang*, edited by Loh Wei Leng et al. (Penang and Kuala Lumpur: Think City and MBRAS, 2013), p. 130.

BIBLIOGRAPHY

Archival Materials

CO273 Straits Settlements, Original Correspondence

CO275 Extracts from Legislative Council papers relating to native states 1873–1896

Annual Report of the Penang Chamber of Commerce and Agriculture 1887–1915

Federated Malay States Annual Departmental Reports 1904–1911

Foreign Office Series Files (FO 422)

Proceedings of the Federal Council of the Federated Malay States for the year 1909–1911

Straits Settlements Blue Books

Straits Settlements Government Gazettes

Straits Settlements Legislative Council Proceedings

Straits Settlements miscellaneous papers and original correspondence

Tabular Statement of the Commerce and Shipping of Prince of Wales' Island, Singapore and Malacca

The Burma Gazette

Newspapers and Directories

Pinang Gazette and Straits Chronicle
Prince of Wales Island Gazette
Straits Times Overland Journal
Straits Echo
The Maulmain Chronicle
The Penang Almanack and Directory for 1876
The Penang Argus and Mercantile Advertiser
The Penang Directory for the year 1874
The Penang Herald

The Penang Times
The Singapore Free Press and Mercantile Advertiser
The Singapore & Straits Directory 1888–1915

Unpublished Works

Airries, Christopher. "A Port System in a Developing Regional Economy: Evolution and Response in North Sumatra, Indonesia". PhD thesis, University of Kentucky, 1989.

Beeman, Mark Allan. "The Migrant Labor System: The Case of Malaysian Rubber Workers". PhD thesis, University of Illinois, 1985.

Cheng U Wen Lena. "British Opium Policy in the Straits Settlements 1867–1910". Academic Exercise, University of Malaya, Singapore, 1960.

Chin Kong James. "Merchants and Other Sojourners: The Hokkiens Overseas, 1570–1760". PhD thesis, University of Hong Kong, 1998.

Cummings, William Patrick. "Cultural Interaction in a Sumatra State: Deli, 1814–1872". Master thesis, University of Hawaii, 1994.

King, Phillip. "From Periphery to Centre: Shaping the History of the Central Peninsula". PhD thesis, University of Wollongong, 2006.

Montesano, Michael. "The Commerce of Trang, 1930s–1990s: Thailand's National Integration in Social-Historical Perspective". PhD thesis, Cornell University, 1998.

Pongsupath, Chuleeporn. "The Mercantile Community of Penang and the Changing Pattern of Trade, 1890–1940". PhD thesis, University of London, 1990.

Prasertkul, Seksan. "The Transformation of the Thai State and Economic Change, 1855–1945". PhD thesis, Cornell University, 1989.

Raman, Santhiram R. "The Economic Basis for the Founding of Penang and the Development of Commerce, 1786–1930". Long Essay, University of Malaya, 1969/70.

Songprasert, Phuwadol. "The Development of Chinese Capital in Southern Siam, 1868–1932". PhD thesis, Monash University, 1986.

Chinese Materials

世界谢氏宗亲第五届恳亲大会纪念特刊 [Special Issue on the 5th World Cheah Clansmen Conference]. *Beima Xieshe Zongci He Xieshe Fuhougong Gongsi* 北马谢氏宗祠和槟城谢氏福侯公司 [North Malaya Cheah Si Chong Soo and Penang Cheah Si Hock Hew Kong Kongsi], Penang, 1989.

王重阳 Wang Zhong Yang. "泰国普吉省华人拓荒史" *Taiguo Pujishen Huaren Tuohuangshi* [History of Chinese Pioneers in Phuket]. 南洋文摘 Nanyang Digest, vol. 6, no. 5 (1965).

方雄普 Fang Xiong Pu. 朱波散记 — 缅甸华人社会掠影 *Zhubo Sanji — Miandian Huaren Shehui Lueying* [Short Essays on the Burma's Chinese Society]. Hong Kong: Nandao Chubanshe 南岛出版社, 2000.

东方日报 *Dong Fang Ri Bao* [Oriental Daily News]

张少宽 Teoh Shiaw Kuan. 槟榔屿华人史话续编 *Binglangyu Huaren Shihua Xubian* [Historical Anecdotes of the Chinese in Penang Book II]. Penang: Nanyang Tianye Yanjiushi 南洋田野研究室, 2003.

———. 槟榔屿华人史话 *Binglangyu Huaren Shihua* [Historical Anecdotes of the Chinese in Penang]. Kuala Lumpur: Prometheus Enterprise Sdn. Bhd. 光燧人氏事业有限公司, 2002.

———. 槟榔屿福建公冢暨家冢碑铭集 *Binlangyu Fujian Gongzhong Ji Jiazhong Beiminji* [Epigraphic Inscriptions of Penang Hokkien Cemeteries]. Singapore: Singapore Society of Asian Studies 新加坡亚洲研究学会, 1997.

李永球 Lee Eng Kew. 移国：太平华裔历史人物集 *Yiguo: Taiping Huayi Lishi Renwuji* [The Chinese Historical Figures of Taiping]. Penang: Nanyang Mingjian Wenhua 南洋民间文化, 2003.

陈耀威 Tan Yeow Wooi. "殖民城市的血緣聚落：槟城五大姓公司" *Zhimin Chengshi De Xueyan Juluo: Bincheng Wudaxin Gongsi* [Blood-related Kin Congregation in a Colonial City: Penang's Big Five Clan *Kongsis*]. A paper presented at the Workshop on Southeast Asian Hokkien Studies 东南亚福建学研讨会, Selangor, Malaysia, 2005.

———. 慎之家塾：室内可移动文物普查 *Shenzhi Jiashu: Shinei Ke Yidong Wenwu Pucha* [Inventory of Movable Artifacts for Private School of Chung Keng Kwee]. Penang: Tan Yeow Wooi Culture & Heritage Research Studio, 2004.

陳達 Chen Da. 浪跡十年 *Langji Shinian* [Ten Years of Floating]. Shanghai: Commercial Press 商務印書館, 1946.

陈剑虹 Tan Kim Hong. 走近义兴公司 *Zoujin Yixin Gongsi* [The Story of Ghee Hin Kongsi in Penang]. Penang: Tan Kim Hong, 2015.

新江邱曾氏族谱 *Xinjiang Qiuzengshe Zubu* [The Genealogy of the Sin Kang Khoo and Chan Clans].

泉州譜牒華僑史料與研究上册 *Quanzhou Pudie Huaqiao Shiliao Yu Yanjiu Shangce* [Quanzhou Genealogy: Overseas Chinese Historical Materials and Studies, vol. 1]. Beijing: Zhongguo Huaqiao Chubanshe 中国華桥出版社, 1998.

槟城龙山堂邱公司: 历史与建筑材料 *Bincheng Longshantang Qiugongsi: Lishi Yu Jianchu Cailiao* [Leong San Tong Khoo Kongsi: The History and Architecture]. Penang: Leong San Tong Khoo Kongsi Publication Committee 槟城龙山堂邱公司出版小组, 2003.

林氏敦本堂暨勉述堂: 壹百週年纪念刊 *Linshe Dunbentang Ji Mianshutang: Yibaizhounian Jiniankan* [Centenary Souvenir of Lim Kongsi Toon Pun Tong and Lim Sz Bian Soot Tong].

石塘谢氏世德堂福侯公公司章程 *Shitang Xieshe Shidetang Fuhougong Gongsi Zhangcheng* [Rules and Regulations of Seh Cheah Kongsi].

颖川堂陈公司: 神主簿. *Yinchuantang Chengongsi: Shenzu Bu* [Tan Kongsi's Record Book of Spirit Tablet]. Compiled in 1969.

槟州華人大會堂慶祝成立一百週年新厦落成開幕纪念特刊 *Binzhou Huaren Dahuitang Qinzu Chengli Yibai Zhounian Xinxia Luocheng Kaimu Jinian Tekan* [Commemorative Publication of Centenary Celebrations and Inauguration of New Building]. Penang: Penang Chinese Town Hall, Binzhou Huaren Dahuitang 槟州華人大會堂, 1983.

南洋名人集传 *Nanyang Mingren Jizhuan* [South Sea Chinese Biography], no. 1, vol. 2.

林孝胜 Lim How Seng. 新加坡华社与华商 [Singapore Chinese Community and Entrepreneurs]. Singapore: Singapore Society of Asian Studies 新加坡亚洲研究学会, 1995.

冯邦彦 Feng Bang Yan. 香港金融业百年 *Xianggang Jingrongye Bainian* [A Century of Hong Kong Financial Development]. Hong Kong: Sanlian Shudian Youxiangongsi 三联书店有限公司, 2002.

柯木林 Kua Bak Lim. 新华历史人物列传 *Xinhua Lishi Renwu Liezhuan* [Who's Who in the Chinese Community of Singapore]. Singapore: EPB Publishers Pte. Ltd., 1995.

苏继顾 Su Jiqing. 岛夷志略校释 *Daoyi Zhilue Xiaoyi* [Translation of the Records of Archipelago]. Beijing: Zhonghua Shuju 中华书局, 1981.

刘朝晖 Liu Zhao Hui. 超越乡土社会: 一个桥乡村落的历史文化与社会结构 *Chaoyue Xiangtu Shehui: Yige Qiaoxiang Cunluo De Lishi Wenhua Yu Shehui Jiegou* [Beyond Peasant Society: History, Culture and Social Structure in a Qiao Xiang Village]. Zhong Shan–Minzu Chuban She 民族出版社, 2004.

Articles

Battersby, Paul. "An Uneasy Peace: Britain, the United States and Australia's Pursuit of War Reparations from Thailand, 1945–1952". *Australian Journal of International Affairs*, vol. 54, no. 1 (2000): 15–31.

Beattie, G.A.C. "A Forgotten Tan Family of Penang and Phuket". A paper presented at the Shared Histories Conference, Penang, 2003.

Blusse, Leonard. "Chinese Century: The Eighteenth Century in the China Sea Region". *Archipel*, vol. III, no. 58 (1999): 127.

Buiskool, Dirk A. "The Chinese Commercial Elite of Medan, 1890–1942". A paper presented in Shared Histories Conference in Penang, 30 July–3 August 2003.

Chen Kuo-Wei and Huang Lan Shiang. "Meaning in Architectural and Urban Space of the Penang Kongsi Enclave". A paper presented at the Penang Story International Conference 2002.

Cushman, Jennifer. "Revenue Farms and Secret Society Uprisings in Nineteenth Century Siam and the Malay States". *RIMA (Review of Indonesian and Malaysian Affairs)* 23 (1989): 1–15.

Drabble, J.H. and P.J. Drake. "The British Agency Houses in Malaysia: Survival in a Changing World". *Journal of Southeast Asian Studies*, vol. Xll, no. 2 (September 1981): 297–328.

Frost, Mark Ravinder. "Emporium in Imperio: Nanyang Networks and the Straits Chinese in Singapore, 1819–1914". *Journal of Southeast Asian Studies* 36, no. 1 (February 2005): 29–66.

Gullick, J.M. "Captain Speedy of Larut". *The Malayan Branch of the Royal Asiatic Society*, vol. 26, part 3 (November 1953): 4–103.

Hillman, John. "Australian Capital and South-East Asian Tin Mining, 1906–40". *Australian Economic History Review*, vol. 45, no. 2 (July 2005): 161–85.

———. "Malaya and the International Tin Cartel". *Modern Asian Studies*, vol. 22, no. 2 (1988): 237–61.

Hussin, Nordin. "A Tale of Two Colonial Port-towns in the Straits of Melaka: Dutch Melaka and English Penang". *Journal of the Malaysian Branch of the Royal Asiatic Society* 75, no. 283 (2002): 65–98.

Khoo Kay Kim. "J.W.W. Birch: A Victorian Moralist in Perak's Augean Stable". *Journal of the Historical Society*, vol. IV (1955/56): 33–47.

Khor Jin Keong, Neil. "Economic Change and the Emergence of the Straits Chinese in Nineteenth-century Penang". *Journal of the Malaysian Branch of the Royal Asiatic Society* 79, part 2 (2006): 59–83.

Loh, Philip. "Social Policy in Perak". *Peninjau Sejarah*, vol. 1, no. 1 (July 1966): 29–38.

Musa, Mahani. "Malays and the Red and White Flag Societies in Penang, 1830–1920s". *Journal of the Malaysian Branch of the Royal Asiatic Society*, vol. 72, no. 277 (December 1999): 151–82.

Myers, Charles A. "The International Tin Control Scheme". *The Journal of Business of the University of Chicago*, vol. 10, no. 2 (April 1937): 103–25.

Pieris, Anoma. "Doubtful Associations: Reviewing Penang through the 1867 Riots". A paper presented at the Penang Story International Conference 2002.

Sinn, Elizabeth. "Preparing Opium for America: Hong Kong and Cultural Consumption in the Chinese Diaspora". *Journal of Chinese Overseas*, vol. 1, no. 1 (May 2005): 16–42.

Smith, Carl. "A Sense of History: Part 1". *Journal of the Hong Kong Branch of the Royal Asiatic Society*, vol. 26 (1986): 213–41.

Stifel, Laurence D. "The Growth of the Rubber Economy of Southern Thailand". *Journal of Southeast Asian Studies*, vol. IV, no. I (March 1973): 107–32.

Tregonning, K.G. "Straits Tin: A Brief Account of the First Seventy-Five Years of the Straits Trading Company Limited". *Journal Malayan Branch Royal Asiatic Society*, vol. 36, part 1 (1963): 79–152.

Trocki, Carl A. "Opium and the Beginnings of the Chinese Capitalism in Southeast Asia". *Journal of Southeast Asian Studies* 33 (2002): 297–314.

Ward, Marion W. "Port Swettenham and Its Hinterland". *Journal of Tropical Geography*, vol. 19 (December 1964): 69–78.

Wong Lin Ken. "The Revenue Farms of Prince of Wales Island 1805–1830". *Journal of the South Seas Society* 19, nos. 1 & 2 (1964/65): 56–127.

Books

Akira, Suehiro. *Capital Accumulation in Thailand 1855–1985*. Tokyo: Centre for East Asian Cultural Studies, 1989.

Allen, G.C. and Audrey G. Donnithorne. *Western Enterprise in Indonesia and Malaya*. London: Allen & Unwin, 1957.

Anderson, John. *Acheen and the Ports on the North and East Coasts of Sumatra*. London: Oxford University Press, 1971*a*.

———. *Mission to the East Coast of Sumatra in 1823*. London: Oxford University Press, 1971*b*.

Austin, Gareth and Kaoru Sugiharn, eds. *Local Suppliers of Credit in the Third World, 1750–1960*. New York: St. Martin's Press, 1993.

Australian Dictionary of Biography, vol. 10. Melbourne: Melbourne University Press, 1986.

Backman, Michael. *Overseas Chinese Business Networks in Asia*. Australia: East Asia Analytical Unit, Department of Foreign Affairs and Trade, 1995.

Barlow, H.S. *Swettenham*. Kuala Lumpur: Southdene Sdn. Bhd., 1995.

Blake, Robert. *Jardine Matheson: Traders of the Far East*. London: Weidenfeld & Nicolson, 1999.

Blandin, J.J. *Crude Rubber Survey*. Washington: The Bureau of Foreign and Domestic Commerce, 1924.

Blythe, Wilfred L. *The Impact of Chinese Secret Societies in Malaya: A Historical Study*. London: Oxford University Press, 1969.

Broeze, Frank, ed. *Gateways of Asia: Port Cities of Asia in the 13th–20th Centuries*. England: Kegan Paul International, 1997.

Brown, Ian. *A Colonial Economy in Crisis: Burma's Rice Cultivators and the World Depression of the 1930s*. Oxon: RoutledgeCurzon, 2005.

———. *Economic Change in Southeast Asia, c.1830–1980*. New York: Oxford University Press, 1997.

———. *The Elite and the Economy in Siam c.1890–1920*. New York: Oxford University Press, 1988.

Brown, Rajeswary Ampalavanor. *Capital and Entrepreneurship in Southeast Asia*. New York: St. Martin's Press, 1994.

Bunnag, Tej. *The Provincial Administration of Siam 1892–1915: The Ministry of the Interior under Prince Damrong Rajanubhab*. Kuala Lumpur: Oxford University Press, 1977.

Burns, P.L. *The Journals of J.W.W. Birch: First British Resident to Perak 1874–1875*. Kuala Lumpur: Oxford University Press, 1976.

Butcher, John and Howard Dick, eds. *The Rise and Fall of Revenue Farming*. New York: St. Martin's Press, 1993.

Butler, Captain J. *Gazetter of the Mergui District, Tenasserim Division, British Burma*. Rangoon: The Government Press, 1884.

Campo, Joseph Norbert Frans Marie. *Engines Power: Steamshipping and State Formation in Colonial Indonesia*. Hilversum: Verloren, 2002.

Cases Heard and Determined in Her Majesty's Supreme Court of the Straits Settlements. Somerset: Legal Library Publishing Services, 1885/90.

Chai Hon-Chan. *The Development of British Malaya 1896–1909*. London: Oxford University Press, 1964.

Chang, Queeny. *Memories of a Nyonya*. Petaling Jaya: Eastern Universities Press Sdn. Bhd., 1981.

Chiang Hai Ding. *A History of Straits Settlements Foreign Trade 1870–1915*. Singapore: National Museum, 1978.

Colombijn, Freek, Martin Barwegen, Purnawan Basundoro, and Johny Alfian Khusyairi, eds. *Kota Lama, Kota Baru di Indonesia Sebelum and Setelah Kemerdekaan* [Old City, New City: The History of the Indonesian City Before and After Independence]. Yogyakarta: Ombak & NIOD, 2005.

Cooke, Nola and Li Tana, eds. *Water Frontier: Commerce and the Chinese in the Lower Mekong Region, 1750–1880*. Lanham: Rowman & Littlefield, 2004.

Courtenay, P.P. *A Geography of Trade and Development in Malaya*. London: G. Bell & Sons Ltd., 1972.

Cowan, C.D. *Nineteenth-Century Malaya: The Origins of British Political Control*. London: Oxford University Press, 1981.

———, ed. *The Economic Development of Southeast Asia.* New York: Frederick A. Praeger, 1964.

———. *Early Penang & the Rise of Singapore 1805–1832: Documents from the Manuscript Records of the East India Company.* Singapore: Malaya Publishing House Limited, 1950.

Cragg, Claudia. *The New Taipans: A Vital Source Book on the People and Business of the Pacific Rim.* London: Century Business, 1995.

Cushman, Jennifer. *Family and State: The Formation of a Sino-Thai Tin-Mining Dynasty 1797–1932.* Singapore: Oxford University Press, 1991.

Debernardi, Jean. *Rite of Belonging: Memory, Modernity, and Identity in a Malaysian Chinese Community.* California: Stanford University Press, 2004.

Dick, Howard, et al. *The Emergence of a National Economy: An Economic History of Indonesia, 1800–2000.* N.S.W and Honolulu: Asian Studies Association of Australia in association with Allen & Unwin and University of Hawaii Press, 2002.

Drabble, John H. *An Economic History of Malaysia, 1800–1990: The Transition to Modern Economic Growth.* Canberra, New York: St. Martin's Press in association with the Australian National University, 2000.

Eusoff, Ragayah. *The Merican Clan: A Story of Courage and Destiny.* Singapore: Times Books International, 1997.

Feldwick, Walter. *Present Day Impressions of the Far East and Prominent and Progressive Chinese At Home and Abroad: The History, People, Commerce, Industries and Resources of China, Hong Kong, Indo-China, Malaya and Netherlands India.* London: Globe Encyclopedia, 1917.

Freeman, Donald B. *The Straits of Malacca: Gateway or Gauntlet.* Montreal: Mcgill-Queen's University Press, 2003.

Fujimoto, Helen. *The South Indian Muslim Community and the Evolution of the Jawi Peranakan in Penang up to 1948.* Tokyo: Institute for the Study of Languages and Cultures of Asia and Africa, 1988.

Gerini, G.E. *Old Phuket: Historical Retrospect of Junkceylon Island.* Bangkok: The Siam Society, 1986.

Hamilton, Walter. *The East India Gazetteer: Containing Particular Descriptions of Hindostan, and the Adjacent Countries, India beyond the Ganges, and the Eastern Archipelago, Together with Sketches of their Various Inhabitants.* London: J. Murray, 1815.

Handbook of the Netherlands East Indies, 1924.

Hayes, M. and S. Smith, eds. *Thai–Australian Relations in the Twentieth Century.* Bangkok: Kasetsart University, 2000.

Helfferich, Emil. *Behn Meyer & Co. and Arnold Meyer: A Company History*, vol. II. Hamburg: Hans Christians, 1981.

The Story of Hokkien Kongsi, Penang. Penang: Hokkien Kongsi, 2014.

Hussin, Nordin. *Trade and Society in the Straits of Melaka and English Penang, 1780–1830*. Copenhagen: NIAS, 2007.

Hyam, Ronald. *Britain's Imperial Century, 1815–1914: A Study of Empire and Expansion*. New York: Palgrave Macmillan, 2002.

Hyde, Francis Edwin. *Blue Funnel: A History of Alfred Holt and Company of Liverpool from 1865 to 1914*. England: Liverpool University Press, 1957.

Jackson, James C. *Planters and Speculators: Chinese and European Agricultural Enterprise in Malaya, 1786–1921*. Kuala Lumpur: University of Malaya Press, 1968.

Jamaluddin, Mon Bin. *A History of Port Swettenham*. Singapore: Malaya Publishing House Limited, 1963.

Jarman, Robert L., ed. *Annual Reports of Straits Settlements 1855–1941*. Slough, Berkshire: Archive Editions, 1998.

Kaur, Amarjit. *Bridge and Barrier: Transport and Communications in Colonial Malaya 1870–1957*. Singapore: Oxford University Press, 1985.

Khoo Kay Kim. *Malay Society: Transformation & Democratisation*. Petaling Jaya: Pelanduk Publications (M) Sdn. Bhd., 1991.

———. *The Western Malay States 1850–1873: The Effects of Commercial Development on Malay Politics*. Kuala Lumpur: Oxford University Press, 1972.

Khoo Su Nin. *Streets of George Town Penang: An Illustration Guide to Penang's City Streets & Historic Attractions*. Penang: Janus Print & Resources, 1993.

Kotkin, Joel. *Tribes: How Race, Religion, and Identity Determine Success in the New Global Economy*. New York: Random House, 1993.

Kunio, Yoshihara. *The Rise of Ersatz Capitalism in Southeast Asia*. New York and Singapore: Oxford University Press, 1988.

Laxon, W.A. and R.K. Tyers. *The Straits Steamship Fleet 1890–1975*. Singapore: Straits Steamship Co., 1976.

Lee Kam Hing. *The Sultanate of Aceh: Relations with the British 1760–1824*. New York: Oxford University Press, 1995.

Lee Kam Hing and Chow Mun Seong. *Biographical Dictionary of the Chinese in Malaysia*. Kuala Lumpur: Pelanduk Publications, 1997.

Leeuwen, Laurentia Magchilina van Lottum-van. *From Source to Scourge*. Rotterdam, Netherlands: University Erasmus, 1992.

Lewis, Dianne. *Jan Compagnie in the Straits of Malacca, 1641–1795*. Athens: Ohio University Center for International Studies, 1995.

Lim Chong Yah. *Economic Development of Modern Malaya*. Kuala Lumpur: Oxford University Press, 1967.

Lim Teck Ghee. *Peasants and Their Agricultural Economy in Colonial Malaya 1874–1941*. Kuala Lumpur: Oxford University Press, 1977.

———. *Origins of a Colonial Economy: Land and Agriculture in Perak 1874–1897*. Penang: Federal Publications, 1976.

Lindeboom, Lucas. *Oude K.P.M. – schepen van 'tempo doeloe' = Old K.P.M – ships from the past*, vol. 1. Bilthoven, Netherlands: Maritime Stichting, 1988.

Loh Wei Leng et al., eds. *Biographical Dictionary of Mercantile Personalities of Penang*. Penang and Kuala Lumpur: Think City and MBRAS, 2013.

Low, James. *The British Settlement of Penang*. Singapore: Oxford University Press, 1972.

Mackay, Derek. *Eastern Customs: The Customs Service in British Malaya and the Opium Trade*. London: The Radcliffe Press, 2005.

Mak Lau Fong. *The Sociology of Secret Societies: A Study of Chinese Secret Societies in Singapore and Peninsular Malaysia*. Kuala Lumpur: Oxford University Press, 1981.

Malayan Cases, vol. I. Singapore: Malayan Law Journal Pte. Ltd., 1939.

Miles, T.A. *Diamond Jubilee of Tin Dredging: The Story of the Creation, Building and Commissioning of the First Tin Dredge*. London: Tin Publications, 1967.

Mills, L.A. *British Malaya 1824–1867*. Singapore: Methodist Publishing House, 1925.

Musa, Mahani. *Kongsi Gelap Melayu di Negeri-negeri Pantai Barat Semenanjung Tanah Melayu, 1821 hingga 1940* [Malay Secret Societies in the Northern Malay States, 1821–1940s]. Kuala Lumpur: Malaysian Branch of the Royal Asiatic Society, 2003.

Newbold, T.J. *Political and Statistical Account of the British Settlements in the Straits of Malacca*. Singapore: Oxford University Press, 1971.

Ng Chin Keong. *Trade and Society: The Amoy Network on the China Coast 1683–1735*. Singapore: Singapore University Press, 1983.

Nonini, Donald M. and Ong Aihwa, eds. *Ungrounded Empires: The Cultural Politics of Modern Chinese Transnationalism*. New York: Routledge, 1997.

Ooi Jin Bee. *Land, People and Economy in Malaya*. London: Longmans, 1963.

Ownby, David and Mary Somers Heidhues, eds. *Secret Societies Reconsidered*. New York: M.E. Sharpe, 1993.

Parkinson, C. Northcote. *British Intervention in Malaya 1867–1877*. Singapore: University of Malaya Press, 1960.

Parmer, J. Norman. *Colonial Labor Policy and Administration: A History of Labor in the Rubber Plantation Industry in Malaya, c.1910–1941*. New York: J.J. Augustin Incorporated Publisher, 1960.

Pronk, Lieuwe. *KPM 1888–1967: A Most Remarkable Shipping Company*. North Turramurra, N.S.W.: L. Pronk, 1998.

Purcell, Victor. *The Chinese in Malaya*. London: Oxford University, 1948.

Puthucheary, J.J. *Ownership and Control in the Malayan Economy: A Study of the Structure of Ownership and Its Effects on the Development of Secondary Industries and Economic Growth in Malaya and Singapore*. Kuala Lumpur: University of Malaya Co-operative Bookshop, 1979.

Raja, Sivachandralingam Sundara. *Perdagangan dan Pelabuhan Bebas: Sejarah dan Perkembangannya* [Free Trade and Free Ports: History and Development]. Shah Alam, Selangor: Penerbit Fajar Bakti, 1997.

Redding, G.S. *The Spirit of Chinese Capitalism*. Berlin: Walter de Gruyter and Co., 1990.

Reid, Anthony. *An Indonesian Frontier: Acehnese and Other Histories of Sumatra*. Singapore: Singapore University Press, 2005.

———. *The Contest for North Sumatra: Atjeh, the Netherlands and Britain 1858–1898*. London: Oxford University Press, 1969.

———, ed. *The Last Stand of Asian Autonomies: Responses to Modernity in the Diverse States of Southeast Asia and Korea, 1750–1900*. London and New York: Macmillan Press, 1997.

———, ed. *Sojourners and Settlers*. Australia: Allen & Unwin Pty Ltd., 1996.

Richmond, Broughton, ed. *Directory of Malaya 1927*. Singapore: Directory of Malaya, 1927.

Rush, James R. *Opium to Java: Revenue Farming and Chinese Enterprise in Colonial Indonesia, 1860–1910*. Ithaca: Cornell University Press, 1990.

Sadka, Emily. *The Protected Malay States 1874–1895*. Kuala Lumpur: University of Malaya Press, 1968.

Saito, Teruko and Lee Kin Kiong. *Statistics on the Burmese Economy: The 19th and 20th Centuries*. Singapore: Institute of Southeast Asian Studies, 1999.

Selected Correspondence of Letters Issued From and Received in the Office of the Commissioner Tenasserim Division for the Years 1825–26 to 1842–43. Rangoon, Burma: Office of the Superintendent, Government Printing and Stationary, 1928.

Silcock, T.H. *The Economic Development of Thai Agriculture*. Canberra: Australian National University Press, 1970.

Smith, Carl T. *Chinese Christians: Elites, Middlemen, and the Church in Hong Kong*. Hong Kong: Hong Kong University Press, 2005.

Song, Ong Siang. *One Hundred Years' History of the Chinese in Singapore*. Singapore: University Malaya Press, 1967.

Stoler, Ann Laura. *Capitalism and Confrontation in Sumatra's Plantation Belt, 1870–1979*. Ann Arbor: University of Michigan Press, 1995.

Straits Settlements Law Reports, vol. 15. Singapore: published for the Committee of the Singapore Bar, 1922.

Tagliacozzo, Eric. *Secret Trades, Porous Borders: Smuggling and States along a Southeast Asian Frontier, 1865–1915*. New Haven: Yale University Press, 2005.

Tan Lye Ho, ed. *Bestowing Luck and Prosperity on All: Hock Teik Cheng Sin Temple*. Penang: Hock Teik Cheng Sin Temple, 2007.

Tarling, Nicholas, ed. *The Cambridge History of Southeast Asia*, vol. II. Cambridge: Cambridge University Press, 1992.

Tate, D.J.M. *The RGA History of the Plantation Industry in the Malay Peninsula*. New York: Oxford University Press, 1996.

The Chronicle and Directory for China, Japan, & the Philippines. Hong Kong: Hong Kong Daily Press Office, 1884.

The Hong Kong Directory and Hong List for the Far East for 1891. Hong Kong: Robert Fraser-Smith, 1891.

The Privy Council Cases: Malaysia, Singapore and Brunei, 1875–1954. Kuala Lumpur: Professional Law Books, 1990.

Thee Kian Wie. *Plantation Agriculture and Export Growth: An Economic History of East Sumatra, 1863–1942*. Jakarta: LIPI, 1977.

Thoburn, John T. *Commodities in the International Economy*. Edinburgh: Edinburgh University Press Ltd., 1994.

Touwen, Jeroen. *Extremes in the Archipelago: Trade and Economic Development in the Outer Islands of Indonesia 1900–1942*. Leiden: KITLV Press, 2001.

Tracy, James D, ed. *The Rise of Merchant Empires: Long-Distance Trade in the Early Modern World, 1350–1750*. New York: Cambridge University Press, 1990.

Tregonning, K.G. *Home Port Singapore: A History of Straits Steamship Company Limited, 1890–1965*. Singapore: Oxford University Press, 1967.

———. *The British in Malaya: The First Forty Years, 1786–1826*. Tucson, Arizona: The University of Arizona Press, 1965.

Trocki, Carl A. *Singapore: Wealth, Power, and the Culture of Control*. New York: Routledge, 2006.

———. *Opium and Empire: Chinese Society in Colonial Singapore, 1800–1910*. Ithaca: Cornell University Press, 1990.

———. *The Prince of Pirates: The Temenggongs and the Development of Johor and Singapore 1784–1885*. Singapore: Singapore University Press, 1979.

Turnbull, C.M. *The Straits Settlements 1826–67: Indian Presidency to Crown Colony*. London: The Athlone Press, 1972.

Twang Peck Yang. *The Chinese Business Elite in Indonesia and the Transition to Independence 1940–1950*. New York: Oxford University Press, 1998.

Voon, Phin Keong. *Western Rubber Planting Enterprise in Southeast Asia 1876–1921*. Kuala Lumpur: Penerbit Universiti Malaya, 1976.

Wang Tai Peng. *The Origins of Chinese Kongsi*. Kuala Lumpur: Pelanduk Publications, 1994.

Webster, Anthony. *Gentlemen Capitalists: British Imperialism in South East Asia 1770–1890*. London, New York: Tauris Academic Studies, 1998.

Winstedt, R.O. and R.J. Wilkinson. *A History of Perak*. Kuala Lumpur: The Malaysian Branch of the Royal Asiatic Society, 1974.

Wolfgang, Franke and Chen Tie Fan. *Chinese Epigraphic Materials in Malaysia*, vol. 2. Kuala Lumpur: University of Malaya Press, 1982–87.

Wong Choon San. *A Gallery of Chinese Kapitans*. Singapore: Ministry of Culture, 1963.

Wong Lin Ken. *The Malayan Tin Industry to 1914*. Tucson, Arizona: The University of Arizona Press, 1965.

———. *The Trade of Singapore, 1819–69*. Singapore: Malaysian Branch of the Royal Asiatic Society, 1961.

Wright, Arnold and Oliver T. Breakspear, eds. *Twentieth Century Impressions of Netherlands India: Its History, People, Commerce, Industries, and Resources*. London: Lloyd's Greater Britain Publishing Company Ltd., 1909.

Wright, Arnold and H.A. Cartwright, eds. *Twentieth Century Impressions of British Malaya: Its History, People, Commerce, Industries, and Resources*. London: Lloyd's Greater Britain Publishing Company Ltd., 1908.

Wright, Arnold, H.A. Cartwright, and Oliver T. Breakspear, eds. *Twentieth Century Impressions of Burma: Its History, People, Commerce, Industries, and Resources*. London: Lloyd's Greater Britain Pub. Co., 1910.

Wright, Nadia H. *Respected Citizens: The History of Armenians in Singapore and Malaysia*. Middle Park, Victoria, Australia: Amassia Pubishing, 2003.

Wu Xiao An. *Chinese Business in the Making of a Malay State, 1882–1941*. London: RoutledgeCurzon, 2003.

Wyatt, David K. *Studies in Thai History*. Chiang Mai: Silkworm Books, 1994.

Wynne, Mervyn Llwellyn. *Triad and Tabut: A Survey of the Origins and Diffusion of Chinese and Mohammedan Secret Societies in the Malay Peninsular 1800–1935*. Singapore: Government Printing Office, 1941.

Yeap Joo Kim. *The Patriarch*. Singapore, 1976.

Yen Ching-hwang. *The Ethnic Chinese in East Asia and Southeast Asia*. Singapore: Times Academic Press, 2002.

———. *Community and Politics: The Chinese in Colonial Singapore and Malaysia*. Singapore: Time Academic Press, 1995.

———. *A Social History of the Chinese in Singapore and Malaya 1800–1911*. Singapore: Oxford University Press, 1986.

Yeoh Seng Guan, Loh Wei Leng, Khoo Salma Nasution, and Neil Khor, eds. *Penang and Its Region: The Story of an Asian Entrepot*. Singapore: NUS Press, 2009.

Yip Yat Hoong. *The Development of the Tin Mining Industry of Malaya*. Kuala Lumpur: University of Malaya Press, 1969.

INDEX

A
Aceh
  Chinese merchants of, 116
  pepper export, 33–34
Algemeene Vereeniging Van Rubber Planters tier Osstkust Van Sumatra (A.V.R.O.S.), 149
Anglo–Dutch Treaty of 1824, 21
Anglo-Oriental Mining Corporation, 141–44
Anthony, Joseph Manook, 28
Anthony, Michael Arratoon, 28
A.V.R.O.S. *See* Algemeene Vereeniging Van Rubber Planters tier Osstkust Van Sumatra (A.V.R.O. S.)
Ayer Kuning (FMS) Rubber Co. Ltd., 147

B
Bangkok-based central government, 6
Ban Joo Hin (Wan Yu Xing 万裕兴), 114–16
Ban Seng & Co., 34
Batavia-East Coast Sumatra shipping line, 114
Behn Meyer & Co., 122
Big Five Hokkien mercantile families, 3–10, 103, 170–76
  affinal kinship of, 51
  agnatic kinship of, 48–51
  coconut trade, 30–32

coolie trade, 39–41
decline of, 175
demise of, 157–59
dominance of, 79–81
economic ascendancy, 171
European proprietors on, 104
family feuds, 159–63
family network of, 57–58
and Ghee Hin, 96–97
implications of Western competition, 129–33
imports and exports, 25–26
interests in Larut, resurgence of, 93
intermarriages, 51–58
methodology and sources, 10–11
opium and, 35–39
pepper and, 33–35
Phuket and, 93–95
revenue farms, end of, 152–56
rice from Southern Burma and, 29–30
on rubber plantation, 145–47
shipping and trading businesses, 114, 116
in sugar estates, 32–33
tin and, 26–29
tin mining interests, Larut and, 87–88
vs. Western insurance companies, 122–29

Western merchants, 105, 106
Western shipping and trading challenge, response of, 117–22
Birch, J.W.W., 90–93
Black Gold, 86
Blusse, Leonard, 2
Bogaardt, Theodore Cornelius, 106
Bowring Treaty of 1855, 75
Brig Emma's shipping voyages and cargoes, 23
British Anglo-Oriental, 173
British norms in land ownership, 156
British plantation rubber production, 147
British Straits Steamship Company, 12, 113, 173
Brown, David, 104
Bunnag family, 55–56
business networks, 170–76
    China, 3–4

C

Calcutta-based Indo-General Tin Corporation, 142
Capel, Victor, 104–5
capital-intensive technological systems, 129
Captain Weber, 28
centralized land policy, 156–57
Chalerm Na Nakhon, 140–41
Chandu (cooked opium), 90, 153, 155, 171
Chandu Revenue Ordinance 1909, 155
Chang Pi-Shih 张弼士, 114
Chaophraya Wongsanupraphat, 157
Cheah Boon Ean, 76
Cheah Boon Hean 谢文贤, 49
Cheah Cheang Lim 谢昌霖, 49
Cheah Chen Eok 谢增煜, 28, 124, 127, 135n26
Cheah Chow Phan 谢昭盼, 22
Cheah Eam, 32

Cheah family, 2n13, 49–50
    intermarriages, 53–55
Cheah Kim Ting 谢金锭, 49
Cheah Kongsi in 1820, 32
Cheah Peck Yee, 38
Cheah Pek Ee 谢伯夷, 71, 75, 76
Cheah Tek Soon 谢德顺, 55
Cheah Tek Swee, 55
Cheah Tek Thye 谢德泰, 55, 128, 145
Cheah Yeam 谢掩, 20
Cheang Hong Lim, 5
Che Ngah Ibrahim, 27, 87–90
Cheng Tee Syndicate, 92, 93
Chettiar, A.M.K. Raman, 131
Chew Choo Heang, 145
Chin Ah Yam 陈亚炎, 63
Chin Ah Yok, 81
China Navigation Company Ltd., 106
Chinese business families, 176
Chinese business networks, 3–4
"Chinese century", 2
Chinese coolies, 29
Chinese family networks, 47
Chinese Immigrants Enactment of 1910, 154
Chinese insurance company, 123
Chinese labour system, 148
Chinese mercantile community, 20
Chinese merchants of Aceh, 116
Chinese Traders Society, 81
Chin Hock Bee, 49
Chip Hock & Co., 109
Chiu Ah Cheoh 赵亚爵, 65
Chiu Sin Yong, 38
Chong Moh & Co., 24, 30, 105
Choo Ah Wat, 80
Choong family, 7
    economic influence, 6
Chop Chip Hock, 28
Chop Eng Hong, 122
Chop Hap Hin 合兴号, 95

Chop Jin Seng 振盛号, 95
Chop Khun Ho, 40
Chop Seng Huat, 40
Chun Bunnag, 94, 95
Chung family, intermarriages, 56
Chung Keng Kwee 郑景贵, 27–28, 37, 56, 78, 80, 87, 88, 97, 159
clan association in Penang, 47
Clarke, Andrew, 90
coastal shipping lines to Sumatra, KPM, 114
coconut estates of Big Five, 30–32
colonial authority, 69
commercial frameworks, 103, 105
commercial rubber cultivation, 146
commodity production sectors, 173
Consolidated Tin Smelters (CTS), 142–43
cooked opium, 171
coolie riot of Taiping (1879), 76–78
coolie trade, 39–41, 171
Cowan, C.D., 15, 16
cross-dialect marriage networks, 56
cross-ethnic marriage networks, 56
Crown Land policy, 152
CTS. *See* Consolidated Tin Smelters (CTS)
Cushman, Jennifer, 5, 21

D

deep-sea harbour, construction of, 158
Deli, pepper export, 33–34
Deli Tobacco Planters' (DPV) Association, 149
dialect factions of Ghee Hin, 64
Drabble, John, 28
dredging companies, 140–42
dredging machines, 164
dredging techniques, 139, 141, 163
Dutch authority, 79
Dutch blockade, 30
Dutch colonial government, 113
Dutch East Indies ports to British ships, 14
Dutch KPM, 113, 117

E

Eastern Shipping Company, 12, 116, 117–22, 129, 131, 158, 160, 173
Eastern Smelting Company, 138, 144
East Sumatra, labourers in, 148, 149
economic depression, 153, 154, 174
Eng Huat & Co., 49
Eng–Moh–Hui–Thye–Kee Estate in Kedah, 145
entrepot trade, 25–26
"ersatz capitalists", or rent-seekers, 176
Estate Labourers (Protection of Health) Enactment of 1910, 154
Eu family, 7
Euro-centric approach, 170
European proprietors, 104
Eu Yan Sang, 7

F

Federated Malay States, 152, 153
Firestone in 1899, 144
Foo Choo Choon 胡子春, 122
Foo Tye Sin 胡泰兴, 54, 87, 124
free trade, 1, 2
Frost, Mark Ravinder, 4

G

Gan Ngoh Bee 颜五美, 38
General Association of Rubber Planters of the East Coast of Sumatra, 149
Ghee Hin, 28, 62–69, 78, 86–90
  Big Five and, 96–97
  camp, 90
  decline of, 79–81
Ghee Hin-Ho Hap Seah league, 88
Goodyear in 1898, 144
government monopolies, rise of, 152–56

Great Depression, 142
Guangdong province, 87
Guggenheim Brothers, 143
guttah percha (local rubber tree), 144

H
Hai San society, 56, 87, 88, 90
Hakka families, intermarriages, 54
Henry Jones & Co., 139
Henry Waugh & Co., 144
Hevea brasiliensis (South American rubber tree), 144
Hock Chong & Co., 117
Hock Teik Cheng Sin 福德正神庙, 81
Ho Ghi Siew 何义寿, 63, 88
Hok Khi, 40
Hokkien families, 1, 3–10
  business networks, 9–10
  dialect networks, 8
  intermarriages, 53–54, 56
Hokkien Kongsi, 5
Hokkien merchants, 20–22, 106, 123
  Singapore, 106–8
Hokkien-owned insurance company, 126
Hokkien shipping companies, 123
Holt, Alfred, 110
Hong Kong-based On Tai Insurance Company, 126
Horseman, Edward, 104
Ho Seng, 78, 93–95
Howeson, John, 141–42
hui, 9, 10, 12, 153–54, 172, 174
Huizhou Hakka, 88
Hup Hin Kongsi, 27

I
immigrant labour force, 171
Immigration Restriction Ordinance, 148
Indian Companies' Act 1866, 123
Indian coolies, 164
Indian immigrants, promotion of, 148
Indian Immigration Committee, 147
Indian labourers, 104
  in East Sumatra, 148
Indo-Malay Red Flag Societies, 12
Industrial Revolution, 86, 103
industries
  rubber industry, 144–52
  tin industry, 138–44
insurance business, 122–29
interconnected economic sectors, 172
intermarriages, 51–53
  Big Five Hokkien mercantile families, 51–58
  Cheah 谢 families, 53–55
  Hakka families, 54
  Hokkien families, 53–54, 56
  Khoo 邱 families, 51, 53, 54–55, 57
  Lim 林 families, 53, 54, 57
  Tan 陈 families, 53
  Yeoh 杨 families, 57
inter-regional shipping line, 114
Itsarathichai, Phra, 75

J
Java-Bengal Line, 114
Java Immigration Bureau, 149
Javanese coolies, 164
Javanese labourers in East Sumatra, 148, 149
Jessen, Hermann, 122

K
Kaw Hong Take, 129
Kean Ann Estate in Province Wellesley, 145
Kedah rice, 29
Kennedy, James Young, 76
Khaw–Australian syndicate, 140
  collapse of, 141–42
Khaw Boo Aun 许武安, 41, 63

Index

Khaw Group, 12, 138, 173
  collapse of, 157–59
Khaw Joo Ley 许如利, 56
Khaw Joo Tok 许如琢, 140–41
Khaw Sim Bee 许心美, 139–40, 145
Khaw Soo Cheang 许泗章, 20
Khean Guan Insurance Company, 124–26, 128, 129
  financial accounts of, 127
  overseas agents of, 130–31
Khie Heng Bee Mill, 32
Khoo Bun Kiad, 38
Khoo Cheng Lim 邱清临, 20, 53
Khoo Eow Chaw, 79
Khoo Eu Yong, 124–25
Khoo family, 2n13, 7
  intermarriages, 51, 53, 54–55, 57
Khoo Guek Chio 邱月照, 32, 48–49
Khoo Hong Chooi, 89
Khoo Hun Yeang 邱漢阳, 38, 49, 145, 161
Khoo Jeow, 30
Khoo Joo Chian, 40
Khoo Kay Chan, 38
Khoo Kay Kim, 15
Khoo Kong Mah, 34
Khoo Kongsi in 1835, 32
Khoo Sian Tan 邱仙丹, 49
Khoo Siew Jin 邱绣巾, 49
Khoo Sim Keok 邱心菊, 22
Khoo Soo Ghee, 79
Khoo Teong Poh 邱忠波, 28, 40, 49
Khoo Thean Poh 邱天保, 49
Khoo Thean Teik 邱天德, 22, 28, 38, 40, 49, 78, 80, 87, 89, 93, 159
Khor, Neil, 7
Kian Bi & Co., 115
Kian Teik-Hai San alliance, 93
Kian Teik Tong 建德堂, 62–68, 73, 75, 81, 87–89, 93–95, 153–54
  camp, 89
  leaders of, 68
Kim Keng Leong & Co., 50–51

King Vajiravudh, 157
kinship ties, 47
Klub Bunnag, 55
Koe Guan & Co., 117, 139
Koh family, 7
Koh Hong Tek 辜鸿德, 129
Koh Lay Huan 辜礼欢, 20
Koh Seang Tat 辜尚达, 38
Koh Seang Thye, 28, 87, 159
Koninklijke Paketvaart Maatschappij (KPM), 105, 113–17
Krabi riot of 1878, 67, 74–76

L

Labour Code of 1895, 154
Labour Enactment of 1911, 154
labourers in East Sumatra, 148, 149
Labourers' Wages Priority Enactment of 1899, 154
Lady Weld, a paddle steamer in 1891, 110
Lan Fang Kongsi of West Borneo, 48
Larut
  and Big Five's tin mining, 87–88
  resurgence of Big Five interests in, 93
Larut Wars, 88–89
Lee Cheng Tee 李清池, 90–92
Lee Cheng Yan 李清渊, 108
Lee Coyin, 63
Lee Ghe Ang, 32–33
Lee Kee, 38
Lee Nie Hee 李乃喜, 64
Lee Phee Ean, 117
Lee Phee Eow, 117
Lee Teng See 李鼎峙, 117
Lee Toh, 38
liberalism, to management, 102–3
Light, Francis, 1, 2, 62–63
Lim Ang Kee 林红柿, 56
Lim Boon Haw, 145, 147, 162
Lim Chin Tsong 林振宗, 50–51
Lim Eow Hong 林耀煜, 50, 117

Lim Eow Thoon 林耀椿, 50, 162, 189
Lim Eu Toh 林有道, 53
Lim family, 2n13, 7, 50
   economic influence, 6
   intermarriages, 53, 54, 57
Lim Hock Seng, 140
Lim It Kim 林乙金, 20
Lim Kek Chuan 林克全, 37
Lim Lean Teng 林连登, 175
Lim Leng Cheak 林宁绰, 30, 37, 50
Lim Mah Chye 林妈栽, 53
Lim Seng Hooi 林成辉, 145, 162
Lim Tek Swee 林德水, 79
Lim Tjing Keh 林清溪, 79
lineage organizations, 48
loans for rubber plantation, 147
Logan, James Daniel, 124
Logan & Ross, 124
London Stock Exchange, 146
Low, James, 30, 32
Low Wei Leng, 7

M
Mahani Musa, 71
Malaya, 86
   freight capacity and rail/land/water cost in, 151
   radical land policy, 156
   railway network in, 150–52
   rubber distribution in, 150
Malaya Secret Societies in the Northern Malay States 1821–1940s (Musa), 71
Malay Peninsula, 109
Malay politics, 90
Malay Reservations Enactment, 157
marine insurance, 123
merchant-trading community in Southeast Asian ports, 20
Miles, Edward Thomas, 139–41
Mills, L.A., 1–2
Mindon, Burmese King, 67
Mohamed Merican Noordin, 55
Mom Chao Vibul Sawatwong, 56
Moulmein rice, 29
Muhlinghaus, Herman, 109

N
Naiyit, a Siamese tax officer, 27
Nakhon, Luang Prachim, 76
Nanyang networks, 4
New Consolidated Goldfield, 143
Ng Boo Be, 161
Ng Chin Keong, 48
Ngee Heng Kongsi of Johore, 48
Nina Merican Noordin, 55
Noordin Estate, 55
Nordin Hussin, 16

O
Ocean Steamship Company Ltd., 106, 123
Oh Wee Kee 胡维期/囲棋, 63, 87
"one-and-all" Perak opium farm system, 90
Ong Boon Eng 王文营, 38
Ong Boon Keng 王文慶, 38
On Tai Insurance Company Limited, 123–24
opium farming system, 92, 171
opium farm rivalry, sworn brotherhood *hui*, 62–680
Opium Régie (or state monopoly), 156
opium revenue farming system, 9, 35–37, 152–55, 158, 171–74
Opium Syndicate, 158
opium trade, 35–39
Ord, Harry, 89, 91

P
Pangkor Treaty of 1874, 90, 92–93
patron–client relationships, 140
Penang
   continuing prosperity of, 14–19
   import and export, 18–19

Penang Argus and Mercantile Advertiser, The, 22
Penang-based Hokkien networks, 10
Penang-based insurance company, 126
Penang-based Western businessmen, 105
Penang-based Western trading, 103
Penang business community, 103–4
Penang-centred economic region, 20
Penang Hokkien merchants, 123
Penang Hokkien vessels, 25
Penang Khean Guan Insurance Company Limited, 12, 122–23, 158, 173
Penang opium revenue farm, 36–37, 70
Penang Opium Syndicate, 57
Penang-oriented Hokkien merchants, 5–6
Penang-oriented network, 114
Penang riot of 1867, 69–74
Penang's merchandise trade, 27
Peninsular and Oriental Steam Navigation Company (P&O Company), 160
pepper trade, 33–35
Perak's major revenue farms and farmers (1880–82), 79–81
Perak War, 77
Phra Borisutlohaphumintharathibodi, 56
Phraya Senanuchit, 56
Phraya Wichitsongkhram, 56, 94
Phuket
  and Big Five, 93–95
  tin mining in, 27
Phuket-based trading, 109
plantation agriculture, 173
plantation coolies revolt of Deli in 1884, 78–79
Pongsupath, Chuleeporn, 6
Prince Damrong, 20, 157
Prince Purachatra, 140
Prince Sommot, 56
Province Wellesley, 32

Q
Quah Beng Kee 柯孟淇, 160

R
railway network in Malaya, 150–52
Raja Abdullah, 89–90
Rangoon-based Tavoy Tin Dredging, 142
Read, W.H., 90
Red Flag secret society, 55
regional business networks, 172
regional shipping services, 106
Reid, Anthony, 2
revenue farming systems, 9
rice trade, 29–30
Robert Kuok Hock Nien 郭鹤年, 176
Ross, Frederick John Caunter, 124
Rotterdamsche Lloyd, 113
Royal Dutch Packet Company (KPM), 12, 105, 113–17, 173
rubber
  distribution in Malaya, 150
  industry, 144–52
  plantation, loans for, 147
  production sector, 173–74

S
San Neng Cantonese, 65
Satupulo Tin Company, 140
Scott, Henry G., 141
Scott, T.G., 141
Section 11 of the Ordinance, 81
Seh Cheah Kongsi, 48
Seh Khoo Kongsi, 49, 53
Seh Lim Kongsi, 53
Seh Tan Kongsi, 48
Seh Yeoh Kongsi, 53, 162
Selangor opium revenue farm, 158
Seng Poh Syndicate, 91, 92

Shanghai-based China Merchants' Insurance Company, 126
shipping agents of Straits Steamship Company, 110–12
Siamese government, 54–56
 opium farms abolishment, 156
Siamese rulers, 38
Siamese Tin Syndicate Ltd., 141
Siam opium farm, 161
Singapore Hokkien mercantile elite, 86, 91
Singapore Hokkien merchants, 106–8
singkeh Chinese, 175
Sin Joo Hin & Co., 30
Sin Neng Cantonese, 64
Sit San, 64, 96, 97
smelting business, growth of, 138
Societies Suppression Ordinance of 1889, 81, 154, 174
Songprasert, Phuwadol, 5–6
Soo Ah Chiang 苏亚昌, 63, 88
South American rubber tree, 144
Southeast Asian ports, merchant-trading community in, 20
Southern Burma and Big Five, rice from, 29–30
S.S. Zephyr, 97
Stepanie Chong Po Yin, 7
Straits Chinese families, 7
 in Singapore, 4
Straits Settlements Government, 148, 153, 155, 164
Straits Steamship Company, 105, 106–13, 117, 158
 shipping agents of, 110–12
Straits Steamship fleet, 123
Straits Trading Company, 12, 106–13, 138, 173
sugar estates in Big Five families, 32–33
Sumatra
 KPM coastal shipping lines to, 114
 pepper export, 33

Sword, James, 109
Syed Mohamed Alatas, 55, 71

T

Taiping coolie riot of 1879, 67
Talerng Tin Dredging, 142
Tamil Immigration Fund, 147
Tan Chuan 陈大川, 65
Tan family, 2n13, 50–51
 intermarriages, 53
Tan Gaik Tam 陈玉淡, 67
Tan Jao 陈锦灶, 95
Tan Jiak Kim 陈若锦, 107
Tan Kay Beng, 145
Tan Keong Saik 陈恭锡, 107
Tan Kim Ching 陈金钟, 5, 90, 91
 involvement of, 89–93
Tan Lian Ky, 95
Tan Lwee 陈雷, 67
Tan Neo Yee or Tan Wee Ghee 陈威仪, 75, 95
Tan Pai Wun, 75
Tan Pheck Kiad, 95
Tan Tam or Tan Cheng (Geok) Tam 陈清淡, 27, 95
Tan Wee Ghee. *See* Tan Neo Yee
Tan Yang Sin, 95
Tan Yit Hoon, 28
Tavoy rice, 29
Tenasserim coast, tin trade of, 14
Thailand, 86
Thammarat, Phraya Nakhon Si, 75, 76
Thio Thiau Siat or Chang Pi-Shih 张弼士, 114, 116
Thomas Barlow & Co., 147
Tiang Lee & Co., 50
tin
 and Big Five, 26–29
 industry, 138–44
 mining, 173
Tjong A Fee (Chang Hung Nan 张鸿南), 38

Tjong A Fie, 145
Tjong Jong Hian (Chang Yu Nan 张煜南), 38
Toa Peh Kong 大伯公, 63, 66
Tongkah Harbour Tin Dredging Company, 139, 142, 158
Touwen, Jeroen, 116
trade, 171
  networks, 58
Tregonning, K.C., 15
Trocki, Carl, 7, 62
Truck Enactment of 1909, 154
truck system, 153–54, 174

V
Virunha, Chuleeporn, 7

W
water-based network, 3
Western agency houses, 145–46
Western and Hokkien merchants, 106
Western competition for Big Five, implications of, 129–33
Western industrial powers, 102–3
Western-inspired revolution, 174
Western insurance companies, Big Five vs., 122–29
Western mercantile elite, 102, 104
Western merchants, 103–5
Western mining enterprises, expansion of, 142
Western-modelled "self-strengthening" strategy, 164
Western shipping companies, 123
  and trading challenge, response of Big Five to, 117–22
Western shipping fleet, 123

Western shipping services, 123
Western smelting enterprise, 138
Western-style bureaucratic frameworks, 103
white gold, 86
  Larut and Big Five's tin mining, 87–88
  outbreak of Larut wars, 88–89
  Phuket, 93–95
  resurgence of interests in Larut, 93
  from Southern Burma, 96–97
  Tan Kim Ching, involvement of, 89–93
Wichitsongkhram, Phraya, 28, 38
Won Bunnag, 55
Wong Lin Ken, 16
Wong Ting Tong, 80, 81
Wu Xiao An, 4–7
Wynne, M.L., 69

X
Xinning Cantonese, 88

Y
Yeap Chor Ee 葉祖意, 175
Yeoh An Yian, 95
Yeoh Cheng Teik 杨清德, 57
Yeoh family, 2n13
  intermarriages, 57
Yeoh Ooi Gark, 161
Yeoh Paik Tatt 杨碧達, 162
Yeoh Tay Thor, 50
Yong Ching Siew, 27
Yoon Ting Hakka, 122
Yoshihara Kunio, 176

Z
Zengcheng Hakka, 88

ABOUT THE AUTHOR

WONG Yee Tuan obtained a PhD in history from the Australian National University. He is Fellow & Head of History and Heritage Research Group, Penang Institute, Malaysia. His main research interest is in the area of the Chinese business history of Southeast Asia, on which he has published several articles in *Asian Culture, Chinese Southern Diaspora Studies, Journal of the Malaysian Branch of the Royal Asiatic Society* and *Archipel*.

IMAGE 1

A Tin Distribution and Smelting Agency Operated by Khoo Low Chang (standing on the left) in Penang

Source: Emil Helfferich, *Behn, Meyer & Co. — Arnold Otto Meyer: A Company History*, vol. II (Hamburg: Hans Christians Verlag, 1983), p. 74. Courtesy of Khoo Salma Nasution.

IMAGE 2
Sir James Hugh Low

Source: Arkib Negara Malaysia (National Archive of Malaysia).

IMAGE 3
Khoo Thean Teik

Source: Taken by the author in Penang with the permission of Boon San Tong.

IMAGE 4
Chung Keng Kwee

Source: Courtesy of Tan Yeow Wooi.

IMAGE 5
J.W.W. Birch

THE LATE J. W. BIRCH.

Source: Arkib Negara Malaysia (National Archive of Malaysia).

IMAGE 6
Loke Yew

Source: Arkib Negara Malaysia (National Archive of Malaysia).

IMAGE 7
Tan Wee Ghee

Source: Courtesy of Tan Yeow Wooi.

MAP 1
Location of Khoo Kongsi and Khoo Thean Teik's Shop Houses

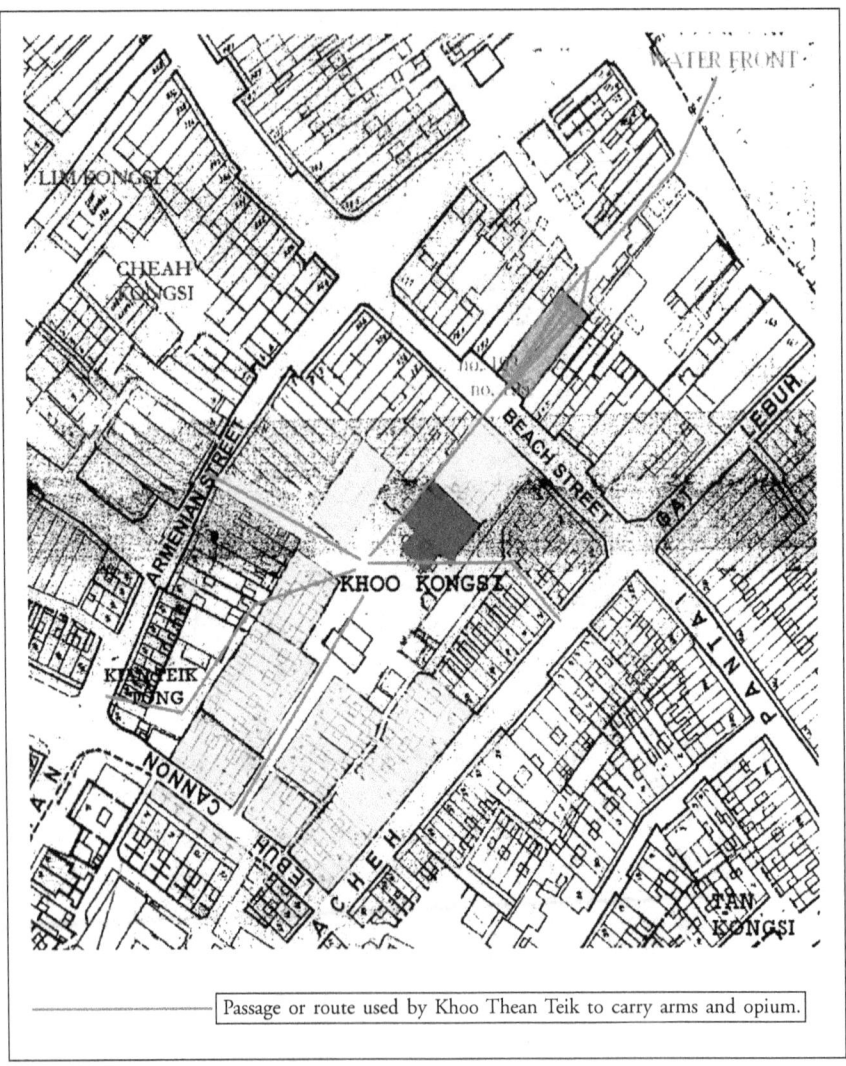

Passage or route used by Khoo Thean Teik to carry arms and opium.

Source: Original map provided by Tan Yeow Wooi Culture & Heritage Research Studio, Penang.

www.ingramcontent.com/pod-product-compliance
Lightning Source LLC
Chambersburg PA
CBHW070029010526
44117CB00011B/1764